MAYAN CALENDAR
ASTROLOGY

Other works by Kenneth Johnson

Jaguar Wisdom: An Introduction to the Mayan Calendar

Mythic Astrology Applied: Personal Healing
Through the Planets
(with Arielle Guttman)

Mansions of the Moon: The Lost Zodiac of the Goddess

North Star Road

The Silver Wheel: Women's Myths and Mysteries
in the Celtic Tradition
(with Marguerite Elsbeth)

The Grail Castle: Men's Myths and Mysteries
in the Celtic Tradition
(with Marguerite Elsbeth)

Mythic Astrology: Archetypal Powers in the Horoscope
(with Arielle Guttman)

Mayan Calendar Astrology

Mapping Your Inner Cosmos

Kenneth Johnson

LUCITA
PUBLISHING

Published in the United States by
LUCITÀ Publishing, an imprint of LUCITÀ Inc.
Sunnyvale, California
http://publishing.lucita.net

ISBN-10: 0-9774035-9-9
ISBN-13: 978-0-9774035-9-2

Library of Congress Control Number: 2011945078

First LUCITÀ Publishing edition 2011.
LUCITÀ and the sun logo are trademarks of LUCITÀ, Inc.

Cover, book design, and interior graphics by Luba Rasine-Ortoleva

Maya day sign illustrations in the chapter headings by Gregorio Kukulcan Itzep Hernandez

The Maya day sign and number glyphs in this book are based on actual Mayan carvings. The graphics have been styled for high quality printing by Luba Rasine-Ortoleva.

The image of the Madrid Codex on the front cover is an artistic rendering of the black & white image sourced from the PDF version of the "Codex Cortesianus," by Léon de Rosny, Libraires de la Société d'Ethnographie, Paris, 1883, pp. 75–76, downloaded from the FAMSI web site on July 7, 2010. <http://www. famsi.org/mayawriting/codices/pdf/madrid_rosny_bb.pdf>.

Visit *www.jaguarwisdom.org* for more information about Kenneth Johnson and his work.

Printed in the United States of America on FSC-certified, 30% post consumer recycled paper.

Las fuerzas del cosmos... no lo vemos no lo tocamos,
pero sí está vivo en nosotros.
Las leyes del Calendario
son fuerzas superiores a las leyes humanas.

We can neither see nor touch the forces of the cosmos,
but it lives within us.
The laws of the Calendar
are forces superior to the laws of humankind.

~ Don Rigoberto Itzep Chanchavac

Contents

Illustrations

A Note on the Spelling of Mayan Words

The way in which Mayan languages are written in our Western alphabet has gone through many changes, especially in the last couple of decades.

The Yucatec Maya words and terms most familiar to non-academic students of the Calendar—especially the names of the day signs—were formerly written in an orthography based on sound values in the Spanish language. Indigenous peoples and scholars have more recently developed new ways of writing Mayan words in their Yucatec form, ways which are not tied to the phonetic values of a specific language (in this case Spanish).

Therefore Yucatec has become Yukatek, Ahau has become Ajaw, Chicchan has become Chikchan, and so on.

While we respect the efforts of so many fine scholars, both indigenous and Western, we also have no wish to confuse the sincere student who is familiar with the older orthography. Therefore, we have retained the common spellings of Yucatec words in this book rather than introduce our readers to an entirely different system.

In the case of K'iche'—which was itself spelled "Quiché" in the former orthography—we have made a different choice. Since most readers are not yet familiar with the K'iche' language, we have chosen to use the newer and more contemporary spellings, as most students are being introduced to the language for the first time.

Acknowledgments

Unlike some other books on "Mayan Astrology," none of the information contained in this volume is my own personal invention. All of the material contained herein is based on my studies with Mayan Daykeepers and shamanic priests in Guatemala, all of whom are well known in the contemporary tradition of the Mayan Calendar. Almost everything I have written here is similar to what you would learn if you had chart readings done by village priests in the highlands of Guatemala.

I would like to thank my teachers. First and foremost, I thank Rigoberto Itzep Chanchavac of Momostenango, who clarified for me the distinctions of meaning between Day Sign, Number, Conception Sign and so on. He also made available to me detailed teachings on the meaning of the numbers and the phases of the sun and moon, none of which have been published before. Since Momostenango is one of the few communities which still keeps both the Sacred Calendar (*tzolk'in*) and the Solar Calendar (*haab*), he is the source for all my information regarding the influence of the Solar Year Lord as well. His son, Gregorio Kukulcan Itzep Hernandez, also an *aj q'ij* (Daykeeper), is the creator of the intricate day sign illustrations used in the chapter headings.

I would also like to thank Roberto Poz of Zunil for introducing me to the esoteric technique known as the Path of Feathered Serpent. A summary of some of his teachings can be found in a book authored by his sister-in-law, Jean Molesky-Poz, and entitled *Contemporary Maya Spirituality: The Ancient Ways Are Not Lost* (Austin, University of Texas, 2006). Thomas Hart's book, listed below, also contains a substantial passage from the work of Don Roberto.

Thanks are also due to Carlos Barrios, whose published writings have detailed the five-sign Tree of Life technique that was originally made popular internationally by the celebrated Mayan priest, Alejandro Cirilo Perez Oxlaj, known to most simply as Don Alejandro.

I take my hat off to Martin Prechtel, author of *Secrets of the Talking Jaguar* (New York, Tarcher, 1999), who taught me the meaning of the intimate connection between the 13 numbers, the Moon Goddess, and the principle of the Divine Feminine.

I also received a great deal of guidance in understanding contemporary Mayan culture from Thomas Hart of Quetzaltenango, author of *The Ancient Spirituality of the Modern Maya* (Albuquerque, University of New Mexico, 2008) and an *aj q'ij* himself.

My personal thanks to my publisher, Birgitte Rasine of LUCITÀ Publishing, and Luba Rasine-Ortoleva, who gave her special artist's touch to the numerous tables, charts, and graphics that you see throughout this book.

Finally, I would have never made it into the highlands and been welcomed there were it not for the extraordinary assistance of Anita Garr, Don Rigoberto's friend, and mine.

Foreword

What you hold in your hands is one of the most comprehensive guides ever written to the rich, intricate system of personal astrology that the sacred Mayan Calendar embodies. With this accessible yet profound book, Kenneth Johnson, author of the well-respected *Jaguar Wisdom: An Introduction to the Mayan Calendar*, takes you deep into the inner secrets of the Tzolk'in, far below the surface of Mayan birth sign calculations. The Mayan Destiny Chart, the all-important Year Lord, the nine-sign horoscope, the solar and lunar cycles, personal compatibility families, composite charts for relationships, and the rare but powerful Path of Feathered Serpent will leave you breathless—and more conscious than ever of the forces that began to shape your life even before you were born.

We live in a world that has no patience for sacred things. Fame, power, and wealth are the ruling values in modern society. Products become obsolete almost as soon as you buy them. You've always got to have the "latest" in everything. Inner peace, tranquility, wisdom, and self-awareness are but an after-thought in the mainstream media. And yet, in our stressful day-to-day existence, we need these sacred things more urgently than ever.

Like the lush jungles of Central America where the Olmecs first began to conceive of a way to intertwine the human experience of time into personal spirituality and everyday life, the Mayan Calendar is both ancient and new, as relevant today as it was centuries ago. Even as new generations arrive, new ideas take root, and new technologies change the way we relate to each other as well as the things we use in our daily lives, the Calendar evolves with us—all of us, no matter where we are in the world. This unassuming tool for measuring time and exploring personal astrology continues to reveal new and surprising linkages, illuminations, and insights into the lifepaths we all travel and the power we each hold over our personal destiny.

No matter who we are or who we want to be, no matter our race, gender, or the color of our skin, the sacred Mayan Calendar envelops us all in the same warm yet demanding embrace: warm because it touches the very core of our souls; demanding because it expects the best of us—and accepts no excuses. Unlike other astrological systems that may relieve us of responsibility for our actions by claiming "it's your fate," the Tzolk'in presents us with a foundation for our lifepath and our personal traits and characteristics, but leaves the ultimate result up to us. As it should. For the intricacy of human thought, emotion, and behavior is far too unique and individual to allow itself to be standardized, constrained, restricted by any system, astrological or logical, Mayan or Western—or any other. As Ken says in Chapter 8,

> We have an archetypal template—our birth day sign and number, and the supporting signs derived therefrom. What we do with it is entirely up to us. ... Mayan astrology, as a whole, is much more shamanic and much less deterministic than anything in the [West].

Reading Ken's books is like diving into one of the deep blue cenotés that interlinks the serene underworld of the Maya lands. The surface looks a picture of tranquility, but mesmerizes you with just a breath of a hint of the extraordinary revelations that you will discover as you dive deeper.

The day sign–number combination that defines our Mayan birth date is but the tip of an entire ocean of profound personal meaning, discovery, and potential that for too many of us, for too long, has been unexplored.

Until now.

Birgitte Rasine
Publisher
LUCITÀ Publishing

On the Nature of Sacred Time

Excerpt from
Jaguar Wisdom: an Introduction to the Mayan Calendar

The Sacred Calendar is about time. We all know what time is—or think we do. It is a succession of dawns and sunsets, days and nights and seasons. We may divide it into hours and minutes, or years and centuries, but we can never step outside of it—except perhaps in moments of special awareness which constitute the peak experiences of life. Time is one of the essential words. Life itself is subject to the regimen of time—not just human and animal life, but the life of planets and galaxies as well. Time is an inescapable fact of existence. Our personal quantum of biological energy will wind down in time, and time will overcome us in the end. We as a species have always been inclined to regard time as a kind of taskmaster, a relentless clock that holds us always in its grasp, ticking away the minutes toward our eventual extinction. Time is the linear reality that gives shape and pattern to our lives, defining our mortality.

According to many traditional societies, there are two dimensions of time: ordinary time and sacred time.

What has just been described is ordinary time.

If ordinary time represents a process to which all of us are subject and before which all of us are ultimately powerless, then sacred time represents cosmic order. It is the foundation of rhythm and motion. It is the glue that binds the universe together. Without the sense of cosmic order implied by this sacred dimension of time, nothing could happen. There would be no loom upon which to weave the tapestry of life. In many ancient mythologies, the gods do their work of universal creation in a world where time does not yet exist. Time itself is the summit of creation, for it is only when time exists that the new-made world is ready for humankind. The creation of time replaces original chaos with cosmic order.

Sacred time exists contemporaneously with ordinary time. It is fashioned of the same elements—seasonal and celestial—that comprise ordinary time. It is simply our altered or ritualized perception of time that allows us to enter its sacred dimension.

When the shaman draws his magic circle, or when a priest approaches the altar to celebrate the mass, he enters ritual space. This is a sacred place where the ordinary laws of reality do not apply. This is where magic happens. The center of the shaman's circle, the altar with its bread and wine—here lies the center of the universe.

We enter ritual space in our daily lives whenever we pray or meditate, whenever we create—in short, whenever we pay homage to the presence of the divine in our lives. For that moment, we are at the center of the universe. Whenever we enter ritual space, we enter ritual time as well. Ordinary time may be going on all around us, but we are no longer a part of it. Our perception of time has changed. It is no longer a mere progression of hours and minutes, but a living, vital, spiritual presence. This is what the sacred dimension of time is all about.

Both ordinary and sacred time are generally measured by the patterns of heaven and earth, for it is these patterns, these constantly recurring cycles, that integrate us with the cosmic order underlying all things. Honoring these recurring changes is yet another way for us to enter the sacred dimension of time. Thus humanity has devised rituals to mark the four major changes of the solar and seasonal year—the equinoxes, when day and night are of equal length, and the solstices, when the sun appears to stand still and then "turn back" to the north or south. Priests and magicians of all cultures have charted the progress of planets and fixed the positions of the stars, for the orderly cycles of the heavens are among the most potent symbols of the cosmic order.

The Mesoamerican spiritual tradition exemplified its vision of the universe in cosmograms, diagrams of the infinite. The double pyramid construction of the Mayan universe was one such diagram; the geomantic city was another. But these cosmograms are essentially static; they are not in motion. The Maya believed that the universe, both human and cosmic, was constantly evolving through different worlds or "suns," different epochs of cosmic time.

They believed that every moment in time was in a state of flux, a shifting tapestry of energies that manifested in earthquakes and volcanoes, in the wars of gods and men and the transformations of the human heart and spirit. Hence the theme of metamorphosis is central to all Mesoamerican mythology. In one story, a deformed and rejected god is transformed into the glorious sun of the new world epoch. In another, the god-king Quetzalcoatl is transformed into the planet Venus. The world is constantly evolving. Human beings must constantly struggle for the sense of universal order and harmony even as they strive toward their own evolution.

To pluck order out of chaos, we must understand the ebb and flow of energy in time, the vast transformations and metamorphoses that make up life on earth. Yet how shall we find the sense of cosmic order in this shifting, restless world of volcanic passions, both human and terrestrial? How shall we sense both the order and the chaos entwined in one vast scheme?

For this, the people of ancient Mesoamerica needed a cosmogram that was fluid rather than static—a cosmogram that moved in time, capable of embodying the flux and reflux of life.

This was the Sacred Calendar.

Kenneth Johnson

Chapter 1

An Introduction to the Sacred Calendar

The Structure of the Calendar

When we talk about the Mayan Calendar, we are really talking about two calendars—one that measures ordinary time, and one that measures sacred time. These two calendars interpenetrate in such a way as to integrate and synthesize the secular and sacred dimensions of reality. In this book we shall be primarily concerned with the measure of ritual time, usually called the *tzolk'in* and sometimes referred to as the Ritual Almanac or Divinatory Almanac.

We do not know what the ancient Maya called this ritual or sacred aspect of the Calendar. Most scholars use the Yucatec term *tzolk'in* (from *tzol* = count and *k'in* = day, hence "count of days"), but this term may not have been used by the Classic Maya and is in fact based on the equivalent K'iche' term *ch'ol q'ij*.[1] The *tzolk'in* is a unique method of reckoning time. It consists of twenty named days combined with thirteen numbers. Each day name is repeated thirteen times during the Calendar cycle, for a total of 260 days (13 x 20 = 260). The twenty days, with their glyphs, directional correspondences, Mayan names, and some of their most common English meanings, are shown in Figure 1 on the next page.

A Language Note

Before we proceed much farther, a few words need to be said about the languages involved with Mayan Calendar studies.

Figure 1. THE NAMES OF THE DAYS

YUCATEC	K'ICHE'	ENGLISH
Chuen	B'atz'	Master of all the Arts, Monkey, Thread (of Destiny)
Eb	E	Road of Life, Path, Tooth, Destiny
Ben	Aj	Resurrection of the Corn, Cane, Reed, Authority
Ix'	I'x	Jaguar, Strength, Vigor, Magic, Sacred Earth
Men	Tz'ikin	Vision of the Bird, Eagle, Wisdom, Fortune
Cib	Ajmaq	Forgiveness, Sin, Pardon, Vulture, Dead Ancestors
Caban	No'j	Vision of the Cosmos, Intelligence, Thought, Wisdom, Knowledge
Etznab	Tijax	Obsidian Knife, Pain, Healing
Cauac	Kawoq	Universal Community, Family, Rain, The Divine Feminine
Ahau	Ajpu	Hunter, Sun, Marksman, Hero, Ancestors
Imix	Imox	The Left Hand, Craziness, Water, Crocodile
Ik'	Iq'	Breath of Life, Wind, Air, Lord Tepeu
Akb'al	Aq'ab'al	Dawn, Harmony, Obscurity
Kan	K'at	The Net, Womb, Heat, Fire
Chicchan	Kan	Feathered Serpent, Snake
Cimi	Kame	Death and Rebirth, Cycles, the Eternal Now
Manik'	Kej	The Pillars of the Universe, Deer, the Four Cardinal Points
Lamat	Q'anil	The Regeneration of the Earth. Seed, Ripeness, Yellow, the Four Colors of Corn
Muluc	Toj	Offering, Payment, Thunder, Fire, Atonement, Suffering
Oc	Tz'i	Law and Spiritual Authority, Dog, Raccoon

Both popular and academic writers have used the Yucatec names for the day signs, though the days are no longer kept in the Yucatan. The *tzolk'in* still constitutes a living tradition among speakers of K'iche', Tz'utujil, Caqchikel, and other highland languages of Guatemala. I learned in the K'iche' language, but have commonly used the Yucatec names for the day signs because they are more familiar to most students.

This can be confusing. For example, the fourteenth day sign is called "Kan" in Yucatec but "K'at" in K'iche', while the fifteenth day sign is "Chicchan" in Yucatec but "Kan" in K'iche'. Even scholars (some of whom are Maya!) get confused between the two Kans.

Even so, and at the risk of causing more confusion, I have provided the K'iche' names for the day signs along with the Yucatec. There are certain meanings attached to the day signs that are typically conveyed through word play or punning in that tongue, so it is important for the reader to have at least a little bit of familiarity with it.

Because the *tzolk'in* is comprised of twenty days but only thirteen numbers, the cycle of days and numbers will soon set up an interlocking rhythm of its own design. The rhythm of the Sacred Calendar is circular; many contemporary Calendar shamans insist that it has neither beginning nor end. It has certainly been the source of much confusion for those who are convinced that the Sacred Calendar "begins" with 1 Imix and must "end" with 13 Ahau, so it is just as well to clear up some of the issues before proceeding.

The *tzolk'in* is a circle, not a straight line. To try to force a "beginning" or an "end" upon the circle of time is to impose our own Western linear concepts onto a world in which they have no place. Imix may serve as a logical "beginning" in certain respects because each of the all-important prophetic cycles called *k'atuns* (19.7 of our years) ended on an Ahau day; therefore, a new *k'atun* always began on an Imix day. But this should by no means be taken as evidence that the *tzolk'in* itself "begins" on Imix.

Some writers have asserted that the Imix beginning represents a "Yucatecan Day Count" based on principles different than the K'iche' count. This is nonsense. The Mayan prophetic writings, the books of Chilam Balam written in Yucatec, always begin the count of the days with Kan (K'at) rather than Imix. The reason is simple. At the time of the Conquest, the Yucatecans were using Type IV Year Lords (see Chapter 5), and Kan was the Year Lord that began the Calendar Round (which is also explained in Chapter 5). The *tzolk'in* days themselves were the same everywhere. If it was 4 Chicchan at Chichen Itza, it would be 4 Chicchan among the Toltecs as well, and 4 Chicchan in the highlands of Guatemala. The day count never changed; it still hasn't.

There is, however, a faction among academic scholars that believes the Maya somehow "lost" two days out of the count at some point in history. In fact, they seem to believe that all of Mesoamerica somehow "lost" these same two days, which in my own opinion requires a gigantic leap of the imagination. In the standard correlation, the GMT or Goodman-Martinez-Thompson count with a correlation constant of 584283, the beginning date of the so-called Great Cycle is August 11, 3114 BC, with an "end date" of December 21, 2012. The other correlation, developed by Floyd Lounsbury, has a numerical constant of 584285, yielding a beginning of August 13 and an ending of December 23.

Thanks to the influence of the late Mayanist Linda Schele, scholars are fond of using the Lounsbury correlation without explaining that they are employing a variant count. Academics are supposed to be rigorous about clarifying their sources, but scholarly courtesy does not seem to be a virtue among Lounsbury's advocates. Therefore even academics often confuse themselves, listing a beginning date of August 13 but an end date of December 21! The Maya themselves emphatically reject the Lounsbury Correlation and live their lives according to the GMT.

Throughout the time that anthropologist Barbara Tedlock spent studying the Sacred Calendar in Momostenango,[2] she never heard a single Daykeeper begin counting from Imix. Current practice among the Maya is as follows:

One may begin counting from the current date, on any given day. One may also begin with the day upon which the current *trecena,* or "round of thirteen days," began, which is to say, upon the day numbered "1" in the current cycle. (And if one happens to start on an Imix day, or if the trecena began with 1 Imix, then this day is a logical place to begin one's count—but not otherwise.)

Some communities have "special" days of initiation which can be regarded as points of beginning, for example 8 B'atz' (Yucatec: 8 Chuen) in Momostenango, or 8 Tz'ikin (Yucatec: 8 Men) in Santiago Atitlan. These vary from place to place.

It should be noted that there is some evidence that the Maya of the Classic Period (c. 200-900 CE) often began their count with No'j (Yucatec: Caban), the sign that ruled the Fourth World in which we now live.

It should also be noted that some of the colonial period Chilam Balam books of the Yucatec Maya begin their count with K'at (Yucatec: Kan), which was the primary day sign among their four Lords of the Year.

In contemporary Mayan spirituality, most Daykeepers have agreed to set B'atz' (Yucatec: Chuen) as the beginning of the count of the days, in accordance with the primacy of that day in traditional K'iche' Maya communities. Since my instructors in the art of Mayan astrology are K'iche', this is the order we will follow in this book— beginning with 8 B'atz', the day upon which the highland K'iche' always celebrate the "*tzolk'in* New Year."

The Meaning of the Calendar

What, then, does the Sacred Calendar symbolize? Why thirteen numbers and twenty day signs? What sort of cycle is this that chronicles the sacred dimension of time?

One clue, of course, lies in the fact that there are thirteen divisions of Heaven in the Mayan cosmos. Therefore, we may say that the number 13, far from being "unlucky" as it is in Western folklore, was to the Maya a symbol of Heaven itself.

Figure 2. THE CALENDAR BOARD

Chuen / B'atz'	8	2	9	3	10	4	11	5	12	6	13	7	1
Eb / E'	9	3	10	4	11	5	12	6	13	7	1	8	2
Ben / Aj	10	4	11	5	12	6	13	7	1	8	2	9	3
Ix / I'x	11	5	12	6	13	7	1	8	2	9	3	10	4
Men / Tz'ikin	12	6	13	7	1	8	2	9	3	10	4	11	5
Cib / Ajmaq	13	7	1	8	2	9	3	10	4	11	5	12	6
Caban / No'j	1	8	2	9	3	10	4	11	5	12	6	13	7
Etznab / Tijax	2	9	3	10	4	11	5	12	6	13	7	1	8
Cauac / Kawoq	3	10	4	11	5	12	6	13	7	1	8	2	9
Ahau / Ajpu	4	11	5	12	6	13	7	1	8	2	9	3	10
Imix / Imox	5	12	6	13	7	1	8	2	9	3	10	4	11
Ik' / Iq'	6	13	7	1	8	2	9	3	10	4	11	5	12
Akb'al/Aq'ab'al	7	1	8	2	9	3	10	4	11	5	12	6	13
Kan / K'at	8	2	9	3	10	4	11	5	12	6	13	7	1
Chicchan / Kan	9	3	10	4	11	5	12	6	13	7	1	8	2
Cimi / Kame	10	4	11	5	12	6	13	7	1	8	2	9	3
Manik' / Kej	11	5	12	6	13	7	1	8	2	9	3	10	4
Lamat / Q'anil	12	6	13	7	1	8	2	9	3	10	4	11	5
Muluc / Toj	13	7	1	8	2	9	3	10	4	11	5	12	6
Oc / Tz'i	1	8	2	9	3	10	4	11	5	12	6	13	7

It is commonly said that the thirteen numbers also correspond to the thirteen joints in the human body. These are: the two ankle joints, the two knees, the two hips, the hands, the elbows, the shoulder joints, and, finally, the neck or thirteenth joint.

The twenty day signs may also be related to the human metaphor, the microcosm as macrocosm. The number 20 was regarded in ancient times as the number of humankind, because it is the number of all the digits—fingers and toes—on the human body. Thus, the equation 13 x 20 unites Heaven with humankind.

Anthropologists working among the contemporary Maya have asked their native colleagues what the Calendar symbolizes. The answer given by Mayan Calendar shamans is remarkably consistent:

It is the term of pregnancy, the cycle of human gestation. This, they say, is the foundation of the Calendar.

Scientifically, we know that the actual period of pregnancy is somewhat longer than 260 days. The 260-day interval is a fair rule of thumb for the period which elapses between the time a woman first misses her menses to the time when she gives birth; hence the *tzolk'in* is symbolic of the gestation period. It is primarily an earthly, human cycle.

Figure 3. THE TZOLK'IN

All the same, various astronomical cycles may have contributed to the overall symbolism of the *tzolk'in*. For example, 260 days is an interval between zenith passages in the Mayan country; the visibility cycle of Venus vis-à-vis the moon can also be expressed as 260 days; and the moon itself has both a thirteen-day cycle of waxing as well as a twenty-day visibility cycle.

Although it is the cycle of human gestation that, after so many centuries, the Maya still cite as the basis of the *tzolk'in*, the gestation cycle itself is yet another metaphor. All the world's great myths are essentially concerned with the journey of human consciousness— the archetypal hero's journey. The Mayan Calendar is no different. Consciousness, like life, must journey from conception to full birth. The day sign Eb signifies "the road"—what other Native Americans have called the Road of Life. In Yucatec Maya, the word *eb* also means "stairway"—perhaps in reference to the stairways that led to the top of Mayan temples on which the ancient kings ascended to the world of the gods. The Calendar, as a symbol of the growth of human consciousness, leads us up the Pyramid of Time. It is the Road of Life, and its roots lie in the eternal journey we all must make, the journey from conception to birth.

Just as Western astrology may attribute various qualities such as the four elements or the three modes and a planetary ruler to each sign of the zodiac, so do Mayan astrologers. Before we begin to examine the meaning of each day sign separately, let us take a quick look at the principal correspondences of the Mayan system.

Of Darkness and Light

The Maya perceive the universe as an energetic whole made up of two opposing but complementary polarities.

Some writers describe this as "dualism," but that is an incorrect term. "Dualism" implies an absolute and irreconcilable difference between two forces such as "good and evil" or "God and the Devil." The Mayan pairs of opposites are more accurately an example of "polarities," meaning that these two forces are opposing expressions of a single, unified force. They mirror each other like opposites, but they are ultimately of the same essence.

Don Rigoberto Itzep Chanchavac of Momostenango gives the following examples:

Winter/Summer	Health/Sickness	Laughter/Weeping
Cold/Hot	Birth/Death	Slowness/Capability
Light/Darkness	Suffering/Joy	Gain/Loss

The concept of polarity permeates Mayan spirituality. In terms of astrology, it is most clearly seen in the idea that day signs are masculine whereas numbers are feminine, but as we shall see, many of the individual day signs embody various expressions of these essential polarities.

Some readers will already have noted that the Mayan concept of polarity is very similar to the Chinese concept of yin and yang, or the Hindu idea of Purusha and Prakriti. Indeed, I have sometimes used the terms "yin" and "yang" in this book, as well as "karma," "dharma," etc. I am not trying to confuse the issues or to precisely equate one cultural expression with another, still less to claim that the ideas of these two cultures are identical. However, Don Rigoberto has often said (and I am paraphrasing):

"Sometimes there are no adequate words in English or in Spanish to express many of the basic concepts of Mayan spirituality. Western philosophical thinking is just too different. I have used Eastern philosophical terms in my own lectures and writings because the Eastern concepts are often much more similar to those of our cosmovision. Since many Western students understand the Eastern terms, their use helps people to comprehend the Mayan concepts."

The Fourfold Universe

The Mayan universe is based upon the concept that there are four essential, meaningful divisions of time and space. Long before the arrival of the Spanish, the cross was a common symbol among the Maya. It represented the fourfold Tree of Life which defined their world view and their universe. If the Calendar is a road of life, then life itself is a medicine wheel comprised of four directions—East West, North, and South.

This concept of the universe or cosmos as a quaternity is virtually universal and can be found in mystical systems all over the planet. Carl Jung taught that the human psyche itself is a fourfold entity—an idea that is worth further exploration.

Each direction also corresponds to:

• The four colors of corn, which also celebrate the four races of humankind;
• The four elements Fire, Earth, Air, and Water[3]

Since each day sign corresponds to one of the four directions, it also corresponds to one of each of the four vital components of our symbolic universe.

Readers who have some previous acquaintance with the Mayan Calendar may be surprised to note that the directions attributed to the day signs here are different than those to be found in other standard works, whether academic or popular. While many Daykeepers acknowledge that the ancient system was different and that things must have changed at some point in the past, they are almost all in agreement in using the directions given here in their contemporary spiritual practice.

The Four Directions and Their Colors

East

East is the direction of sunrise and of the spring. It is a symbol of beginnings, of the energy that gives birth to action and idea, just as the energy within the greening earth gives birth to the flowers of spring or the first rays of the rising sun give birth to a new day. East is the heavenly face of the Celestial Serpent, and red is the color associated with the eastern direction. When a Mayan shaman faces East, he is facing his future, in both the spiritual and material sense. Thus he attributes both his destiny and his physical children to the East.

West

West is the direction of sunset, the direction of autumn. In the West, all things come to an end; creatures die, just as the sun takes its nightly death when it dips below the western horizon, or as the leaves die and blow away in the fall. But what seems to be the end is, in fact, only one stage in an eternal process. Souls will be reborn in Heaven even as the earth will be reborn in spring.

An action or idea which has its birth in the East may dip below the surface of the symbolic western horizon and experience an Underworld sojourn, but it will arise again reborn. Hence West is the direction of transformation, the Underworld face of the

Celestial Serpent. This is the place of the ancestors, of all who have come before us and, if we are facing East, those who stand behind us to give us their support.

Both black and purple are colors associated with West. In Aztec poetry, "the red and the black" is a metaphor of wholeness, of completeness. It signifies the polar opposites of East and West, and hence the process of birth, transformation, and rebirth. On the cross of the four directions, the East–West polarity forms the horizontal arm, like a road. Among North American tribes this horizontal arm finds its equivalent in the Medicine Wheel as the "Good Red Road," the medicine path. This is the road that leads from birth to spiritual transformation, the Road of Life.

North

Another arm of the directional cross runs from North to South. In Classical times, North was equivalent to "above" as well as to the northern direction, hence symbolic of the place of the sun at zenith. Like West, it was associated with the ancestral spirits who have departed this world. The road to the Underworld is the road to the north of the sky. Hence north has the meaning of wisdom, the wisdom we acquire from the ancestors. Its color is white.

When the Mayan shaman stands facing east, the North is on his left. As in other mystical systems around the world, the left is the feminine side. Hence, to the contemporary shaman, this direction can also represent women, relationships, and marriage.

South

As with the North and its symbolism of "up," the South was anciently equivalent to "below" as well as to the southern direction. It was symbolic of the mysterious generative power that comes from beneath the soil and makes the plants sprout and grow. Its color is yellow, the color of the growing corn. South is symbolic of the generative power that gives life to all things. Facing East, the shaman has the South on his right side. Thus the South symbolizes male energy, the strength and abundance of one's family line.

Figure 4. THE DIRECTIONS OF THE DAY SIGNS

DAY SIGN	DIRECTION	COLOR	ELEMENT
Chuen / B'atz'	East	red	fire
Eb / E'	West	black	earth
Ben / Aj	North	white	air
Ix / I'x	South	yellow	water
Men / Tz'ikin	East	red	fire
Cib / Ajmaq	West	black	earth
Caban / No'j	North	white	air
Etznab / Tijax	South	yellow	water
Cauac / Kawoq	East	red	fire
Ahau / Ajpu	West	black	earth
Imix / Imox	North	white	air
Ik' / Iq'	South	yellow	water
Akb'al/Aq'ab'al	East	red	fire
Kan / K'at	West	black	earth
Chicchan / Kan	North	white	air
Cimi / Kame	South	yellow	water
Manik' / Kej	East	red	fire
Lamat / Q'anil	West	black	earth
Muluc / Toj	North	white	air
Oc / Tz'i	South	yellow	water

In addition to these basic correspondences, there are many others, some of which have uses in shamanism and magic, others in traditional medicine. The list which follows is as complete a rendering as I have been able to acquire over the years.

When Does the Day Begin?

Of all the questions I have received over the years, one of the most common is:

What time does the Mayan day begin?

Figure 5.   CORRESPONDENCES OF THE DAY SIGNS

DAY SIGN	ANIMAL	MEDICAL	BOTANICAL
Chuen / B'atz'	monkey	veins	carnation
Eb / E'	bobcat	soles of feet	pine
Ben / Aj	armadillo	spinal column	sugar cane
Ix / I'x	jaguar	blood	white rose
Men / Tz'ikin	quetzal	eyes	sunflower
Cib / Ajmaq	vulture	female sexual organs	violet
Caban / No'j	gazelle	brain	basil
Etznab / Tijax	wolf	teeth & tongue	mallow
Cauac / Kawoq	lion	heart	maguey
Ahau / Ajpu	eagle	chest	horsetail
Imix / Imox	fish	muscles	cypress
Ik' / Iq'	weasel	respiratory system	mint
Akb'al/Aq'ab'al	fawn	stomach	cinnamon
Kan / K'at	lizard	rib cage	marshmallow
Chicchan / Kan	serpent	nervous system	blackberry
Cimi / Kame	owl	fingernails	grapefruit
Manik' / Kej	deer	hands	olive tree
Lamat / Q'anil	rabbit	sperm & eggs	corn leaves
Muluc / Toj	shark	ears	grape leaves
Oc / Tz'i	tepezcuintle	nose	lily

This question is pertinent to all studies in Mayan astrology because it has a bearing on the most essential question of all: *What is my day sign?*

I have seen a great deal of speculation from Western "scientific" types who want to find an exact moment, down to the nano-second, when the day begins. They have developed all kinds of interesting theories! Unfortunately, none of these are even remotely Mayan, conceptually speaking. In order to understand the Mayan concept of the days, we need to understand a bit of the language as well. The word for "day" (*k'in* in Yucatec or *q'ij* in K'iche') is exactly the same as the word for "sun." If I am talking about "this day," I use the word *q'ij*. If I want to remark that the sun is hot today and point at that orb in the sky, I also use the word *q'ij*.

The words are the same because, in Mayan thinking, a day is defined as the course of the sun through the four stations of midnight, dawn, noon, and sunset. Here again we see the essential Mayan world view of a fourfold universe coming into play. It should also be remembered that in Mayan thinking "north" is the same as "up," and "south" is the same as "down." Thus dawn = east, noon = north, sunset = west, and midnight = south. We live in a fourfold reality, which is not merely static but forever in motion.

This is how it works. I am writing these words on the day 11 Chicchan. When the sun goes down this evening, it will mark the moment at which the energy of the day 11 Chicchan crosses into the Underworld, the world of the ancestors and the spirits. The deeper it travels into the Underworld, the more its energy shall wane. As soon as the sun is down, the energy of the next day, 12 Cimi, will begin to make itself felt. The Daykeepers will light candles and burn incense in their shrine rooms to honor the advent of the day to come, 12 Cimi. There is no "exact" moment when this takes place. Don Miguel Vicente began his observances as soon as the sun dipped below the horizon. Don Rigoberto Itzep preferred to wait until it was fully dark. It's a matter of personal preference.

As the sun travels farther into the Underworld, the energy of 11 Chicchan becomes less and less powerful as its essence surrenders to the overwhelming forces of the darker half of the eternal polarity. Somewhere round about midnight, the growing energy of 12 Cimi will become stronger and more powerful than that of the waning 11 Chicchan.

Scientific minds in search of an "exact moment" for the shifting of the days may perhaps be frustrated with such vagueness, but this is the real Mayan perception of the matter. It is a process rather than an event. Mayan Daykeepers always calculate horoscopes based on a midnight transition between the days, just as we do. Their reasoning and their world view may be somewhat different, but the result is the same. One should always use midnight as the astrological definition of a day, just as we do here in the west. Don Rigoberto once remarked that people born shortly before or after midnight often partake of the qualities of both day signs, much like those born upon a "cusp" in Western astrology.

By the time dawn arrives, 11 Chicchan will have disappeared completely. 12 Cimi will rule the day alone until sunset, when it too shall pass into the Underworld, and the energy of a new day will begin to make itself felt.

What About Time Zones?

Another frequently asked question is: *Should I define midnight in terms of my local time zone, or should I adjust it to the time zone for Central America (equivalent to the American CST)?*

This question has a bearing on an even more important philosophical issue: Is the Mayan Calendar indicative of a global energy, a planetary rhythm geared to the rising and setting of the sun wherever we may be in the world?

Or is it a kind of time pulse which emanates specifically from the Mayan lands and has a distinct geographical locus?

I wish I could answer these questions clearly and unequivocally, but I cannot. I would be dishonest if I were to tell my readers that Mayan Calendar astrology is a cultural monolith, etched in stone with absolute agreement among all practitioners. This would be very far from the truth. There are just as many "topics of lively debate" in Mayan astrology as there are in Western astrology.

This particular issue is one such topic. No consensus exists among Daykeepers. Don Rigoberto feels that the day signs should be calculated according to your local time zone, wherever you may be in the world. Don Audelino Sac believes that one must use Central American time and adjust your calculations accordingly. I don't remember that I ever asked Don Roberto Poz how he felt about it.

I encourage students to experiment in this respect. If you come across a birth date which would change according to the time zone, try it both ways. Explore your feelings and your intuition about it. What do you think works best?

How to Find Your Day Sign and Number

Consult the Mayan Calendar Tables at the back of this book. Let us assume that you wish to find the day sign for an individual born August 18, 1961. Begin by finding the year 1961 in the Mayan Calendar Tables. Running your finger down the list of dates, you will note that August 9 was 1 Etznab, while August 22 was 1 Chuen.

Next, consult the Calendar Board diagram, which can be found either on page 10, page 189, or page 231 in Appendix B. Locate 1 Etznab and count forward by counting down: August 9 is 1 Etznab, August 10 is 2 Cauac, and so on until you reach August 18, which will be 10 Manik. If you were born in late February or early March of an even-numbered year, be alert for leap year days! 10 Manik is the day sign for any individual born on August 18, 1961.

You can easily photocopy the Calendar Board wherever it appears in this book, and keep it on your desk for easy reference.

Chapter 2

The Day Signs

The day signs of the Sacred Calendar are the archetypes of the Mayan people—indeed, of all the people of indigenous Mesoamerica, for they were shared by cultures from central Mexico to Honduras. Like all collective archetypes, they are too complex to be reduced to a few mere words. Each one is a myth unto itself.

Contemporary Western astrologers have debated whether their own art originated as a technical language or whether it has its roots in the infinite storehouse of myth. None of the Mayan astrologers with whom I have spoken expressed the slightest doubt on this question. Your day sign is your personal myth, your archetype.

As well as detailing the personal characteristics that exemplify natives of each day sign, we shall also examine the symbolic and mythic background of each of the signs. For those who have read my previous book, *Jaguar Wisdom*, let me remark that the approach in this present book is quite different from the previous one. In that volume, I explored the day signs from a cross-cultural perspective that included all the different cultures of the wider Mesoamerican sphere—the Aztecs and Toltecs as well as the Maya, and even the Pueblo people of the American Southwest. In this book, I will focus on the meanings attached to the day signs by Mayan astrologers currently working and practicing among their own people. All of the material here is completely new.

One's archetype is also deeply related to the Mayan concept of the human soul. According to the Maya, each human being is born with two souls. One of them is known as the *uxlab*. The Spanish word *anima* is often used to describe this aspect of soul, since it is identical to what Catholic Christians perceive as the soul. It is invested in the body and in breathing. It remains within the body until the moment of our death.

The second aspect of the soul is quite different. In the K'iche' language, it is called *uwach uk'ij*, which literally means "the face of his or her day." In other words, this is the energy template or imprint of the Sacred Calendar day upon which we are born. My *uwach uk'ij* is Imix; I have an Imix soul because I was born upon that day, and I share a common bond with all others born upon Imix. My best friend was born upon Cimi; she has a Cimi soul and is bonded in soul with all those who share the same *uwach uk'ij*.

Sometimes the Maya use the word *nawal* to describe this aspect of the soul. The word is borrowed from the Nahuatl word *nagual*, but it should be emphasized that this word means something rather different to the Maya than it means in Carlos Castaneda's well-known books or even in most anthropological literature. Castaneda uses the word *nagual* to describe the "non-ordinary" aspect of reality; this perception of reality is "left-handed" in the sense that it is vested in the left side of our body. We shall deal with a parallel concept among the Maya later on. Many anthropologists use the term *nagual* to describe one's "spirit animal" or "animal totem." While the Maya do in fact recognize a specific animal totem for each of the day signs, this is not always the same as what they mean when they use the term *nawal*.

The word *nawal* can have many meanings. In general, it could be said to mean "a spirit." This can be almost any kind of spirit, including an ancestor spirit or personal guardian spirit. It can be the patron deity or spirit of a particular aspect of life or profession—we shall cite any number of examples in the course of this chapter. Most importantly for our purposes, a *nawal* is the spirit inherent in a day sign, any day sign in fact. Since we all have a particular day sign upon which we were born, we all have a personal day sign *nawal* as well. Our *nawal* is our day sign soul, our spiritual essence, our archetypal imprint. This is the soul which dreams; it should be emphasized that dreaming is an important part of the spiritual path to most Daykeepers. The *anima* may be vested within the human body, but the *nawal* is not. It can roam freely through the astral world while we are asleep.

Though the "face of one's day" may be described as a *nawal*, there are subtle distinctions between the *nawal* and the *uwach uk'ij*. While all living things possess a *nawal* or spiritual essence, only human beings possess the *uwach uk'ij* or day sign soul. Though Westerners may ask an astrologer to cast a horoscope for their dog, the Maya would never do so. A dog may have a *nawal*, but it doesn't have a day sign soul. The day sign soul is one of the things which distinguish human beings from other beings. We all have a *nawal* based upon the day sign of our birth, but the quintessentially human aspect of our *nawal* distinguishes us from other living creatures, and thus is also called by a more specific name, the *uwach uk'ij*.

Day Signs as Sun Signs

I am often asked: Is your day sign more important than your number, or are both factors of equal importance? Here, the answer is fairly unequivocal:

> *The day sign of one's birth is the single most important factor in a Mayan horoscope. The numbers serve to modify and personalize the energy of the day sign, but it is the day sign which constitutes one's most essential archetype.*

In the Western world, it is normal for one to ask: "What's your sign?" In response to such a question, a person will usually answer simply with her or his sun sign, i.e. Aquarius, Sagittarius, and so on. Very few people will give a detailed answer such as: "The Sun is in Aquarius with a Gemini Moon and Cancer rising."

I can attest, from personal experience, that it is just the same among the Maya in Guatemala. I know the day sign of birth for almost all of my Mayan friends, but I only know the number of birth for about half of them. If someone asks, "What is your *nawal*?" the customary reply will be (in K'iche'), "I was born on Imox," or "My *nawal* is Tz'ikin." Occasionally someone will answer in more detail and say, "I was born on 8 Tz'i," but not always. The *nawal* or day sign is commonly taken as the core factor of any Mayan horoscope.

The Pop Wuj, *Epic of Creation*

The full meaning of the day signs cannot be understood unless we understand the tale of the Hero Twins, as recorded in the *Popol Vuh* or Book of Counsel, now usually written *Pop Wuj*. Though the first manuscript, written in Ki'che', dates only from colonial times, the stories contained within its pages can be found in painting and sculpture during the time of the Classic Maya, and even in pre-Classic times. These stories clearly constituted the most important myths of Mayan civilization. The day signs of the Sacred Calendar figure powerfully in the myth of the Hero Twins. Early artistic representations of this myth are found at Izapa c. 200 BCE, and perhaps even in a series of recently discovered paintings at the very ancient site of San Bartolo (c. 300 BCE).

Many people simply do not care for mythological stories; therefore I have included the story of the Hero Twins and the essentials of the *Pop Wuj* in Appendix A. The reader is encouraged to study it in order to gain a deeper appreciation of the day signs.

In the description of the day signs which follows, some readers may be surprised to see that I have used different, and more impressionistic, translations of the meanings of the signs. In the earliest edition of my previous book, *Jaguar Wisdom*, I used English renderings of the common Aztec meanings, e.g. "Wind" for Ik, "Vulture" for Cib, and so on. While it is true that these same natural forces and animals still constitute part of the meaning of the day signs, I want to emphasize the word *part*. The full meaning of each day sign is much too complex to be expressed through a single word describing an animal or a force of nature.

The fact that the Aztecs used such names for the days tells us something about the world view of Aztec culture, but can be a source of confusion when it comes to understanding the day signs themselves. The translations I have given, such as "The Vision of the Bird" for Men or "The Universal Community" for Cauac are based on information received from a charming Maya woman in Chiapas who prefers to remain anonymous.

Getting Started: The Astrological Significance of the Day Sign

The day sign of your birth constitutes your *nawal* and "the face of your day." It is your archetypal imprint or spiritual identity. Unlike other factors we shall discuss later, the day sign is an inner influence rather than an outer one. It is the symbolic core that underlies your outer personality, not the personality itself (that is comprised of the day sign's number and the Year Lord). Thus the day sign or *nawal* may not always be the first thing that people notice about you; its power lies under the surface, deep in your innermost heart.

Chuen
(B'atz')
Master of all the Arts

The day sign Chuen or B'atz' is symbolic of the deity that the *Pop Wuj* calls the "Maker and Modeler," the deity that created Earth and Sky. This day symbolizes human origins, as well as being a continuation of the past; this is why K'iche' Daykeepers insist that it is B'atz', rather than Imox (Imix in Yucatec), which begins the count of days. New *aj q'ijab,* or Mayan priests, are initiated on the day 8 B'atz', which thus serves as a beginning date for the 260-day cycle as a whole.

Chuen signifies the gestation period in the womb—hence the *tzolk'in* itself, for the gestation period is one of the primary metaphors of the calendar and its meaning. The 260 divining seeds are thus also under the influence of Chuen, which thereby represents the future. Time is the movement of Ajaw, which is the K'iche' word for the Divine Power.

This day sign represents the energy that oriented the first wise ones to form humanity; it is the warp and woof from which the Maker and Modeler wove the thread of all our lives. As it is the beginning, so it is also the end of the universe. In this respect, Chuen is symbolic of time itself, its development and its movement.

Among the Maya, weaving is one of the most complex and beautiful of the arts. It is the epitome of "women's wisdom." The blanket you purchase in the marketplace is a symbolic universe unto itself, for the entire cosmos is said to be like a tangle of threads which must be "unbundled" in order to be woven into a harmonious universe. The world we live in is an orderly pattern, a beautifully woven blanket; but the Underworld below us, Xib'alb'a, is a tangle of chaotic threads, primal and as yet without order. The paths of the planets, of the sun and moon and stars, are a part of that majestically woven pattern. The tangled threads of the Underworld touch our own world in many places, like conduits of energy between one world and the next. These are the places of power, the sacred places alive with magic.[1]

We weave words in the same way that we can weave a blanket. Maya priests are, by their very nature, prayer-makers, for all ceremony is attended with prayer. To pray is to speak with the greatest eloquence of which we are capable; the *Pop Wuj* tells us that the Gods created human beings so that we might sing out in praise of the divine force that created us. To weave our prayers with words of supreme eloquence is yet another way of weaving a sense of implicate order into the cosmos.

In the *Pop Wuj*, the day sign B'atz' is also represented by Jun B'atz' and Jun Chowen, the twins One Monkey and One Artisan.[2] In the beginning, they were of human form. They were the first practitioners of the arts; it was they who kept our First Grandmother amused when the Hero Twins were in the Underworld by playing their flutes for her, singing songs and painting pictures. The younger pair of Hero Twins was mistreated by these half-brothers, who were jealous of them and who egotistically conspired with our First Grandmother to make sure the younger brothers would receive no food at the family hearth. Instead, the Hero Twins were forced to provide food for all the others.

In the end, they got even. They coaxed One Monkey and One Artisan into a tree, ostensibly to retrieve some birds killed by the Hero Twins but stuck in the branches. No sooner had the two artists ascended than the tree magically began to grow into the sky, leaving One Monkey and One Artisan stranded. Then another magical transformation occurred: they turned into monkeys. They finally succeeded in getting down from the trees and returning to the home of their grandmother, but First Grandmother just laughed at their ridiculous appearance. They retreated back to the sanctuary of the forest, and remain monkeys to this very day. Despite the fact that they were humbled and turned into animals for their envy of their brothers and their excessive egotism, they were nevertheless prayed to by the flautists and singers among the ancient people, and the writers and carvers prayed to them as well. Chuen is still regarded as the *nawal* of artists and of all the arts, especially weaving.

Upon this most auspicious day, we may voice our intent that all we have requested from the universe may be freely given to us. This is an auspicious day for all artistic projects. In fact, it is an auspicious day to begin projects of any sort, for this day sign represents "the thread of life," the weaving of the loom of existence. Thus this is the best day to "weave" any matter or project to its perfect completion, as well as to untangle or "unweave" any problem. It is also one of the best days to attract a love partner into one's life and upon which to be married.

Chuen Natives

Those born under the day sign Chuen spin the thread of life with skill and grace. There isn't much that they aren't good at. They can be lucky with money and lucky in love all at the same time. In keeping with the symbolism of thread and weaving, there is a Mayan saying about these folks to the effect that they can "roll things up" with great ease. They can have anything they want, and they expend less effort in getting it than most people.

They know things without needing to be taught—including deep, metaphysical, spiritual things. Most of them have a mystical streak to them, even if it is often well disguised by their practicality. Painful, existential doubt about the existence of a divine power just isn't their style. They can easily perceive and flow with the balance between the material and the spiritual aspects of life.

True to the myth of the monkey twins who were patrons of the fine arts to the ancient Maya—and the monkey is still regarded as the animal totem associated with this day sign—Chuen natives often show significant talent for one or more of the fine arts; they can become excellent painters, writers, and musicians. At the same time, they are well grounded in reality, with less of a tendency to be as "spaced out" as other artistic types. Their combination of cleverness and insight makes them good at business. They are effective and efficient at making plans. Even though they seldom run into many obstacles on their road to success, they are tenacious in tackling the problems that they do encounter.

Chuen is considered one of the best days upon which to be married, so it ought not to be surprising that those who are born upon this day are fortunate and enthusiastic about human relationships. Their biggest problem in this area of life lies in the fact that they seek and expect perfection. After all, they quickly get the point of any endeavor and have a natural ability to untangle the complex weaving of existence, shaping their lives successfully and "rolling up" everything in their path. They have a tendency to expect the same from a partner, and can quickly become disappointed when other mortals don't have as easy a time with the game of life as they do. But once they make a commitment to a relationship, they will work hard to make it a successful one, bringing to it the same combination of talent and enthusiasm that they bring to everything else.

The same unrealistic desire for perfection that may cloud their human relationships sometimes applies to almost any aspect of life, and herein lies the dark side of this most fortunate of day signs. Blessed with the ability to sail through life with ease, they just don't understand why other people sometimes have difficulties getting by. Like the monkey twins of the ancient myth, Chuen natives can be a bit arrogant and egotistical; they can be quite dismissive and have little patience with those less fortunate than themselves—which is almost everyone. Because their mythic totems are twins, they can manifest a great deal of duality—twins are associated with the number two, and hence with the primary Mayan dualities of dark and light, woman and man, moon and sun. Chuen people can have a Jekyll and Hyde streak that shifts from their charming, talented, and giving side to their egotistical arrogant side in a hot minute. Sometimes that strong Chuen personality is just too much, and other people can easily perceive them as overbearing.

They place a high value on family and community, and tend to become more and more active in social and civic affairs as they mature and grow older. More often than not, they will end up as the leaders and authority figures of their own family systems—the matriarchs and patriarchs of the clan. This is equally true of their role in society at large. They often develop into community leaders.

Many Chuen natives have more energy and power during the night than during the day.

Eb
(E)
The Road of Life

To the Maya, time is "a man walking along the road." In a Mayan creation tale dating from perhaps the late 16th century, four Maya women see a man's footprints along a path. They proceed to measure the footprints "in accordance with the Word of the Mistress of the World." By so doing, they create time, the Sacred Calendar itself.[3] To the Maya, all of time is perceived as a path. The gods walk the path; so do human beings. In that sense, the path of time is the road of history as well.

This day sign is the path of destiny, the Road of Life. In Yucatec, this sign is called Eb, a word which means a stairway or a ladder, as if we were climbing to the top of a pyramid, one which symbolizes the structure of the heavens in ancient myth. The day sign Eb represents all the mystical paths or stairways that lead between the heavens, the world, and Xib'alb'a. It is the spiritual path which we walk. Many Native American traditions refer to the path of human life as a road; this same metaphor is a part of Mayan spirituality, and a spiritual teacher is often known as a "Road Guide." This day sign is the *nawal* of all such travelers and all such guides, as well as of all the roads upon which we walk in the course of our lives. It is, in and of itself, a kind of benediction.

Another commonly known meaning of this sign is "the tooth," and teeth are an esoteric symbol for all the things which mark our path along the Road of Life. Eb is also sometimes taken to symbolize "human being" as well, since the Maya regard the teeth as a particularly human thing, and one which distinguishes us from the gods.

Author Martin Prechtel tells the saga of "The Toe Bone and the Tooth,"[4] in which the primordial Goddess is slain and dismembered. Only a few bones remain, among which are a toe bone (the toes help us to walk the Road of Life) and a tooth. Her human lover—for all men are ultimately the lovers of the Goddess—tries to chant her back to life because he possesses her toe bone and tooth. But instead of restoring the Goddess to her original unity, he creates a new and beautiful creature—a human woman.

When the Hero Twins set forth to challenge the Lords of the Underworld, they travel the path of the Milky Way or road of souls, following it through the sky until they reach a crossroads, and then they take the dark or black road that leads to Xib'alb'a. This crossroads is the place where the ecliptic and the Milky Way cross at the Galactic Center. The starry path of the Milky Way is the White Road or *saq b'e*; a yellow (sometimes said to be green) road follows the ecliptic eastward while a red road follows it westward. The dark swathe of sky which we call the Great Rift in the Milky Way and which marks the Galactic Center is known among the Maya to this very day as the black road or the Road to Xib'alb'a, and it is this road

that the Hero Twins choose. This is yet another meaning of the day
sign Eb.

As above, so below.… the road to the Otherworld lies not only
in the heavens above us, but upon the earth as well. Throughout
the Yucatan, there are the remains of ancient causeways made of
white stone. These are also known as "white roads," (*sac beob* in the
Yucatec plural), and may have been intended as earthly counterparts
for the Milky Way—and perhaps for other celestial pathways as
well. Traveling in perfectly straight lines along the geomantic energy
paths of the Mayan world, they may have linked one sacred site
with another.

On this day we give thanks for the Road of Life upon which
we continually walk, for this sign represents the Road itself. It is the
best possible day upon which to begin a journey. It is also a most
favorable day for the initiation of any business manner or for the
signing of contracts.

Eb Natives

Eb natives have an innate curiosity about the world around them
which makes them perpetual students of life. The most common
expression of their curiosity is through travel; those born on the
day of the Road of Life often seem destined to walk that road
perpetually, and they are among the most enthusiastic travelers of all
the day signs. In the human body, this day sign corresponds to the
soles of our feet, upon which we walk. These natives are blessed—
or cursed—with the spirit of adventure; perpetually restless, they
enjoy taking the path untrodden. Sometimes their questing spirit
leads them to take risks. They make some of the best merchants and
traders that you will ever meet.

Their wanderings and their explorations frequently endow
them with wisdom. Their life experience and good nature can turn
them into genuine sages in their later years; they may develop into
guides for the road as well as travelers upon it. Because of their
concern for social and political values in the world around them,
they can become political leaders in their own right.

Those born on an Eb day are endowed with a large number
of good qualities. Eb natives commonly enjoy a long, healthy life.

They work hard at whatever they turn their hands to, and they work with a cheerful good will. Kind hearted and generous, they like people and sincerely enjoy helping others. They need to learn to trust, however, as that is something that does not come naturally to them. They also need to learn to see the positive side of situations and events around them, for they have a naturally suspicious quality when it comes to human nature. They want to like you, but they don't know if they can trust you. Their vigilance serves them well when they are traveling, but not so well when dealing with friends and family.

They make good parents, and over the course of time they acquire the kind of life wisdom which is meant to be shared with others. Natural story tellers, Eb natives have the gift of gab. They were born to serve as subjects of fascination to their grandchildren. They frequently have good taste in art, and many of them are collectors.

They tend to have numerous relationships in life, for their restless spirit is seldom satisfied with a single relationship. They are explorers of the human heart, just as they are explorers of the world around them. Because of their intrinsic good nature, most of their relationships will be fortunate, though one could not exactly describe them as the most faithful of partners. They tend to have more friends with members of the opposite sex than with their own, which is another reason for their many relationships. But they gain a great deal from seeing things from a different perspective, and it is usually a positive experience for them to favor the company of the opposite sex.

While the road is beautiful in its own right, it helps to have somewhere to go. Without a goal in mind, Eb natives can become more than a little aimless and wander without a clear sense of direction. They may be as cheerful and enthusiastic as ever, but they have no destination in mind. They need to keep the end of the road in sight, and to have a goal to strive for.

Perhaps their worst qualities arise when they invest themselves too strongly in their opinions, always needing to be right. In these cases they may easily become argumentative, even combative. They can be highly manipulative as well.

Their animal totem is the bobcat and their bird is the thrush. Eb natives can most often be found far from the place of their birth. They flourish in foreign countries and make cheerful, successful expatriates.

Eb is one of the four Year Lords. As well as those born on an Eb day, those born in an Eb year will also manifest many of the qualities of this day sign.

Ben
(Aj)
The Resurrection of the Corn

As the Hero Twins, Junajpu and Xb'alanke, are about to journey into the Underworld to challenge the Lords of Death in a game of handball, they each plant an ear of corn in their grandmother's patio. They tell her that if the corn withers, it means they are dead, but if it sprouts again, they are once more alive.

The corn withers when the Hero Twins die, but then returns to life when the Twins travel the paths of the Underworld and conquer death.

This day sign is the inner voice and the spiritual intent of our First Grandmother, when she prayed for a sign that her grandsons had survived their trials in the Underworld. In fact, the K'iche' word itself, *Aj* (pronounced "ah" with a very slight guttural "k" sound at the end), appears in this passage of the book and is part of a language pun intended to draw the reader's attention to the fact that the sacred *Pop Wuj* is discussing the metaphysical meaning of this day sign.

This is a day sign of strength, of resurrection, of the triumph of life over death. This sign symbolizes the cornstalk (a stalk of sugar cane in some Mayan communities), a pillar, or world tree that connects heaven and earth. It symbolizes all the seven virtues that are entwined with strength, triumph, resurrection, and the union of heaven and earth.

The seven virtues of Mayan philosophy are elemental principles—in contrast to the seven sins or "shames," which are symbolized by purely human failings. The four elements—Fire, Earth, Air, and Water—are regarded as "virtues." Their energy is pure. In Mayan thinking, the divine principle in nature can be expressed in terms of the polarity of Heart of Sky and Heart of Earth; these too are counted among the seven virtues. Finally, there is the Center, the place where the world pillar or world tree is planted (just like the cornstalk in First Grandmother's house). This vital center of all things, or *axis mundi*, is the seventh virtue. Throughout the world's mythologies, this central axis is symbolized by a great tree that connects the various worlds. The World Tree is the center of all things, and it is the essence of this day sign.

The Aztecs also linked this day sign with resurrection and the triumph of life over death, for they associated this sign, more than any other, with Quetzalcoatl, the Feathered Serpent—although the contemporary Mayan tradition is different in this respect, assigning the Feathered Serpent archetype to the day signs Chicchan (K'iche': Kan) and Ik' (K'iche': Iq').

Though the Feathered Serpent has been worshiped all over Mesoamerica since earliest times, the Aztecs reverenced the memory of a Toltec spiritual teacher, Topiltzin Quetzalcoatl, who was said to have been born upon this day (Acatl in the Nahuatl or Aztec tongue) and who may have been regarded as an incarnation or avatar of the deity Feathered Serpent. The legend asserts that he preached a religion of light and higher consciousness; but the people of that time and place were not ready to receive his message, and he was cast out. It is said that he was immolated upon a funeral pyre, and that he rose to the sky as the planet Venus—which, with its appearances and disappearances, is yet another symbol of resurrection and rebirth, of the journey to the Underworld and back again. Some believed that

Topiltzin Qutezalcoatl would one day return—and in a day and year associated with the day sign Ben or Aj. This belief may have contributed greatly to the downfall of the Aztecs, for Cortez arrived at the time that had been prophesied.

Ben is considered one of the best days upon which to deal with matters of the home. After all, the Hero Twins planted their regenerative cornstalk in the home of First Grandmother; in and through the home, their resurrection was known and perceived. This day is the very *nawal* of the home, and especially of the children within it, for our children are none other than ourselves reborn; they are living symbols of our power to regenerate and renew ourselves, for they are created from our own vital energy, which they carry with them into the future, into eternity.

Ben is a day to give thanks for the place in which we live; it is connected with the nourishment and flourishing of all things related to the home, whether human, animal or plant. It symbolizes the energy and vitality of life itself. It strengthens the family system and lends vital energy and power to all matters within one's household. It is the day *par excellence* to pray for the health of children.

Ben Natives

Ben people are decisive and authoritative, and mostly cheerful. In Mayan communities, the local civic council often works in collaboration with a council of indigenous town elders. These Native leaders carry a staff; the ones that I saw were usually tipped with silver and sporting a tassel. The staff is the symbol of the council member's authority, and some K'iche' Daykeepers say that the day sign Aj represents the staff carried by these village leaders; one of the most common K'iche' meanings of the word *aj* is as an honorific title referring to someone's profession (as in *aj q'ij*, meaning one whose profession is the day, i.e. Daykeeper). It is this sort of localized, community-focused sense of authority which is so characteristic of the day sign Ben. The medical correspondence of this day sign is the spinal column through which the majestic serpent energy flows.

Natives of Ben are capable of living fully and completely in this world; they are masters of the physical plane. But their talents extend far beyond the merely physical. At best, they may see far enough to perceive worlds beyond this one; Ben natives are known for their clairvoyant abilities. Many of them are endowed with an authentic sense of vision. Their tendency toward deep thinking makes them great researchers and scholars, and they can do well in academia if they choose to follow that direction in life. They also make excellent psychologists; both Sigmund Freud and Carl Jung were born upon the day 10 Ben. Nor do these people lack the drive and commitment necessary to turn their dreams into reality; Ben natives are fiercely passionate about their ideals and desires, and their passionate commitment endows them with the energy to achieve things.

With so much energy at their disposal, it is interesting to note that few Ben natives will appear on a typical list of "famous people" born under particular day signs. This is partly because they avoid the spotlight and prefer to work at home and behind the scenes, albeit with great authority. They are not big travelers; this day sign is the *nawal* of hearth and home, as well as of the children in one's house. Ben natives like to stay at home and usually favor their place of birth. Another reason that they so seldom show up on "famous people" lists is because of a peculiar tendency that they have to be ignored or unnoticed by those around them. They may often feel that they are "tilting at windmills," with no one in sight with whom to share their great dreams.

Often, it is necessary for them to learn to focus their considerable energies in one place. Without a "guiding star," they can change like the wind, moving from one project to another, good at starting things but not very good at finishing them. But a great vision has its price, for we may sometimes envision more than is good for us; these people have a tendency to be greedy; nothing is ever enough. Sometimes they take life so seriously that they appear withdrawn and peculiar to others.

They can be so intensely passionate about a cause that they lose their practicality, becoming insensitive to the needs of others and consequently impossible to deal with. They can be overly emotional, tempestuous characters. Their desire for justice and harmony can become obsessive, and their search for perfection may be both a blessing and a curse. At worst they are unable to manifest their talents and thus they sometimes live in poverty, but they usually prevail in the end, like the resurrected corn.

Rich or poor, they typically have a talent for matters of the home, as well as for understanding and relating to children and nurturing the growth of plants. While this concern for hearth and home is characteristic of both sexes, the Ben women in particular will often have a special gift with both children and critters.

Ben natives are nature lovers. Their animal totems are the armadillo and the honeybee.

Ix
(I'x)
The Jaguar

This is the sign of the Jaguar; it is a feline and an essentially feminine energy. The jaguar is the most powerful animal in the jungle; in the deep shadows of its forest world, it is a kind of deity. Like the jaguar that is its animal totem, this day sign is filled with spiritual potency, strength, force, and vitality. It is symbolic of Mother Earth, the Sacred Earth, which, in our own culture, we call "Mother Nature." There is nothing about the energy inherent in the day sign Ix that is not wholly and completely natural. It is the sign of raw animal vitality.

This day sign also represents an aspect of the sacred energy embodied in the element Water, which of course is an important part of the world of nature. There are several signs that partake of different aspects of the energy of this element (see also Imix, which symbolizes oceans, and Muluc, which symbolizes rain).

Ix is specifically associated with fresh water, the water of springs and rivers and streams. This is the water that emerges from Sacred Mother Earth to give life and sustenance to us all.

Ix is often said to be the day sign associated with Mayan (as opposed to Catholic) altars. It should be remembered that while some Mayan altars are erected in family shrines in private homes, others are comprised of natural features in the landscape, usually rock. As the day sign of Mother Earth or Mother Nature, Ix represents all such natural altars as well as the vital, earth-centered energy that they emanate. It is the primal source that u nderlies and activates the planet's geomantic grid of power. It is the very body of the Earth Mother.

In terms of the mythology of the K'iche' epic *Pop Wuj*, the day sign I'x is symbolic of the first Four Fathers of humanity, the *B'alameb'* or Jaguar Men. It was they who guided the people in ancient, primordial times, and who led them upon their migrations or journeys in search of the light; it was they who lit the fires and sang the prayers when the light finally dawned and the sun took its place in the sky to shine down upon a new world, the world we still live in to this very day.

Each day sign partakes of the eternal polarities of existence, and thus has its negative as well as its positive manifestation. In that context, this day sign is connected with the so-called Seven Sins or—to use a more precise and accurate translation of the Spanish term used often by the Maya, *siete sinverguenzas*—the Seven Shames. The Mayan concept of "sin" is quite different than the Seven Sins of Catholic Christianity, and the "shames" are usually listed as follows: excessive pride, ambition, envy, lying, criminal activity, ingratitude, and ignorance.

Note that the so-called "sins" so common in Christianity, Hinduism, etc. that relate to the consumption of food or enjoyment of human sexuality have no place in the Mayan cosmo-conception. Unlike other religious traditions, Mayan spirituality does not regard the human body and its needs as essentially negative, something unpleasant from which we must turn away. The human condition is seen as essentially positive; thus the "sins" or "shames" involve inappropriate or ungrateful behavior in terms of the community and our dealings with the other human beings with whom we share this blessed, earth-centered existence.

To put it in a different way, we may say that Ix is the *nawal* of many powerful and important things, of altars and sacred space; it is the whole exquisite world of plants and flowers and rocks that the Tz'utujil Maya of Santiago Atitlan refer to as the Blossoming World. And thus, by the magical alchemy of opposites and polarities, Ix is also the *nawal* of all those shameful behaviors that prevent us from interacting in a spirit of gratitude and graciousness with the natural world, both earthly and human, that surrounds us.

Those who keep the Days always set aside a special place or household altar for prayer, meditation, incense, candles, and so on. This is the day to give thanks that we have created such a sacred place in our lives. It is a day we may fruitfully devote to introspection and meditation, if the opportunity is there. It is also regarded as a favorable day to practice any kind of divination. Since this day sign is filled with so much vitality and strength (the strength of nature itself), it is an excellent day to ask for fortitude, both physical and mental.

Ix Natives

As is clear from everything written above, Ix natives have a special relationship with Mother Earth. Since all good things come from the Earth Mother, these people, with their deep connection to the source of our being, often become quite wealthy, sharing in Her abundance.

As we shall see (in the next chapter), all day signs are masculine or yang from the point of view of Mayan cosmovision, while all numbers are essentially feminine or yin. Nevertheless, within the parameters of this cosmic duality, there are certain day signs that have a more "feminine" tone than others. Ix has a very feminine energy; even the men will seem somewhat androgynous, while the women will be very feminine indeed, often bewitchingly so. Both the women and the men are said to make especially good parents.

All the same, one should not mistake their feminine nature for "softness." On the contrary, it is the eternal strength of the Earth Mother that is represented by this sign, and Ix natives are typically agile and clever and endurable. They are energetic and passionate, with great reserves of natural strength. They have an abundance of vigor and energy with which to pursue their goals, and they often seem to be specially endowed with all kinds of practical abilities.

Though their connection with the earth makes them realistic, they are also capable of dreaming great dreams and acting upon them courageously. Sometimes they need to learn how to take a wider vision; they can be so "earth-centered" and pragmatic that they may try to deny their magical side, but it usually catches up with them. Despite their enormous stamina, which seems rooted in Mother Earth herself and equally inexhaustible, Ix natives sometimes tend to have health issues. These are challenges and "wake-up calls," however, which are designed to make them aware of the mystic or the healer within them. They will need to access their own personal magic in order to remain healthful. Then they are free to become the shamans and magicians that they really are.

If they are capable of dreaming great dreams and confronting great obstacles with courage, it is also true that they may sometimes pursue their goals to the point of recklessness or even silliness. They can be vain and quick-tempered. They like to be the center of attention. Ix natives possess great personal power. It is always a temptation to wield as much power as we possibly can, and these natives may sometimes go too far in that quest, becoming cruel and unbalanced (Richard Nixon was born on an Ix day).

At the worst, they can lean toward what we have called the Seven Shames, since this day sign is also the *nawal* of these difficult aspects of life. Ix natives can be proud, envious, ungrateful and deceitful. However, some Daykeepers have remarked that these issues often center around those who were born on 7 Ix. This is only partly due to the fact that there are seven such "shames." As we shall see when we study the symbolism of the numbers, 7 has more than a few difficulties attached to it. Those born upon 7 Ix may need to steer a more rigorous, fiercely honest course through life in order to access their true nature. Other numbers, like 1, 2, 6 and 8 are more likely to show the positive attributes of this sign without as much effort.

As participants in the geomantic grid of power which flows through Mother Earth, Ix natives often have a special relationship with sacred sites, especially those involving ceremonial centers, temples and pyramids from whatever culture or civilization. They can gain great energy from visiting sacred places.

They are good with animals, too, and of course their totem is the jaguar.

Men
(Tz'ikin)
The Vision of the Bird

Once, in the earliest times, the people wandered in dim light, guided by the Fathers, the four Jaguar Men. The Morning Star, Venus, cast a faint light, but it was the light that precedes the sun, the early pre-dawn light, for as of yet there was no sun. The Jaguar Men burned copal incense and prayed, and the gods sent them the sun. As they witnessed that first glorious sunrise of the Fourth World, our present world,

> *...the animals, small and great, were happy. They all came up from the rivers and canyons; they waited on all the mountain peaks. Together they looked toward the place where the sun came out.*
>
> *So then the puma and jaguar cried out, but the first to cry out was a bird, the parrot by name. All the animals were truly happy. The eagle, the white vulture, small birds, great birds spread their wings.... They were overjoyed....* [5]

This day symbolizes that first cry of delight at the rising of the sun. In some traditions, it is said that the *maq'uq'* or quetzal, rather than the parrot, was the first bird to sing out. To the Aztecs, this day sign was the eagle, whose voice is powerful and distinctive. Both the eagle and the quetzal may be taken as the totem animals of this day sign, which, in any case, represents the cry of joy and wonder at the beauty of the world and the precious light of day. Many Daykeepers think of this day sign simply as "the bird" without distinguishing between species. (This is what the K'iche' word *tz'ikin* actually means.)

Birds live in the sky; the eagle flies high above the world. Thus this sign mediates between the human world and the divine world of *Tz'aqol B'itol*, the Maker and Modeler. It represents space, sky, light, clouds, and the purity of the cold air above us.

The day sign Men is both warm and cold. It is the polarity of yin and yang, sky and earth. It is the warmth of Heart of Sky, Heart of Earth, and some would say that it is the mediating principle between these two polarities as well. [6]

The K'iche' word for this day sign, *Tz'ikin*, clearly embodies the meaning behind the symbol. While the word may simply mean "bird," one may also etymologize the word *tz'i* as "authority," while *q'in* means Father Sun, hence *Tz'ikin* is the Authority of the Sun. Don Rigoberto calls this day sign the guardian of the sun and of cosmic space, for it is the great intermediary between the worlds; the joyful cry of the bird as it flies through cosmic space nurtures the power of the sun and preserves its purity. The sunflower is the botanical correspondence for this day sign.

Flying high above the world, the eagle sees all things clearly. Seeing, he cries out for that which he desires. So do we, the members of the human tribe. We may cry out for love, for a vision, or for prosperity.

Most mortals cry out for prosperity first and foremost. Thus Tz'ikin is the *nawal* of economic well-being and good fortune. Unlike some spiritual traditions, Mayan spirituality does not regard material prosperity as essentially undesirable or "non-spiritual." Economic well-being is a valuable tool that helps us to manifest our dreams, our visions, and to bring our highest aspirations into reality.

Upon this day, we may thank the universe for whatever prosperity we currently enjoy while honestly expressing the intention that more abundance may enter our lives. This is the best of all possible days upon which to begin a business venture, or to bring one to completion and fruition.

This day is as fortunate for love as it is for money; it is also appropriate to pay attention to relationship issues on Men days.

Pay attention to dreams as well, for this is a day upon which one may experience powerful and important revelations through dreams. Sometimes our visions are worldly ones, tied in to our desire for prosperity. Sometimes our visions partake more of the Otherworld than of this one. The day sign Men, like the eagle flying above us, can see into both worlds. In this day sign, we encounter visions that encompass both heaven and earth.

Men Natives

Natives of the day sign Men "cry out" (like the quetzal or the eagle) for just about everything; they seek all good things, material and spiritual. This is one of the day signs especially associated with breadth of vision, for the eagle can see great distances when he is far above, in the clouds. In fact, in the human body this day sign corresponds to the eyes. These folks usually get what they ask for; this is a fortunate day sign.

One will often see it written that natives of Men are "lucky with money" and destined to become rich. This is often the case, but not always. As one Daykeeper told me, "These keywords for the day signs simply identify the *issue*. With Tz'ikin people, money is the issue. Whether or not they are successful with it is due to their own choices in life."

Natives of Men are most likely to be successful when they are their own bosses. They are fiercely independent and don't take orders well from others. They don't do well with rules and regulations and get very frustrated if forced to punch a time clock and answer to other people. If they are allowed to make their own way in life, they are capable of developing any number of talents which will bring them success and prosperity. They are often gifted in a variety of arts, and usually in mercantile enterprises as well. They are clever, accurate, honest and truthful; many of them are eloquent as well, and their gift for words helps to make them good intermediaries between opposing points of view. Let us remember that one of the essential meanings of this day sign has to do with the position that birds occupy, midway between heaven and earth, between the gods and the mortals. Natives of Men can be natural mediators.

Most natives of this day sign are very sociable and popular, with lots of friends. They can be the life of any party. But this easy-going good cheer can be one of their greatest obstacles to success, just as it can be one of their greatest assets. They are somewhat erratic and get bored easily, in which case they may simply walk away from projects without bothering to bring them to completion. Their social butterfly tendencies can make them both eccentric and forgetful. They sometimes exaggerate and can be both lazy and irresponsible. They love to be flattered and can easily be taken in by those who stroke their big egos.

They are commonly said to be fortunate at relationships—and they may have many relationships in the course of a lifetime. They have a need to experience the energy of the opposite sex, whether as friends or lovers, and they usually do it quite well. But the same drawbacks that apply to other areas of their life can also extend to their relationships. They sometimes tend to be players, libidinous and not terribly reliable.

But perhaps their most negative quality is a tendency to become pessimistic when the world does not respond immediately to their visions and great dreams. They need to keep their spirits up and not become discouraged.

More often than not, Men natives simply need time. They may not be willing to settle down and "get serious" until later in life; but when they finally do so, they can focus on manifesting their vast dreams and visions, bringing the world of the divine down from the clouds to land upon the earth gently and successfully. It is beneficial for them to be in the mountains and other high places physically, too, for it inspires them and connects them with their true inner nature.

Cib
(Ajmaq)
Forgiveness

In one of the Yucatec prophetic books, the Chilam Balam of Chumayel, it is written: "On 6 Cib the first candle was made; it became light when there was neither sun nor moon." 7

A candle may be lit for many purposes. In Mayan ceremony, candles are offered up to the *nawales* of the day signs; they are lit in remembrance of the spirits of our ancestors as well. In the Catholic churches, Mayan people often light votive candles when they pray for forgiveness, on account of their wrongdoings.

All of these meanings are inherent in the day sign Cib. The word itself means "wax" in the Yucatec language. Before the coming of the Spanish, there were no candles; wax was symbolic of the industrious bee, which is still one of the animal totems associated with this day sign. When seen from that perspective, it is important to remember that Cib represents the sacred energy of the element Earth, which thrives and hums like a beehive. Cib is the day sign of Mother Earth, who gives us our life. Without our ancestors, for whom we burn candles on Cib days, we would not be here. They have become part of the earth itself, part of the nourishment that sustains us.

Another animal totem for Cib is the vulture. The vulture, an eater of carrion, disposes of the garbage accumulated in our lives, just as we burn away the spirit of our misdeeds with candles and pray for forgiveness. While the K'iche' word *ajmaq* can literally mean "sinner," or to be more culturally precise, "master of sins," this day sign is more often said to refer to the forgiveness rather than the commission of misdeeds. Ajmaq, above all other signs, is symbolic of "karmic clean-out." [8]

As we have seen, the day sign Ix is said to be the *nawal* of the so-called Seven Shames or Seven Sins: excessive pride, ambition, envy, lying, criminal activity, ingratitude, and ignorance. Both Ix and Cib could be regarded as *nawales* of these challenging aspects of life, though perhaps from a different perspective.

Cib is related to the myth of 7 Macaw, a character in the *Pop Wuj* who exemplifies the Seven Shames. The macaw bird was perched on top of the tree standing at the center of the universe, the world tree that forms the axis of all being. From his lofty vantage point, looking down upon the world below him, he began to assume that he was God. But he was mistaken. Only Ajaw is God. The macaw was deluded by pride, ambition, and ignorance. The gods sent the Hero Twins to dislodge him from his perch, causing him to see that, in reality, he was only a silly bird.

It is said that the first human beings could see all things clearly. Their perception was so extraordinary that they were like the gods themselves. And yet human beings had been created to sing out with song and poetry in praise of the gods—not to challenge them by setting themselves at the same level. Thus the gods created "sin" or *maq*, a curtain of smoke that hides us from the presence of Ajaw—or, in the poetic words of the *Pop Wuj*, the gods breathed a cloudy mist on the mirror of our consciousness that serves to obscure our vision. If we were able to clean the mirror, we would see the world as the gods see it. Instead, we are mortal. We are human. We must struggle with the Seven Shames that keep us anchored to our Mother the Earth, and be grateful for each moment of clear perception that allows us to see the world through the eyes of gods, the world as it truly is.

This is in part a day of the Otherworld. It is good to remember friends and family members who have passed away from us, and to light a candle or two in their memory. If there is anything for which you seek forgiveness, today is the day to ask for it; the ancestors are listening, and incline themselves favorably to our affairs. This day is the day, above all others, to ask forgiveness for any of the Seven Shames or Sins that may afflict us.

Cib Natives

Natives of the day sign Cib usually give the appearance of being extremely clever, which in fact they are. They possess boundless curiosity about the world around them; at best, they are interested in almost everything. It may be difficult to notice how deeply they are exploring people and situations all around them; Cib folks tend to be "the quiet type." They observe things without drawing undue attention to themselves. They are typically shrewd and astute; consequently they may be fortunate with money. They are inherently analytical and not easily fooled.

A great many of their interests—and they always have many interests—are the result of the influence of past lives. Cib is one of the signs most closely associated with the ancestors, and Cib people are often acting out themes and situations from their karmic past. Sometimes these past issues can arise with startling vigor and unpleasantness—Cib people are said to be among those most often afflicted with religious fanaticism or, in the opposite mode, atheistic cynicism. At the very least, it may be said that they have a predisposition to be dissatisfied with the religious path of their upbringing. They are eternal seekers. At best, their search is conducted with tolerance for others and equanimity towards all rather than with fanaticism.

They take great pride in their accomplishments. They are prudent and have a powerful sense of responsibility, and may even be overly responsible, obsessed with details. Their innate conservatism about life usually keeps them fairly healthy. They don't take many risks with their bodies. They take things slowly in life and usually get what they want.

Despite the somewhat introverted tone so common with natives of Cib, they tend to have quite a few relationships in the course of a lifetime. Their gentleness and quiet charm makes them a favorite with others.

Responsibility can be an "issue." While Cib people are often overly responsible and even obsessive, they can also be among the first to be irresponsible as parents or unfaithful in relationships. In fact, they are somewhat notorious among the day signs when it comes to walking the straight and narrow path in their relationships (the female sexual organs are sometimes said to be the medical correspondence of this day sign). This is a challenge for them, though there will of course always be some who meet the challenge successfully.

Irresponsibility and adultery may not be their only vices; it is with good reason that this day sign is associated with the seven shames. Too often, Cib's innate sense of pride becomes inflated into vanity and conceit, and as has been remarked elsewhere, pride and its inevitable consequences (such as ambition, envy, and a tendency to stretch the truth for one's own purposes) are regarded as particularly difficult human traits by the Maya. Cib natives can retreat within themselves, enclosing themselves in a shell and refusing to share their feelings or thoughts with others. This makes them seem gloomy rather than charming, and they can indeed be depressive.

One of the best things about this sign of "forgiveness" is that even among those who stumble into any number of indulgences, there is something in their intrinsic good nature which allows them to shed all their wrong-doings like a suit of ill-fitting clothes. Many Daykeepers say that their sins will always be forgiven them.

Since Cib is the sign of forgiveness, forgiveness can be one of their best qualities. Some will need to learn this skill over the course of time. Many of them, especially the overly responsible types, sometimes have difficulties accepting the faults of others. But in time, they almost always learn the virtue of tolerance, even if it takes them until later in life. Just as the word *cib*, in Yucatec, may symbolize a candle, they almost always achieve a certain modicum of "inner light" in the course of their lives.

Caban
(No'j)
The Vision of the Cosmos

In the Nahuatl tradition, this day sign was called Earthquake, although the actual word, *ollin*, signifies "movement" in general, and is etymologically related to the Nahuatl word for "heart," thus signifying a heartbeat or natural human rhythm. While Caban may still be regarded as the *nawal* of earthquakes and seismic disturbances, in the contemporary tradition the real "movement" or pulse is mental and intellectual. This ought to be seen from the general quality of movement associated with the human heartbeat, for the heart and the mind are inextricably linked—or, at least, they should be.

This sign symbolizes wisdom and ideas. It is the *nawal* of intelligence. The K'iche word for this day sign, *No'j*, actually means "thought," and is the word used in ordinary conversation to describe our thoughts and our ideas. Another keyword for this day sign, though somewhat overly simplified, might be "the Thinker."

But human ideas may be either positive or negative, and our thoughts often race back and forth without clarity or anchor, especially if they are disconnected from the ultimate, primal rhythm of the human heart. In Mayan folklore, there is a character called Juan No'j who exemplifies the mind's "trickster" nature. [9]   He appears as a dapper fellow, both courteous and clever, who typically offers us everything we want, especially money. But he will sell your soul to the devil sooner or later.

The mind can play tricks on us and get us into trouble. In

order for the mind to function properly, for our thoughts to become good and useful ideas that benefit not only ourselves but the larger community of which we are a part, we must learn to clarify our thinking. We have already seen (in Cib, above) that the Maya believe the first human beings could see all things clearly, like the gods. In order that we might not challenge the gods rather than worship them, the gods breathed a cloudy mist on the mirror of our consciousness that serves to obscure our vision. If we were able to clean the mirror, we would see the world as the gods see it. The day sign Caban teaches us to act with patience and pure intent in order to gain wisdom. Thus this sign symbolizes our aspiration to seek wisdom from Ajaw, for only Ajaw is truly wise.

One of the associated meanings of this day sign is "incense," and the Chilam Balam books say that "incense is the brains of heaven." One of the forms of incense most often used in Mayan ceremony is copal; our thoughts, prayers, and intentions rise to Ajaw with its smoke. This is why incense is associated with our *no'job*, our thoughts, and why it is part of the symbolism of this day sign.

This day sign also has a connection with the *tz'ite* tree, the seeds of which are used for divination—seeking answers to our problems from Ajaw, from the source. The divinatory ritual is another way in which we may seek the wisdom of Ajaw. Some Daykeepers assert that this is the best of all possible days upon which to consult a shaman who is adept at divining with the *tz'ite* seeds, and to ask Ajaw for answers to the questions that confront us in life.

Upon this day, we may ask the universe to grant us creativity in all our endeavors, and the intelligence to find solutions to all our challenges. We strive to realize the talents inherent within us. This day enlivens the intellect and enhances the eternal quest for wisdom.

Upon this day, we seek the contact with the divine energy that serves to clean the mirror of our consciousness. The energy of this day gives us a special gift to develop new ideas, new inspirations.

If the exigencies of daily life make it impossible for an apprentice to be initiated as an *aj q'ij* on the traditional day 8 B'atz', the day 8 No'j may be substituted.

Caban Natives

This is the sign of the Thinker. These people are creative and thoughtful and abundantly clever. They know how to analyze and dissect things with their minds. At best, their ideas are eminently practical and their problem-solving techniques are workable; this gives them natural leadership ability, whether in civil or spiritual matters, and they frequently become pillars of their communities. This is a very masculine sign, and its natives have a masculine tone regardless of their own gender.

Caban natives know how not to sweat the small stuff. They can exemplify tremendous patience, and they don't waste time worrying unnecessarily about trivial matters. So broad is their vision that they may occasionally neglect the details; there is a certain naiveté about Caban natives that renders them quite unaware of the ill intentions of others. Even when they blunder, their temperament is noble and high-minded. They are oriented towards the future, and frequently impatient of the present with all its "silly demands." Because they prefer the realm of the mind, they tend to live lives of extreme simplicity. They usually don't need to struggle much to meet the essentials involved in keeping themselves alive; prosperity comes naturally to them.

Needless to say, they love to read, and it is through books and other studies that they glean some of their best ideas. All the same, they should not be mistaken for the kind of dreamy intellectuals who accomplish nothing. To Caban natives, an idea is only important if they can make it manifest in reality. They are just as likely to express themselves through the arts as they are through politics or community service; their essential creativity and breadth of vision is often beautifully realized through words or music.

They have one of the best relationship records of all the day signs. They usually make wise choices in love, and they are able to weather the challenges that all relationships bring, remaining faithful and dependable throughout the years.

While Caban natives are good-hearted folk who tend to be greatly admired by the societies in which they live, they do have their darker, less developed side. Their quest for truth sometimes manifests as the kind of brutal honesty which is just plain tactless and hurtful. Though they do indeed value ideas that can be turned into reality, some of them simply lack the talent to make it all happen. Lost in their dreams and visions, they miss the practicalities necessary to turn inspiration into reality. They are not always the strongest of people, either; many of them possess a fragility that makes them go all to pieces when their grand plans don't work out. Some can be a bit overly proud of their clever ideas and their intellectual magic; vanity and self-importance are among their worst faults.

Knowledge and wisdom are two different things, it is true, but Caban people have a wonderful talent for pursuing the kind of knowledge that leads to genuine wisdom. It is no wonder that they tend to be so well liked by all those around them.

Their animal totems are the industrious woodpecker and the swift gazelle. It will surprise no one to discover that in terms of the human body, Caban is associated with the brain. They do well in high places filled with clear air and beautiful clouds; Caban natives were born to be close to Ajaw above us.

In general, the Maya prefer days with middle numbers, especially in terms of ceremony. In personal astrology, it is a bit more complicated. In any case, Caban has so much positive energy that it is one of the signs that does well with the higher, occasionally more difficult numbers. People born on 12 Caban can be quite unique.

Caban is one of the four Year Lords. As well as those who are born upon this day, those who are born in a Caban year will manifest many of the qualities of this day sign.

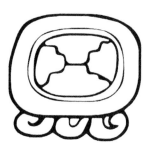

Etznab
(Tijax)
Obsidian Knife

Though many day signs vary in their names and meanings throughout the wider world of Mesoamerica, Etznab is almost universally perceived as a knife of flint or of obsidian. The black volcanic stone obsidian was connected with the Aztec deity Tezcatlipoca, who is known in the Classic Maya period as Kauil and in the *Pop Wuj* as Tohil. His Aztec name means "Smoking Mirror," and we shall hear more of him later on. Some have called him the dark god of human sacrifice. Others have called him a healer, a *curandero* or patron of *curanderos.*

In the *Pop Wuj*, the Hero Twins must endure many tests and challenges during their sojourn in the dark Underworld of Xib'alb'a. They are forced to spend the night in a number of different "houses," all of which are controlled by the Lords of the Underworld and all of which are fraught with peril. One of the most difficult such houses is called Chaim Ha or Razor House, a dark cave where sharp knives fly through the air. This day sign, symbolized by an obsidian knife (*chay*), represents the experience of Chaim Ha, the place of punishment or flint stones. Seen from the vantage point of its darker side, this day can be the *nawal* of suffering and of sudden death.

And yet, as the Hero Twins discover, the same knife that slashes our skin can also be used to supply us with food. They pacify the flying knives by reminding them of that fact, and therefore they emerge from their trial the next morning, whole of body and soul, the knives of suffering and sudden death transformed into an agricultural tool or, at best, into the scalpel of the healer.

The day sign Etznab embodies this very same duality. If it is a sign of suffering and wounding, it is also one of the quintessential signs of healing. It is the day sign of surgeons and physicians; or, among more traditional societies, of *curanderos* and folk healers. The obsidian knife cuts away disease. Tezcatlipoca, the God of the Smoking Mirror, has two faces. The mirror can be clouded, as we have seen (in Cib and Caban, above). Or it can be clear, reflecting the light of reality as it truly is.

The hieroglyph for Etznab is, in and of itself, suggestive of duality, and there are several polarities or dualities embodied within the symbolism of this day sign. It is said that Etznab is one of several day signs that embodies the basic polarity of woman and man, and though its most important medical correspondence is that of the teeth and the tongue, on an esoteric level it is symbolic of human sexual organs.

Etznab is also a day sign of both knowledge and misinformation. While the K'iche' name of this day sign, Tijax, reminds us of the word *tij*, implying a struggle, there are also associated words like *tijoj*, the verb meaning "to teach," and *tijobal*, meaning a classroom or school. At its best, this sharp knife cuts through illusion and ignorance, honing the fine edge of our thoughts into true wisdom. In this respect, Etznab is indeed a sign of education and teaching. But true to the duality inherent within the sign, information also has its dark side. Etznab can all too easily become a sign of gossip, malicious talk, quarreling, and "disinformation" pure and simple.

Etznab is the warrior and the healer. It is our choice as human beings as to how we shall use its energy. It is not a matter of destiny; we have the freedom to walk towards the darkness or towards the light.

The Daykeepers have named various different animal totems for this sign, including the toucan, the owl, and the wolf.

Etznab has a special connection with the mineral world, and with stones. Certain healers use stones, especially quartz crystal, as instruments of seeing, or even medical diagnosis (see Cauac, below). In terms of the physical world around us, Etznab also has a special connection with caves and with lightning storms.

The world is full of potential roadblocks and accidents. Upon this day, we pray for safety from all harm, and for the resolution of all conflict. This day has a special connection with healing and is favorable for health matters and the curing of disease, for the obsidian knife is capable of cutting away all evil, everything unhealthy. It is an auspicious day for all those involved in the healing professions. It is a day to resolve quarrels.

Etznab Natives

Interestingly enough, the official birth certificate of the revolutionary leader Che Guevara gives his birth date as a Muluc (Toj) day. But according to his mother, the birth certificate was incorrect, and he was in fact born on an Etznab or Tijax day.

One suspects that his mother must have been correct. Etznab is the warrior, always fighting for a cause, struggling valiantly until the bitter end. But Etznab is also the sign of the healer; Guevara was a medical doctor as well as a revolutionary. His colorful, adventurous, but frequently inconsistent and downright contradictory career is an almost perfect archetype of this day sign's inherent qualities.

These people are born contenders, always fighting for a cause. Unfortunately, they often pick the wrong cause, thereby acquiring a reputation as quarrelsome, contentious, angry individuals. They are certainly quick to anger, which can get them into a great deal of trouble. Much of their apparent quarrelsomeness comes from the fact that, beneath the surface, they are fragile and easily hurt. Consequently, other people take advantage of them, and they can become the subject of gossip, the first ones to get fired, or the victims of theft. It is also said that Etznab people are also notorious gossips and busybodies, frequently meddling in other peoples' business. They can be fussy, demanding, and downright absent-minded.

They don't do well with relationships. The women and the men both tend to be shy of commitment. Having such strong personalities, they frequently seek partners who are somewhat submissive in nature.

In the body, Etznab symbolizes the teeth and the tongue. The verb *tij* also means "to eat."

But the blade has two edges. These people make tremendous doctors and healers. Etznab is, par excellence, the sign of the surgeon. The obsidian knife cuts away disease and cleans out all that is in need of regeneration.

Some natives of this day sign are frail and prone to ill health. But there is a reason for this; their illnesses serve as an incentive, brought to them by their destiny, to learn the nature of true healing. If they can heal themselves, they can heal others. This is the archetype of the Wounded Healer.

Etznab natives can be extraordinary seers, and they often have an almost magical talent in their hands. One would not expect such visionary or mystical talents to appear among warriors, fighters, and contenders. But those born under Etznab will fool you. They can be both. Despite their cantankerous side, most of them are genuinely kind-hearted, with a great ability to care about others. They simply get worked up and cranky more easily than other folks. Their lives often seem subject to impulse; they can change course overnight. They are the ones who like to dance in lightning storms.

It has been noted that the duality of woman and man is one of the various polarities embodied in this day sign, and that in some sense it represents the human sexual organs. Many Etznab women are quite beautiful.

Etznab people also have a gift as educators, and can be intellectually astute. They make excellent journalists, linguists, and publishers. At best, their well-honed intellect makes them supremely rational, logical, able to mediate between opposing sides (duality again). But their "cutting edge" talents can make them somewhat devious as well, and endow them with a talent for intrigue; James Bond was probably born on an Etznab day. Needless to say, they make excellent politicians as well, thanks to their ability to manipulate the polarities and dualities of human existence.

At their very best, the natives of Etznab have the gift for being both intensely rational and able to access deep reserves of intuition.

Cauac
(Kawoq)
The Universal Community

This day sign is one of great potential as well as of great difficulty. In most Mesoamerican societies, it symbolized a rainstorm; it is still sometimes called the *nawal* of thunder. One of its animal totems, the turtle, is a water animal.

Rain can nourish us and cause the plants to grow; it feeds the Blossoming World. It can also inundate us with floodwaters and hence overpower us. Like the rain itself, this day sign both nourishes and inundates.

In the *Pop Wuj*, humanity's first Four Fathers, the Jaguar Men, burn copal incense as an offering when they call upon the sun of this Fourth World to rise for the first time. Clouds and clouds of incense took flight toward the heavens at that moment. In mythological terms, Cauac symbolizes this first great offering. It is the spirit in which we make sacrificial offerings, the spirit of resolution and reconciliation that blesses us and nourishes us when we surrender. It is the altar or table upon which those offerings are made.

As we have mentioned elsewhere (see the descriptions for Ix and Cib), the Mayan concept of wrongdoing or "sin" is inextricably linked with the way in which we relate to our community. This day sign is the very archetype of the community itself. Sometimes it is called "the universal community," and sometimes it is even referred to as "the celestial home of the gods." It is all about the way in which we interact with everything around us—people, earth, animals, and the Divine.

When it is said that Cauac symbolizes trouble and difficulty of all kinds, or that it is the *nawal* of all manner of disputes, we should see this in its proper context, which is a social one. The difficulties and misunderstandings ruled by this day sign are those that set us apart and separate us from the larger community. At the very heart of any community are the home and the family; Cauac is said to have a special connection with domestic and marital problems. The feuding wife and husband are out of harmony with the sense of community implied by this day sign.

But Cauac also points the way to the resolution of our difficulties. As we have noted above, this day sign is symbolic of that first great offering performed by the four Jaguar Fathers at the beginning of the Fourth World of time. Hence it symbolizes the kind of sacrifice, the kind of union with others through which we may most easily achieve our own personal sunrise, the end of our troubles and travails. Cauac takes us outside ourselves and reminds us of the unity of humankind.

It has already been noted (see Ix) that the Calendar embodies a cosmic polarity wherein signs are masculine while numbers are feminine, although certain day signs are quintessentially feminine in tone. Cauac is one of these. The sense of community and communion is founded in the feminine principle. The wife and/or mother is the very heart of the household. In fact, in the Yucatec language, the words for "home" and "mother" are the same; only context distinguishes between using the word *na* to mean a house or the mother who lives in and manages it. Since hearth and home are the center of any community, whether small or planetary, Cauac may be taken as the day sign of the Eternal Feminine. It is strongly associated with midwives and female healers; it is their special day, and the day of women in general. The traditional garments (*traje*) worn by Maya women are sometimes taken as yet another image or symbol for this day sign.

Since this day is associated with midwifery, it is likewise associated with childbirth. It is sometimes believed among the Maya that the midwives of ancient time used quartz crystals as divinatory instruments to see within the mother's womb and judge the growth of the fetus; Don Rigoberto believes that the hieroglyph for this day sign may be a kind of portrait of the developing child. In that sense, this supposed sign of "difficulties" is one of the most positive signs of all, for it symbolizes both the miracle of birth and the Feminine Principle that makes birth possible.

In terms of correspondences in the human body, Cauac is the heart itself. It is also strongly associated with *koyopa*, the "body lightning" or "lightning in the blood," the primal energy which vivifies all things (see Chicchan).

Upon this day, we may pray that there will always be harmony in our home lives and among our friends. Cauac is auspicious for all matters regarding health and healing, especially healing modalities associated with women's wisdom such as herb-lore and midwifery. This is the day associated with quartz crystals and their healing power. Like Caban, it is one of the days that are strongly linked with the *tz'ite* seeds used in the Mayan divination ritual.

Cauac Natives

Many challenging statements have been made about natives of the day sign Cauac. They are often said to be troubled and harassed by their own karma, and to live lives of confusion. But as often as not, these troubles are purely and simply a result of the fact that Cauac natives are extremely sensitive; and their sensitivity is in fact one of their best qualities.

These people are intelligent and imaginative. Their intrinsically "feminine" and intuitive nature often endows them with artistic talent; Cauac natives can be fabulously creative.

For the most part, they are good-natured, caring, extremely friendly, and kind. While it is often believed that they have many emotional difficulties, they seldom have major financial problems, and more often than not their material circumstances are quite comfortable.

Cauac people value human relationships. Friends and family matter more to them than achievement in the outside world. They are not terribly ambitious and tend to conform to predominant social mores. If they become leaders, they will act in terms of the community and its values rather than blazing new trails for new minds.

Their sense of community, which leads them to value others so highly and to care deeply for those around them, has a downside. They are extremely attached to their families, whether for good or for bad, and find it difficult to abandon the family system and seek their own individual destinies. Even if they travel widely, they will always long for hearth and home, and they will always return to their roots. They are extremely sensitive to gossip and sometimes too concerned about what other people think of them. They are just as likely to gossip as to be gossiped about, and they have an annoying tendency to poke their noses into other people's business, much to the chagrin of those who are the objects of their attention. They can strangle their children with "smother love," always believing that they are acting in someone else's best interest.

Their close family ties get them into trouble in relationships as well. Despite the fact that they are extremely romantic and relationship oriented, they often have trouble in this department of life, because they have great difficulty mediating between the demands of the relationship and the original family, especially their mothers. No one wants to compete with Mom, especially if she is the mother of a Cauac native. Cauac people are well known for their domestic difficulties and marital problems.

This sign is very feminine, and women respond to it better than men. Cauac women make excellent midwives; in fact, Cauac is the very archetype of the midwife, and, in a larger sense, of the Divine Feminine principle in human nature. Women who are born under Cauac tend to have a very traditionally feminine appearance; there aren't many tomboys in this crowd.

Cauac men may seem androgynous and possess a gift for communicating with women. They have a sense of intuition that is quite feminine as well; at best, they are positively psychic. Despite their talent for communicating with the opposite sex, they often experience the marital difficulties so characteristic of this day sign, and typically because of their attachment to the birth family or the mother. They are productive and talented in whatever profession they choose, and often have a gift as craftsmen of one type or another.

Cauac natives can sometimes have health difficulties. In Mayan society, chronic health problems are often regarded as a message that the person is destined to take the healing path. This is certainly true of those born under Cauac; as we have noted, they are said to make the best herbalists and midwives. They are also very psychic and clairvoyant, and especially prone to receiving messages through the "lightning in the blood" or through dreams.

Ahau
(Ajpu)
The Hunter

The glyph for this day sign represents Ajaw, the divine perceived as the radiant sun. Ahau or Ajpu has the deepest mythical associations of any of the day signs, since almost the entire myth of the Hero Twins is to be found within its symbolism. Most especially, this is the sign of the Hero Twin who was transformed into the sun.

In the beginning was the first set of twins, One Junajpu and Seven Junajpu. They played handball with such vigor that they attracted the attention of the Underworld Gods. They were commanded to enter the dark realm of Xib'alb'a, there to play handball with the Lords of Death. But it was a ruse, a trap. The Hero Twins were killed. The severed head of One Junajpu was hung in the World Tree. This day sign is the *nawal* of the sun, and the sun is the face of One Junajpu hanging on the World Tree.

His sons were Junajpu and Xb'alanke. This is their sign as well. They were skilled blowgun hunters who fought with and destroyed a number of dangerous cosmic monsters; the circular mouth on this day sign glyph is symbolic of the Hero Twins as blowgun hunters.

In time, the younger generation of Hero Twins was likewise commanded to appear before the Lords of Death and play handball. They had learned from their father's mistakes; they survived the five deadly trials and won the handball game against the Underworld Lords. But the gods of death were less than honest; they sacrificed the Hero Twins even though they had won the game honestly.

But the Hero Twins were nothing if not shamans; they rose again, returning to the Underworld disguised as wandering minstrels. They tricked the Underworld Lords in their turn, subjecting them to a sacrifice from which there was no resurrection. They had triumphed.

As they left the Underworld, they made offerings at the grave of their uncle, Seven Junajpu. This was the beginning of the rites to the ancestors, whose day sign this is. The ceremonies associated with the Day of the Dead or *Día de los Muertos* were originally celebrated on Ajpu days, and in some traditional Mayan communities they still are.

As an emblem of the sun, Ahau is also a symbol of wholeness, of completeness. The sun makes four stations in the course of a day; midnight, sunrise, noon, and sunset. Thus it establishes the four directions, the symbolic template of completeness. One may easily expand this daily cycle to encompass an entire year: winter solstice (south), spring equinox (east), summer solstice (north), and autumnal equinox (west). One may, in fact, expand the fourfold metaphor unto the vast reaches of cosmic space: the celestial equator or ecliptic, often perceived as the Road of Life, conjoins the Milky Way, often perceived as the Road of Souls, in two places, thus dividing the heavens into four quarters. This is yet another meaning of Ahau.

As Maya writer and philosopher Lem Batz has pointed out,[10] there are various Ahau symbols throughout the different Mesoamerican civilizations. The glyph we see here is the ancestral face. Ahau can also be conceptualized as a decapitated head; this is One Junajpu sacrificed by the Death Lords, his head hanging in the World Tree. [11] Among the Aztecs, this day sign was called Flower, which is yet another symbol of Ahau; in ancient times, the ancestors were perceived as flowers blossoming on the branches of the World

Tree. Sometimes this concept, as a mathematical zero and also a symbol of mathematical infinity, is represented by a seed. In all contexts, the symbol represents both the infinite subatomic void of zero as well as the infinite vastness of the universe. It is beginning and end; it is all things and nothing.

This is a day sign of lordship and leadership, of struggle, heroism, and hunting. It is a sign of the eternal struggle between life and death, and of life's eventual triumph through perpetual rebirth.

This is a day to express the intention that we remain safe, that our homes be filled with harmony, and that those who have passed before us be remembered. This day brings us especially close to our ancestors; they stand near to us, and whisper in our ears. Because this day is symbolically linked with the mythic Hero Twins, it may endow us with courage, valor and heroism. Thus this is an excellent day upon which to express one's intention to cultivate wisdom, talent, and physical fortitude.

Ahau Natives

Ahau is the sign of the hunter, but what these individuals hunt for is Spirit. Their archetypal progenitors, the Hero Twins, were courageous and valorous; Ahau natives are often brave and powerful. They are natural warriors, fighting for a cause. Ahau natives somehow manage to be soft, generous and good-hearted while at the same time embodying principles of powerful leadership.

This is the sign of the Hero Twins, the mythic progenitors who became the new sun and the new moon after they had passed through the tests and challenges of their shamanic passage through the Otherworld. Ahau natives also have to face many tests and challenges in life; this is not an especially easy destiny. Their heroism consists of meeting those challenges. Their biggest obstacle is that they may be blinded by their own light and in love with their own talent; they have a powerful egotistical streak. They believe in themselves, sometimes too much so. Convinced that they are always right, they sometimes need to learn the hard way that this is not always true. There may be more than one answer to a question and more than one truth; Ahau people sometimes have difficulty accepting this fact.

If they are warriors, they are also mystics. The Hero Twins were our "first ancestors". A close relationship with the ancestors exists among the natives of the day sign Ahau. These people have natural mediumistic or shamanic abilities. They can be among the finest psychics, clairvoyants, and diviners. Sometimes, their connection with the "otherworld" is their biggest obstacle in relating to "this" world. They are often a bit "spaced out," as well as subject to morbid apprehension about signs and omens. If they can clear the fog away from the mirror of their perception, seeing through the metaphysical haze of their omens, they can become true spiritual leaders, which is their ultimate destiny. This is the day sign associated with the sun itself; Ahau people were meant to shine. They were meant to achieve great things. They tend to have a positive outlook on life.

These folks are naturally artistic. The Hero Twins masqueraded as strolling performers; Ahau people often have theatrical abilities. They can be discriminating connoisseurs of food and wine as well. Like most natural artists, Ahau people also tend to be romantics. As such, they may have many relationships. If they are not paying attention, they may find themselves looking back later in life, regretting great loves now lost to them. They would do well to pay attention to their relationships instead of taking them for granted.

Though essentially kind-hearted, Ahau natives may have difficulty with the faults that typically form the dark side of courage and bravery; they can be belligerent, domineering, and aggressive. They can also be manipulative. Since they are warriors by nature, they are accustomed to prevail in all matters; they can become quite cranky when things don't work out the way they wish. They have a tendency to act on impulse, to leap before they look. At worst, they can become violent. They spread their energy too thinly by taking on too many projects at once.

Some Daykeepers say that the animal totem of Ahau is the majestic eagle. Others say there isn't an animal totem; that this is the *nawal* of the human being, symbolic of all that the human spirit was meant to embody. This is the day sign of the sun, triumphant.

Imix
(Imox)
The Left Hand

In ancient Mayan mythology, the tree at the center of the world grew from the back of an enormous caiman who slumbered in the depths of the primordial sea.[12] This mythic figure, which appears so often in Mayan iconography, is sometimes called the Earth Monster. Imix is the day sign of that primal, pre-conscious beast, and therefore it is symbolic of the beginning of life and of existence.

Since the Earth Caiman sleeps in the depths of the primal sea, this is also the day sign governing the sacred energy inherent in the ocean. Each of the four elements (Fire, Earth, Air and Water) has at least one governing day sign or *nawal*. The element of Water has three. While Ix governs the fresh running water of streams and Muluc is symbolic of the rain, it is Imix that rules over the world's great oceans. This watery day is an excellent time to pray for rain— something rather uncommon in highly industrialized, technology-driven societies but quite normal among the Maya even today.

Because the sea is vast and filled with infinite variety, Imix has a multiplicity of animal totems. All the creatures of the sea are connected with this day sign: the dolphins and whales are among its animal manifestations, as are fish of all kinds.

The ocean is a universal symbol of the collective unconscious or group mind that underlies all of humanity. Here, in the depths of the collective mind, lie the visions, the dreams, and the pre-conscious yearnings that underpin the lives of all of us. Imix symbolizes this aspect of the human mind, and this is why we call it the day sign of the Left Hand. As among many other traditional cultures, the Maya associate dreams and visions with the left side or feminine polarity, similar to the yin principle of Chinese philosophy, and the light of rational consciousness and ordinary reality with the right side or masculine polarity, similar to the yang principle.

One Daykeeper says: "...there's a grandfather long ago who clashed with Xib'alb'a, so his arm was removed. For three days the arm of a grandfather called Ajpu was removed. It was hung in the kitchen where the smoke of the fire comes out. Afterward, when our grandfather managed it, his arm was brought and put back on... It was the left arm, so this is a bit of an idiot."[13]

This would seem to refer to the story in the *Pop Wuj* wherein Junajpu loses, then regains an arm in a struggle to defeat Wuqub Qak'ix, the Seven Sins, whose name also signifies 7 Macaw. However, the story does not specify that it was his left arm or that it no longer functioned properly after it was restored.

Be that as it may, the contemporary meaning of this day sign stresses the fact that the world of reason and practicality is frequently at odds with the world of dreams and visions. Hence the judgment: "so this is a bit of an idiot." When we are deeply under the influence of this visionary, oceanic, pre-conscious side of human nature, we may seem to be at odds with all things reasonable. This is why this day sign is sometimes perceived as an embodiment of madness or lunacy. Imix represents that aspect of human nature that can be more than a little bit crazy. And yet it is only when we set aside the dictates of "ordinary reality" that we are able to lift the veil between the worlds and see into other realities. Some of these alternate dimensions may be treacherous and drive one mad; others are sources of authentic wisdom. Ultimately, the right hand and the left hand were not designed to be at odds with each other, but to cooperate.

The world is filled with psychological perils and stresses. Upon this day we pray for good mental health, both for ourselves and for all those around us. We pray that our dreams and visions may bring us beauty and wisdom rather than delusion and craziness. This day has a strong connection with water; to be close to a flowing river or stream or the ocean is beneficial upon this day. This is yet another day to pay attention to potential wisdom from our dreams.

Imix Natives

Some would say that these are the crazy ones. The *zeitgeist* or "spirit of the times" may easily sweep them off their feet, spin them around, and send them wandering off without direction. Imix people like mystical things, but may be more attracted to the magical than the genuinely spiritual.

And yet it is equally likely that they will develop into artists, poets, mystics and visionaries.

Imix natives tend to be homebodies. They don't exert themselves much; they work to live rather than live to work. They can be downright lazy, yet somehow they always seem to land on their feet financially. They can be very eccentric; at worst, they are genuinely cranky and silly.

They are a gentle lot, very loving and romantic. Unfortunately, they also have a reputation for being libidinous and not in control of their passions. Their relationships tend to be wild and passionate, like some grand love story in a movie or a Gothic novel. But despite their romantic peccadilloes, they seldom have difficulty in finding relationships, and they are frequently quite fortunate in that regard.

Their close connection with visionary reality makes them seem highly charismatic to more ordinary minded folks. They often have a powerful hypnotic quality. In fact, it is commonly said among contemporary Daykeepers that Imix natives are capable of actually hypnotizing other people. This is a sword that cuts two ways. An Imix native could develop into a genuine hypnotherapist, one who uses her or his power to aid more worldly folks. On the other hand—for Imix is symbolic of nothing if not the duality of human existence—the Imix person could just as easily use such power to manipulate the hearts and souls of others for more selfish purposes.

It is part of their life's journey to gain control over their extraordinary psychic perceptions and turn their powers to actions that benefit others. Imix people can easily become confused, adrift in the deep waters of the collective unconscious. They can be indecisive and wavering, doubtful of their own perceptions. If they lack spiritual and psychological maturity, they are likely to become deceptive, sneaky, underhanded and dishonest. They are quick-tempered. Their intrinsic laziness leads them to take advantage of more hard-working day signs. Some are genuinely loony; the mystical "left side" of existence overwhelms their rational consciousness completely and leaves them lost in the cosmic ocean without vessel or anchor. Imix natives may seem, at first glance, to be among the most highly organized individuals you have ever met—perhaps even obsessively so. Don't be fooled: their desire to compartmentalize everything into neat little categories is their own way of dealing with a reality which is less "real" to them than the world of visions and dreams.

At their best, these natives are able to see through the worlds and bring the uncanny beauty of the "left side" into manifestation here on earth. They are clairvoyant and adept with dreamwork. At best they are true visionaries, fearless guides to the other worlds which resonate all around us.

Some have said that young Imix people tend to attract the interest and attention of older people, while older Imix folks exercise an equal fascination on the very young.

Imix natives do best when they live near the ocean. They draw power and inspiration from it. Because whales and dolphins are their animal totems, they may have a special relationship with these magical beings.

Ik'
(Iq')
The Breath of Life

This powerful day sign is, at the same time, one of the most spiritual and one of the most potentially dangerous.

We have already encountered Feathered Serpent (the Aztec Quetzalcoatl) as a symbol of rebirth and resurrection (see Ben). But this all-important deity has a number of aspects. A bit later on (see Chicchan), we may consider Feathered Serpent as a metaphor for the powerful and mysterious energy in the body called *koyopa* or "lightning in the blood." But here, in the day sign Ik, the Feathered Serpent appears as a god of the wind.

The creation of all things is described in the opening pages of the *Pop Wuj*. Here, Lord Feathered Serpent (Tepeu Q'ucumatz in the K'iche' language) emerges as part of the creative energy of the universe itself.

The Maya typically describe creation as an interplay of positive and negative polarities not dissimilar to the Chinese concept of yin and yang. At its most fundamental level, the Divine is called Tz'aqol B'itol, the Architect and Maker. [14]

This duality of creation can also be expressed as "Heart of Sky, Heart of Earth." The term Heart of Sky refers to the god known as Hun Rakan—or, to use one of the few Mayan words that has been adopted into English, "Hurricane." [15] This deity is the primal spirit of the wind and the air. If Lord Feathered Serpent is an aspect of the day sign Ik' as god of the wind, so is Hun Rakan, the Heart of Sky. As the creative power of the air, Ik' represents the Breath of Life itself, a force which has many similarities to the Hindu concept of *prana*, which is yet another metaphor for breath or air as the creative energy of life.

As we have noted, each of the four elements has at least one day sign which symbolizes its essence or *nawal*; Ik' is the day sign which rules the element of Air. It is also said to be symbolic of one of the B'alameb' or Four Fathers of Humanity; the father called Majukutaj in the *Pop Wuj* is yet another mythic reflex of Ik'.

The primal creative entity known as Heart of Sky is said to have three aspects, one of which is called Nim Kaqulja', which could perhaps best be translated as "Great Thunderbolt." This particular aspect of Hun Rakan or Heart of Sky is also said to be associated with the day sign Ik'. It may be said to symbolize "the power of nature" and has a certain relationship to the *koyopa* or "lightning in the blood," a concept which we shall explore at more length a bit later on (see Chicchan and also Chapter 3, "The Meaning of Numbers").

The concept of Feathered Serpent as a deity of wind and the sacred breath of life is one that is found throughout the entire world of Mesoamerican spirituality. The "T" which appears as part of this day sign's hieroglyph is commonly seen in the form of windows and doorways; there are T-shaped windows as far south as Palenque and T-shaped doorways as far north as Chaco Canyon in New Mexico. The same hieroglyphic element is also found on the ceremonial garments of present-day Pueblo Indians; I have seen many headpieces used by Pueblo women in the Corn Dance which bear the "T-shape" of the day sign Ik'.

But the same wind that breathes life into our nostrils may also be a destructive power. After all, this day sign is the origin of our word "hurricane." The wind that nurtures and vivifies us may also become one of the most destructive forces on earth. The Breath of Life may manifest as a raging hurricane. Ik' is one of the four Year Lords; and, according to the Maya, it is the most potentially dangerous of the four. During an Ik' year, one may expect events that batter the world with the force of a tropical storm. This is a year the Maya associate with revolutions, insurrections, and political disturbances of all kinds.

Among its many other meanings, the name of this day sign, which is *iq'* in K'iche', is also the common term for the lunar month.

Ik' is the wind that sweeps clean our house and our body. Upon this day we ask for the strength, the vitality, and the commitment to carry on in our chosen work. This is a day for the removal of negative energy and illnesses; in terms of healing, it favors the resolution of psychological problems, especially those that arise from angry emotional states.

Ik' Natives

There are a number of animal totems associated with this day sign: the hawk, the weasel, and the bobcat are among them, but most especially, this is the day sign of the hummingbird.

The hummingbird may be tiny, but its energy is powerful and impressive. The rapid-fire action of its wings requires more power than that bestowed upon any other bird. Hummingbirds are aggressive; larger birds stay out of their way.

It is just the same with people born under this day sign. While it is true that this is the sign of the breath of life, those who are born under the power of this *nawal* can blow in all kinds of directions— some of which are better than others. When these people begin to blow like a hurricane, it is best to stay out of their way. It is said that they often become political leaders, even military dictators. They bluster more than any other day sign. I knew a K'iche' couple who, when their Iq'-born (Yucatec: Ik') son began to manifest the mischievous qualities associated with his day sign, decided: "We have never had to apologize to our neighbors for anything, but now we shall probably have to get used to doing so!"

Ik' natives are impulsive and have a tendency to change horses in midstream. They can shift from their "breath of life" personality to their "hurricane" personality within a few minutes. All the same, there are few who will manifest only the darker, more intense sides of Ik's characteristics. In fact, there is a built-in factor in many Ik' natives which acts as their "saving grace": when they stray from the spiritual path and begin to work from their darker, more manipulative side, they become ill, and will continue to have health problems until they find their way back to the light.

And for these natives, the light is indeed powerful. At its best, this is the breath of life, the breath of spirit. Many of these folks are absolutely brimming with cosmic energy, and some are truly spiritual.

Their positive qualities include confidence and self-assurance. As an element, air is considered very mental, just as it is in Western astrology. These people rely on their brains. They are extremely smart. They tend to be very good with math, and hence they make excellent investors or stockholders. They are also very good with words. They have a vivid imagination, and can sometimes mistake their great dreams for hard realities.

Clever and adaptable as they are, Ik' natives are very good at tackling difficult topics or arts of all kinds and acquiring proficiency in such things. They have excellent good taste and appreciate the exotic. They are among the strongest, toughest, and most resilient of all the day signs. They can navigate through almost any situation. Their powerful energy tends to insure that they will become successful at something.

Iq' is the common word for a lunar cycle in the K'iche' language, and most Daykeepers assert that Ik' natives have a special connection with the moon. Obviously, these are extremely moody folks, and the rising and falling of their extreme moods may have a great deal to do with the moon's phases. More than other people, Ik' natives should become aware of how their energy and personality change with the Moon. For contemporary Mayan teachings about the symbolism of the monthly lunar cycle, see Chapter 6.

Ik' is one of the four Year Lords. As well as those who are born on this day, those who are born in an Ik' year will manifest many of the qualities of this day sign.

Akb'al
(Aq'ab'al)
Dawn

In the interval between the end of the Third World and the beginning of this, our present Fourth World, there was a time of darkness. During this time, our Four Jaguar Fathers led the first people away from Tulan, and, according to the *Pop Wuj*, for a long time they wandered in darkness. In other versions of the story, the early people wandered through a kind of half-light, with only the dim glow of the Morning Star to guide them.

The *Pop Wuj* tells us that they gathered upon the mountain called Hacavitz, where they wept to see the light of Venus, the Morning Star. The Four Jaguar Fathers made an offering, burning so much copal that great clouds rose into the sky (see Cauac). At last, the sun rose upon the Fourth World. Birds and animals cried out for joy, and so did the people, laughing and weeping at the same time.

This day sign personifies that "dawning" which is so important in all of Mesoamerican myth. In a sense (since the word *aq'ab* actually means "night") this day sign is symbolic of the polarity of night and day, darkness and light. Many Mesoamerican myths refer to that "in-between time" when the early people wandered in a world illuminated only by stars; some scholars refer to this as the "auroral" phase of Mesoamerican myth. [16]

But this primal event, the dawning of the sun of the Fourth World, is not a concept limited to some mythic era, long ago and far away. It is, in fact, eternal, part of the ever-recurring cycle of human existence. To the Maya, each day is like a blossoming plant, and the dawn is the first sprout, emerging from the dark womb of night and ready to flower. The dawn is Sun Father's arrow, shot forth as he appears in the first moments of ruddy light, an arrow that coaxes the new life of a new day from the waiting earth. [17]

In love and romance lies the renewal and the continuance of human life. Each new love is like a new dawn, capable of bringing to light a new world in the form of a child. The same primal force that coaxes new life from the Blossoming World each day also coaxes forth feelings of passion, of love, of the magnetic attraction between woman and man. While some Daykeepers may practice brief periods of abstinence in order to build up energy for a particular ceremony, it cannot be said that Mayan spirituality has any special reverence for the kind of life-long celibacy that is so important in Hinduism or in monastic forms of Christianity. Instead, the joyous interplay of the sexes is celebrated, and this day sign is symbolic of romance, which dawns like a glorious sun on each new day of human existence.

As a matter of fact, real love is sometimes too important to be left to the devices of shy, inexperienced young lovers. In some Mayan communities, there are shamanic specialists called "marriage singers," who pave the way for the dawning of love by communicating between the families of young lovers, singing the praises of their romance and making all things joyful between the families and anyone else involved. Among the K'iche', the marriage singers typically choose an Aq'ab'al day to do their work. It is also said that those born upon an Aq'ab'al day are likely to have a talent which, if they are shamanically inclined, may help them to become excellent "marriage singers."

This day symbolizes both darkness and dawn; hence it is a day of new beginnings. It is the *nawal* of clarity or light, the day to ask for the occurrence of the light in all things. Upon this day, we express our intention always to think and act with perfect clarity. It is a special day for those who set the bones of the sick and the healers with natural plants. Needless to say, it is also perhaps the most favorable for day for love and marriage (though Chuen is also very good, especially for the actual marriage ceremony). An Akb'al day can also be quite favorable for finding a job. If the exigencies of daily life make it impossible for an apprentice to be initiated as an *aj q'ij* on the traditional day 8 B'atz', the day 8 Aq'ab'al may be substituted.

Akb'al Natives

We have already noted that all day signs are masculine on the level of metaphysical polarities; at the same time, we have encountered certain day signs that are imbued with a definite feminine quality, notably Ix and Cauac. Natives of Akb'al tend to have a feminine, or at least androgynous, energy regardless of their own gender. Their good looks will often last a lifetime. Though there are, of course, exceptions to every rule, Akb'al people can frequently appear eternally youthful and seem never to age.

Their magical and highly attractive appearance is matched by an equally charming personality. Akb'al people are very eloquent, and sometimes very wise. They are pleasant, popular, and enjoy being helpful to others. In fact, one could truthfully say that many Akb'al people are blessed with a "caretaker spirit" that naturally seeks to be of service.

Indeed, Akb'al people can sometimes appear to be blessed with a surplus of virtues. They are typically very optimistic and cheerful. They have the brainpower of the seasoned intellectual without slipping into unreality; their intellectual smarts are matched by a strong dose of realism and common sense. Sometimes they are so fortunate in life that they appear to be blessed with what we would call "dumb luck."

But there is another side to these cheerful souls. At times they can be intensely private, even secretive, and place a high value on solitude. Other people may find their moods confusing, uncertain as to whether they are dealing with a jolly extrovert or a dreamy, artistic introvert.

In fact, Akb'al people embody both of these polarities. Let us remember that this is the day sign of the "in between" times, the half-light of early dawn or late twilight. Some say their power animal is the bat, which also haunts the in-between times. Others say it is the macaw, because this was one of the birds that cried out at the first sunrise. The fact is, Akb'al people slip in and out between the polarities of life—the day or night, the dawn or dusk—with practiced ease.

It can sometimes even be noted that Akb'al people often have their own "power times," and that these are the in between times of dawn or dusk.

At their worst, Akb'al people can be slippery characters for whom the boundaries of truth and falsehood are muddy and unclear. Their charm may sometimes seem frivolous or insincere. Those born on 13 Akb'al in particular are sometimes said to have a passion for the darker side of magic. Like all "in-betweeners", they need to make choices.

Since this is the day sign of love and romance par excellence, these folks are very romantic and relationship-oriented. But passionate and gorgeous though they may be, they often have difficulty finding a partner because they are such extremists in love. The downside of their romanticism is unbridled passion. They can be among the most promiscuous or unfaithful of all day signs. Nevertheless, they are also fortunate in love almost beyond all other signs. Despite their peccadilloes, their long search for the right partner will most likely bear fruit someday—whether they seem to others to be deserving of such good fortune or not. They're lucky.

They are not always appreciated in their own place of origin, and thus can often be found traveling widely in search of a place to make their mark in the world.

Every Daykeeper is a prayer-maker, and every prayer-maker a poet. We have already remarked that, in Mayan society, those born on an Akb'al day are said to make excellent "marriage singers" because of their verbal eloquence. In a wider, cross-cultural context, this means that they often make excellent writers.

Kan
(K'at)
The Net

When Blood Woman, daughter of the Underworld, first escaped to this earth and told First Grandmother that she was pregnant with the Old Wisdom Crone's grandchildren, Grandmother Ixmukane was not inclined to believe her. She gave her a net and told her to go and gather corn. Blood Woman found only a single clump of corn growing in the field to which she was sent, but her magic was so strong that the cornsilk from a single ear of corn grew into many, many ears of corn, filling the net. Grandmother Ixmukane was so amazed that she went to examine the fields herself and saw the imprint of Blood Woman's net. Knowing that her sons, the first pair of Hero Twins, were also the planet Venus, and knowing that Venus would return from the Underworld on a day called K'at in K'iche' (*k'at* means "net"), she realized that Blood Woman was telling the truth. A new pair of Hero Twins would soon be born.

At its best, the day sign Kan represents the abundance of corn in Blood Woman's magical net; this is indeed a day sign of abundance and potential prosperity. Among the Aztecs, this day sign was called the Lizard. The association between the lizard and the power of fertility is one that runs strong and deep in Native American culture. The Pueblo peoples of the American Southwest, who have been deeply influenced by the Toltec Tradition of ancient Mexico, regard the lizard as a symbol of growth, sexuality, and life-giving rain. Lizards, common themes in the rock art of Arizona, New Mexico, and Utah, are typically found in contexts suggesting fertility. In the Yucatec books of Chilam Balam, Kan is often listed first among the day signs, associated with all manner of growth, pleasure, and good things in general, and having a strong connection with the sacred *ceiba* tree which represents the very Tree of Life, source of all abundance.

But there are many things that can be carried in a net. When the Maya go to the altars to make offerings, they carry incense and copal in a net. In this case, the net symbolizes the heavy load of our karma, our mistakes and our wrongdoings for which we must atone by making prayer, making offerings, and asking for pardon. The day sign Kan may often have a great deal to do with our own human tendency to become entangled in the "net" of our karma. It is sometimes said to be the *nawal* of prisons, a place where one may become deeply "entangled" indeed if we fail to recognize and harmonize our failings.

If we neglect to burn away the karma which we carry entangled in our net bag of life, the consequences may be unpleasant indeed. Because Kan is such a "fertile" sign, it has a special connection with sensuality, and as often as not it may symbolize wrongdoings and indulgences specifically sensual in nature.

We burn our offerings of candles and copal in a fire, and the day sign Kan is one of the days that embody the sacred energy inherent in fire. This is not the "sacred fire" which plays such a powerful role in the Mayan Fire Ceremony, and which shall be discussed under the day sign Muluc. Rather, Kan represents the quieter fire of the family hearth, the fire in which we cook our food. This, too, is part of the symbolism of Kan as a day sign of abundance, prosperity, earthly wisdom and earthly growth. And even though this day sign may not symbolize the magical flames of the Fire Ceremony, it is still true that fire is the purest of all the elements. Unlike air, water, and earth, which can all be polluted by the unconscionable actions of humankind, fire is always pure. The simple fire of hearth and home may play just as much of a role in purifying our lives and burning away the contents of our karmic net as does the more sacred fire of ritual.

Upon this day, we express our intention always to have understanding. It is a favorable day upon which to pray for abundance, as well as for the safety and well-being of all those who are incarcerated in prisons and jails. It is a day in which that which was all tangled up as if in a net may at last become untangled. It is also a day upon which healing ceremonies and practices are sometimes performed, especially if the necessary healing is psychological in nature.

Kan Natives

The natives of Kan love to fight for a cause; at times they can be truly noble in spirit. They care deeply about liberating other people from difficulties and entanglements. In fact, some Daykeepers say that these people are born to free others from the prisons of their own making, whether visible or invisible.

There is frequently more than just a touch of bohemian eccentricity about Kan people, for they follow the beat of a different drummer and are born non-conformists. They are highly energetic and frequently become wealthy as a result of their efforts.

Despite their nonconformist tendencies, they are usually quite orderly and well organized. I know one Kan woman who, surprised on her way to the hospital, gave birth in the back of the family car—but remembered to look at her watch so that she could give her astrologer an exact birth time for her daughter.

These folks are just plain sexy. Unfortunately, they often have trouble curbing their instincts. They perceive the world largely through their senses and emotions, and these are the vehicles with which they seek to explore life. Filled with endless curiosity, their willingness to experiment often leaves them with a host of difficulties. This includes money as well as love. Thus they can be tied up in a "net" of difficulties, and if you are deeply involved with them, so can you. Because they believe that they can be helpful (due to their innate sense of idealism), they are always trying to fix things. This can make them meddlesome. Other people get tangled in their net.

Because of their emotional and sensual nature, they are highly sensitive and can easily fall victim to nervous troubles and anxieties of various kinds. The solution to their jittery nerves usually involves finding the right person with whom to share their life, someone who can keep them always feeling safe. Despite their tendency towards passionate peccadilloes, they make excellent partners—among the best of all the day signs. Their sensuality tends to make them highly attractive to others.

Since Kan is the *nawal* of prisons, it should be noted that they can tend to be a bit lawless—perhaps because of their non-conformism and their endless tendency to experiment. They can be nervous, irascible, materialistic, and arrogant.

At worst, they can be greedy, stingy, and shallow. This, of course, also makes them somewhat boring. As with any other sign which carries the symbolism of prosperity and abundance, they can be dreadfully materialistic. As remarked above, they are typically very well organized, but sometimes they may be so well organized that they can become obsessive as well. They bring in a great deal of karma from past lives and will need to stay high-minded in order to "burn it away" and clear the soul.

Kan is a better day for women than for men; Kan women are both sensual and nurturing at the same time. Because they are weavers of webs—whether of magic or of karma—the industrious spider is one of their animal totems, in addition to the lizard. This is one of the day signs which is said to produce excellent doctors, healers, midwives, herbalists and so on. It also produces skilled gardeners. Kan natives are never better than when they are digging in the earth.

Chicchan
(Kan)
Feathered Serpent

This is Feathered Serpent once again (see Ben and Ik), but this time envisioned as the primal force of the universe itself, as warmth, as the all-encompassing energy that enlivens both Heart of Sky and Heart of Earth.

The energy symbolized by Chicchan is sometimes known to the contemporary Maya as *koyopa*. This word may refer to the sheet lightning we see playing over lakes and mountains on stormy nights, but from an esoteric point of view it refers to the "body lightning" or "lightning in the blood," a powerful energy within the human body which Don Rigoberto believes may very well be identical to the Sanskrit *kundalini*. Both are connected with serpent imagery. Yogic texts describe the *kundalini* as the "serpent power." Bolts of lightning are regarded by the Maya as "sky serpents." In fact, in the form of the language used during the Classic Period (200-800 CE), the word *kan* meant both "serpent" and "sky" or "heaven."

Some people (including natives of the day sign Chicchan) are born with the *koyopa* or lightning soul fully activated; other people either develop it or have it awakened through powerful spiritual experiences. Some people never experience it at all. If the *koyopa* is awake, the gods themselves may contact us directly, using the *koyopa* energy as a communicative medium between their world and ours. Anyone who undertakes the path of becoming a Maya priestess or priest will of course have a teacher, a "road guide." Part of the training for such a sacred office consists of the awakening of

the *koyopa* or lightning soul. The shamanic teacher or road guide
is typically an expert diviner, healer, and dream interpreter, for the
koyopa energy manifests itself powerfully in all these arts. We shall
learn more about *koyopa* when we investigate the inner meaning of
the thirteen numbers.

Thus Chicchan is the Creator, the Founder, the *kundalini* coiled
at the base of the spine. The awakening of this energy is both a death
and a mystical rebirth as is clear from the stories and symbolism
regarding this aspect of Feathered Serpent.

One contemporary Daykeeper says: "The plumed serpent
made itself seven times like a plumed serpent, and seven times it
made itself like a spirit, flying in the air. Because the Holy Spirit
nowadays—this is Kan. Because we all have a spirit. We don't see
it, but because of it, we walk, because of it, we speak—an angel's
spirit… The plumed serpent has wings, it flies; we all have it." [18]

The reference to the seven transformations of Feathered
Serpent is from the *Pop Wuj*. These transformations take the form of
a journey to the Underworld and back, a saga of death and rebirth.
Carlos Barrios, in a different interpretation of the same myth, says:
"Q'uq'umatz went down to the underworld to demonstrate his
greatness. After seven days, he became a snake; after seven more
days, he became an eagle; after another seven days, he became a
jaguar; finally, seven days later, he became a pool of blood that was
poured on both the eagle and the snake." [19]

Upon this day we assert that vitality, clarity and understanding
shall be made manifest *right now*. Because this day sign has a
connection with the inner fire or *koyopa*, it is also a day upon which
one may build both physical and spiritual strength.

In times past, many of the village Maya regarded Chicchan as
a somewhat dangerous day sign, strongly associated with the arts of
black magic. And yet its intense energy may also symbolize the more
positive forces that we call magical.

It is sometimes said that Chicchan is the *nawal* of the creation
of man and woman, and thus it is a most favorable day for sexual
matters as well. This too is similar to the symbolism that pertains
to the Sanskrit *kundalini*. Kan days (the K'iche' equivalent of
Chicchan) are considered so powerful that high-numbered Kan

days (primarily 10 and 12) are used to initiate the highest Maya priests of all, those with special psychic and spiritual gifts.

Chicchan Natives

Strong and powerful, these serpents like to go to extremes. Chicchan natives possess abundant energy and are very active—though they are also easily distracted. At their best, they exemplify a search for the deepest levels of truth; their energetic connection with the *koyopa* or *kundalini* and hence with the mysteries of the universe virtually guarantees that they will be seekers of wisdom. Often, this quest for wisdom gives them a scientific bent; science, at its best, is another form of seeking out the ultimate truth of reality, which attracts mystics as well.

At best, this eternal quest for knowledge makes Chicchan people extremely honest and sincere. They make natural educators and can frequently be found in teaching positions, and people look up to them as authority figures because of their intense energy. Despite the fact that other people do perceive them as authoritative, there are many, perhaps most Chicchan natives who like to exercise that authority from behind the scenes. They avoid the limelight, preferring the status of "power behind the throne."

Their active *kundalini* force makes them excellent psychics or healers. In fact, they can be the most psychically powerful of any sign. In the physical body, Chicchan corresponds to the nervous system, which houses and carries the powerful energy of the Feathered Serpent. They like to read and are good with computers. Many of them are naturally endowed with an innate gift for cybernetic technology.

Though they often seem very reserved and unable to express themselves, they are usually lucky in love, or at least very likely to have numerous, intense relationship experiences. Chicchan people possess a very powerful and intense sexual energy, and many will be drawn to them because of this energy. Mae West, Marilyn Monroe, and Angelina Jolie were all born upon Chicchan. Some natives of this day sign are just as powerful intellectually as they are sexually. With its deep need to investigate the mysteries of the universe, Chicchan is the archetype of the "sexy scientist."

At worst, Chicchan natives can be conservative, bossy, and can lord it over other people to the point of oppression, often without even realizing it. They like to test people and may be addicted to comfort. Their desire for perfection and total knowledge tends to make them somewhat obsessive. While many individuals will be satisfied merely with a comfortable life, Chicchan people are compulsively driven to seek ultimate answers.

A word should probably be said about village traditions among the Maya that assert that Chicchan natives are among those most likely to become powerful sorcerers. In our own society, people who actually practice "black magic" may be relatively rare, but the energetics involved—i.e. the use of personal charisma and power to bend others to one's will—are of course a universal phenomenon. With all that natural psycho-sexual and "magical" energy, Chicchan natives are indeed more capable than other people of mobilizing such forces and using them to dominate and control those around them, but this is not very common, and represents the most negative manifestation of this day sign.

Their surplus of cosmic energy usually keeps Chicchan natives extremely healthy and vital, thus endowing them with great longevity. Needless to say, the snake is their animal totem. All are fierce but most are good. They're just very intense.

Cimi
(Kame)
Death and Rebirth

In the *Pop Wuj*, the Lords of the Underworld become annoyed when they hear the first pair of Hero Twins playing a vigorous game of handball in the world above them. They imperiously demand the presence of these Twins, whom they challenge to a handball game, with their lives as the stakes. But first, the Twins must undergo a series of challenges placed upon them by the Gods of Death. They fail to pass the tests, and are killed as a result. In time, the second pair of Hero Twins, children of one of the first pair (see Ben and Kan), once again play handball and once again are summoned by the Death Gods. But these Hero Twins are clever; they outwit their challengers and survive to play the game. But the Gods of Death don't play fairly. They cheat at the game and the Hero Twins lose their lives as a result.

But once again they outwit the Lords of Xib'alb'a, the Underworld, for they are revived by a magic spell, and they return to trick the Lords of Death, sacrificing the sacrificers and thus conquering Death itself (see Ahau).

This day sign is often referred to simply as "Death," and with all these mythic associations—not to mention a symbolic connection with owls, cemeteries, and so on—it is no wonder that many Westerners cringe at the thought of being born upon such a day.

And yet the Maya themselves tend to see this day sign as a positive force. Why?

To the Tz'utujil Maya of Lake Atitlan, the word *camic* means both "Death" and "the Eternal Now." As Martin Prechtel writes, "….in Mayan, Now means Death."[20] The Eternal Now is like an *axis mundi* or world center. Both the Past, comprised of that which has been and gone, and the Future, yet to come, are anchored to the central tree of the Eternal Now. Living, as we do, in the Eternal Now, our eloquent poetic words and our beautiful lives feed the Past and thus create the blossoming of the Future. If the Gods become drunk with our beauty, we heal the Past and make it new. Thus is the Future created. In fact, the word for the grammatical "present tense" in some Mayan languages is *kame* or *kamic* as well.[21] Death is the present moment, and death can only happen in the Eternal Now. It cannot happen at any other time. Death transforms the Present into the Past, giving birth to the Future. If we live a life of true beauty and eloquence, our death will feed the soil of the Present and thus allow us to participate fully in the creation of the Future. Therefore we are not fully "cooked" in the glorious oven of human life until we die; death completes us.

This is the esoteric meaning of the day sign called Death. This is why Death, much against our own Western expectations, is one of the most positive day signs of all. Since this is a very positive sign, it has a deeper mythic relationship with the paradise side of the Underworld rather than fearsome Xib'alb'a. This is a day of communication with the ancestors and with unseen worlds.

In Mayan thinking, this "day of death" is one of the best days upon which to be married. Why? When two people unite in marriage, the ancestors are always involved. One ancestral stream is linked in union with another. When we marry into another family, our ancestors become married as well. Because a marriage often produces children, the life of the community becomes weighted in the direction of life rather than death. The eternal balance of the two is disturbed. Thus the Maya, ever mindful of the Gods' command that we live life with true poetic eloquence, appoint certain individuals as "marriage speakers." They communicate between the two families, and they celebrate the union to the entire village by way of beautiful songs and poems. Because the Gods love to consume our eloquence, the Gods of the Underworld become so intoxicated with beautiful words that they surrender unto life, relinquishing the balance between this world and the Otherworld in a joyful acceptance of the blossoming of human existence.

Upon this day we pray that we and those dear to us have long life. If we are aware of someone who is mortally ill, we may ask for the rest and peace of the dying person. This day is also favorable for healing and for the protection of travelers. It is the day to remove negative energies from people. There is a special connection to the world of the ancestors on this day; communication with other realms is possible.

Cimi Natives

Natives of Cimi are more often than not kind, generous, and good-natured. They are humble and obedient, sometimes to their own detriment, and they can be very strong when facing adverse circumstances. They are charismatic but cautious. They are clever and sociable but may sometimes seem a bit emotionally fragile, and have dreams and aspirations that could never work out in reality. They often take the blame for things they didn't do, and thus earn the dislike of others, usually undeservedly.

Natives of Cimi often have a psychic bent because of their Otherworldly symbolism. They can be skilled forecasters or diviners, though they need to overcome a certain amount of self-absorption and learn to serve others in order to reach full manifestation of their talents. It is said that Cimi natives, more than any others, have a natural connection with the ancestors, and are able to receive powerful messages through the karmic stream of the past.

Much like natives of Akb'al, they are verbally eloquent and make good writers. They tend to be very feminine as well. Women tend to like them, whether they themselves are male or female. This is one of the signs that has a very feminine or androgynous appearance regardless of gender.

In fact, it sometimes seems as if the Gods of the Otherworld have endowed these citizens of the "eternal now" with a kind of eternal youth. Cimi people can be truly ageless and give the appearance of being "forever young."

Cimi natives often have a rather introverted nature; in a very real sense, their power place is their own home and they can be quite grumpy when they do not have a comfortable home place to retreat to. Despite this "homebody" tendency, many are great travelers who are destined to wander the world. In addition to their own homes, they also draw power and energy from "sacred sites" such as temples, pyramids, and ruins. While most people do their wandering in youth, Cimi natives are more likely to travel later in life.

These people are lucky in love. Their youthful beauty and feminine power of attraction serves them well when it comes to finding life partners. All the same, and somewhat by way of contradiction, Cimi people often choose to spend their later years alone.

They may sometimes be terribly self-absorbed and at worst they can be vindictive. Sometimes they are impractical, full of illusions, and emotionally weak, scorned by others because of their laziness, and suffering thereby. Their lives are intense and full of many dramatic events because they bear the burden of much past-life karma. Though they are blessed with good health and longevity, many are likely to experience the power of the Death Gods all too forcefully in the form of losing many loved ones.

Despite their numerous ups and downs, Cimi people almost always land on their feet and seem to be under divine protection, although one of their life's lessons is not to take their luck for granted and always to be thankful for their good fortune. In the final analysis, their road of life is blessed by the spirits of the ancestors, and they seldom fail to manifest what they really need in life.

Their totem animal, not surprisingly, is the owl.

Manik'
(Kej)
The Pillars of the Universe

The animal totem for this day sign is the deer. To the Maya, the deer was not perceived in terms of a soft dappled fawn but as a mighty stag, lord of the forest. The deer was one of the most powerful of all animals. When the conquistadors first arrived in the Mayan country, the natives thought that their horses were a close relative of the mighty deer, so they called it by the same name. In fact, to this very day, the K'iche' word *kej* means both horse and deer.

The deer is sometimes said to hold up earth and sky; it is the guardian of the forests and of nature in general, symbolic of all the raw power inherent in wild nature itself. This power can be equated with the natural energy that moves and animates the four directions or four quarters of the universe, the Medicine Wheel.

According to the Maya, we live in a fourfold world, a fourfold reality. In this universal quaternity is embodied the energy of the four elements, and the four manifestations of human beings: physical, mental, emotional and spiritual. Interestingly enough, Jungian psychology also asserts that the human psyche is composed of four elements or functions.

Manik' is said by the Daykeepers to be the day sign of the four corners of the universe, the four pillars of the world. There are many other fours in the Mayan cosmovision. A day is comprised of the four stations of the sun: dawn, noon, sunset and midnight. This metaphor may be expanded to encompass the four stations of the year, the solstices and equinoxes. There are four colors that symbolize the four cardinal directions—red in the east, black in the west, white in the north and yellow in the south. These are also the four colors of corn; according to the *Pop Wuj*, the perfected humans who were created at the dawning of the Fourth World were formed out of corn. The Daykeepers say that this is why there are four colors of humanity.

In the migration legends of the *Pop Wuj*, the original people were led by four men. These first forefathers were created directly by the gods, who also created their four wives. Thus the four is doubled in terms of yin and yang to equal the number eight, and it is upon days numbered 8 that the most important rituals are performed by contemporary Daykeepers.

Manik' is the *nawal* of all kinds of four-footed animals. As such, it has a strong connection with the natural world in general, as does the day sign Ix (q.v.). Manik' is the strength and power associated with the wilderness and all its beauty. In particular, it represents the rain forest, the source of our planet's oxygen.

Manik' is also the *nawal* of the Mayan religion, which is likewise founded in the principles inherent in nature itself. This is the day of the *aj q'ijab* or Maya priests, symbolizing power, authority, hierarchy, and force.

As we have noted, Daykeepers experience their first initiation on the day 8 Chuen. But the day 8 Manik' is important as well, for it is upon this day that the *chuchq'ajawib* or "mother-fathers" undergo initiation. These are high-ranking Maya priests who are the caretakers of their community; they act with the nurturing qualities of a mother and the authority of a father. If the exigencies of daily life make it impossible for an apprentice to be initiated as an *aj q'ij* on the traditional day 8 B'atz', the day 8 Kej may be substituted.

In ancient codices, the gods of the sacred hunt are frequently shown with scorpions' tails, and these tails end in a human hand. The hand at the end of the scorpion's tail is the same hand we see in the glyph for this day sign; it is the hand of the hunter. This meaning of the glyph reinforces Manik's connection with the natural world. Contemporary Daykeepers also see another meaning in this glyph: This is the hand in which we hold all the potential power of the fourfold universe in its infinite complexity; it is the natural power within us waiting to spark into action and purpose.

This day sign is sometimes said to have an association with the planet Saturn.

Upon this day, we pray for harmony among one and all. This extends to the natural world around us as well as to other human beings; one gains great power and energy if one is able to spend this day in nature or in the wilderness. This is a day to honor priests and shamans, as well as one's mentors—especially those who have passed away from us. Thus it is also a day of the ancestors; in Guatemala it is also regarded as a day upon which one pays honor to those within our own spiritual lineage. On Manik' days we may pray for the strength to bear with all our difficulties in life, for there is great strength in this day sign.

Manik' Natives

In most cases this day sign has a very positive energy; as was said about Chicchan, all are fierce but most are good. They are clever and have good ideas. They usually seem to be lucky, though in fact this luck is actually a native talent for "thinking on their feet."

This is a very masculine sign; Manik' people have a strong masculine energy regardless of their own gender. The natives of Manik' are strong, powerful, perhaps even domineering. Because of their inherent power, they are natural leaders who have an almost unlimited potential for good or for evil. They are not the type to remain behind the scenes. They like to be acknowledged for their leadership skills and powerful ideas, and will push themselves to the forefront of any enterprise. You may not always know that they are doing it; they hide their true strength and energy behind a passive demeanor. Some of them appear to be shy, though for the most part they are simply reserved. Both women and men are true romantics and are often bohemians, frequently with an artistic flair or talent. There is genuine sensitivity underneath all that energy.

Manik' natives have a passion for causes; they can be dedicated seekers of truth and justice. In many cases, they have better success standing up for others than they do for themselves. Despite all that strength and energy, they can be self-effacing to the point of losing their own sense of direction. Nor are they always the rugged individualists that they appear to be. There is frequently a strong attachment to the family of their birth, as well as to the family they create for themselves. This attachment to family can manifest itself in their lives either as a strength or a weakness.

They are strong, brave, but often very refined at the same time. The men make excellent bosses and authority figures; they may also be gifted as spiritual guides and teachers. While some Manik' men can be very pushy, it is the men rather than the women who are prone to hide their true strength and energy by taking a more gentle, negotiative stance.

Manik' women are intense; they have a very masculine energy and are able to assume great responsibilities and occupy important positions. They are affectionate and appreciative, but must often make sacrifices to achieve their goals. They tend to dominate their husbands. They often seek fame; Manik' women are seldom happy staying tied to the home front, but long for the power that comes from assertive activity in the outside world. Unless they are careful, they may end up as truly overbearing personalities who lord it over all those around them.

Manik' people have a tendency to become involved in very intense and obsessive relationships. Though they will work harder than most day signs to preserve a relationship which is important to them, they do have "wandering eyes." They also have the cleverness to get away with almost anything, including bouts of infidelity.

Despite their close family ties, Manik' people tend to be wanderers. They often feel unappreciated in their native environment, and seek out new worlds to conquer in the most literal way, by carving out a niche for themselves far from their place of origin.

Their mythic role as the archetypal guardians of the wild needs to be taken seriously. In order to maintain their equanimity, Manik' people need to be in nature. A walk in the woods or a hike in the mountains is the best way for them to get all that intense energy under control and in balance.

Manik' is one of the four Year Lords. As well as those who are born upon this day, those who are born in a Manik' year will manifest many of the qualities of this day sign.

Lamat
(Q'anil)
The Regeneration of the Earth

Like Manik', this day sign also exemplifies the fourfold world we live in. If Manik' is the symbol of the four directions of the universe, Lamat represents the four colors of corn, which are in turn symbolic of humanity and its four colors—red, black, white, and yellow. As such, it is all about creation, the "cosmic seed that the creator planted" on this day when the primordial polarity mentioned in the *Pop Wuj*, called B'itol and Tz'aqol (the Creator and Maker, or Maker and Modeler) "sowed life in the universe and placed man on this planet." It is the creative energy of Mother Nature herself. The K'iche' name for this day sign, Q'anil, is derived from *q'an*, the common word for the color yellow, and it means a "yellowing" or a "ripening," the ripening or maturation of crops, of human beings, and of ideas.

Lamat signifies the seed, corn, pride, harvest, and food. It is the *nawal* of all kinds of animal and vegetable seeds. It is the day of fertility and harvests, abundance, prosperity; this is an auspicious day for initiating any planting or business negotiation. Lamat is the archetype of the seed that sprouts after being planted in the rich earth. As with the earth, so with the human beings who live upon her body. This is a day sign of reproduction and birth, and thus a very sensuous, even sensual sign.

Lamat is rich with abundance. In the Aztec version of the Sacred Calendar, the totem animal for the day sign Lamat was a rabbit, a common symbol of fertility. The rabbit associated with this day sign was known in Aztec myth as "the rabbit in the moon,"[22] for he was the servant of the Aztec Moon Goddess, she who invented alcoholic drinks. The rabbit mixes up the liquor; sometimes Lamat is abundant to the point of excess. The Mayan Moon Goddess Ix Chel is also frequently depicted with a rabbit as a companion.

The glyph for Lamat is one of the principal symbols of Mayan Spirituality. A Lamat glyph is laid out upon the ground in sugar to form the basis for the altar in the Mayan Fire Ceremony. Instead of the square frame shown here and in most glyphs from the codices, the Fire Ceremony altar is enclosed within a circle, which represents the circle of Time itself, the endless round of the days of the *tzolk'in*. The cross is, of course, the symbol of the four directions that make up a wholeness, and of all its nuances—the colors of corn, of humanity, the four elements, and so on.

Within each quadrant is depicted yet another circle. Those who are familiar with the Chinese yin-yang symbol which is so important in Taoism will know that it represents yin within yang and yang within yin—in other words, the opposite energies of the universal polarity are not disconnected or separate, but include each other and interpenetrate with each other. In this Mayan symbol, the circles within each quadrant convey the same message. The four directions of the Medicine Wheel and of the world we live in are not isolated or separate forces; rather, each direction contains within itself yet another circle of wholeness, or completeness.

This day sign may also be said to have an association with the planet Venus, for during the Classic Period and in the Post-Classic codices of Yucatan, the Lamat symbol also signifies Venus. The codices make it clear that the rising and setting times of Venus were an important indicator of agricultural cycles and rainfall to the ancient Maya.

This is a wonderful day for farmers or simple planter box gardeners, for upon this day we ask that the world may be made to blossom and be made fertile. We may plant ideas and projects as well as flowers; any relationship or business venture that begins on a Lamat day will usually turn out favorably. In some Mayan traditions, the day 8 Lamat is one of special importance. This is the day to celebrate the abundance of the cornfields. In keeping with the principle that what pertains to the earth likewise pertains to those who live upon it, it is also a day for celebrating pregnant women. We, as humans, participate in the abundance of the world; we are not separate from it.

Lamat Natives

This is a very fortunate sign; its natives are intuitive, kind, generous, and good-natured. Most of them have very gentle dispositions; they are adaptable, adjustable, and they assimilate easily. They have a marvelous talent for manifesting anything that they truly desire; all they really need to do in order to make it happen is to be patient.

They are not very adventurous and don't like to take risks. They are better off partnering with someone who does enjoy the adventurous side of life, then relaxing and focusing on the basics. But despite their desire for serenity, many of them will experience numerous ups and downs in life; in time some of them will acquire wisdom thereby. Their children are likely to be among their most powerful teachers—although many Lamat people do not have children, despite this day sign's inner connection with fertility and abundance. Because they are such dedicated caretakers, they have trouble letting go of their children and allowing them to experience life for themselves. Learning this lesson can cause them a lot of stress and strain.

Lamat natives have access to the deep inner knowledge of things; this knowledge is innate within them, and it is a karmic inheritance. In order to nurture their inborn wisdom, they simply need to remain calm and balanced. The best way for them to do this is through contact with the beauties of nature and authentic wisdom traditions. Lamat people should make a habit of reading plenty of books; it will reawaken what they already instinctively know. They need tranquility and security in order for their wisdom to flourish; otherwise they may fall victim to their dark side.

As might be expected, this "sign of abundance" is very fortunate when it comes to relationships. There are a few traits they need to watch out for; they sometimes have a tendency to "dump" on their partners, expecting other people to take responsibility for them. Sometimes their "abundance" spills over into promiscuity.

At worst these people can be egotistical, neurotic, and eternally restless. They may become victims of passion; hence they generate conflict and sow discord. Their biggest potential difficulties in life come from illness and drunkenness. Their extreme sensitivity makes them an easy target for all kinds of anxiety-related problems, and with the *pulque*-stirring rabbit in the moon as their animal totem, they have a predilection for intoxicating substances of all kinds. This is the day sign of the "jolly drunk" who just can't resist any kind of temptation. Elvis Presley and Jimi Hendrix were both born under the sign of Lamat.

Lamat people must learn to believe in themselves while at the same time not taking it all too seriously. If they can do this, they can weather any storm and meet any challenge. Despite their softness and their sensitivity, they have a strong inner core.

Their innate spiritual access to the world's wisdom makes them great historians. They should focus on acting as caretakers for their community, whether in a material or spiritual sense, for one of their greatest gifts is their ability to care about others.

Muluc
(Toj)
Offering

When the "original people" first left Tulan, they wandered in the darkness, guided only by the dim light of the morning star. Their leaders were the B'alam'eb, the four "Jaguar Men" who, along with their wives, were the forefathers of humanity. These leaders were in constant communication with their guardian deities, the most important of whom was Tohil or Tojil, the patron deity of the forefather named B'alam K'itze'.

The original people wandered until they reached the mountain called Hacavitz. It was here that the forefathers made their offerings to Father Sun at the dawning of this new World Age. When the sun first rose upon the Fourth World, the gods of the forefathers were changed into stone. To this day, Mayan altars and sacred places in the wilderness are often places of stone.

This sign is dedicated to the god Tojil or Tohil. Its K'iche' name, Toj, contains part of the name of the god. In the ancient form of the Mayan language that was spoken in the great cities of Tikal and Palenque, this deity was called Kawiil (or K'awiil). One of his legs takes the form of a serpent and he holds a scepter. In central Mexico this same deity was called Tezcatlipoca or Smoking Mirror. While Tezcatlipoca was sometimes regarded as a god of magic and sorcery, he was also renowned as a god of healing. Contemporary Aztec healers still reverence Tezcatlipoca as the archetypal progenitor of their art.

This important day sign participates in the sacred energy of two different elements, Water and Fire. In terms of Water, Toj represents the rain that nurtures the earth. To the Aztecs, this day was known as "Rain" and was symbolic primarily of water.

In terms of Fire, its connection with the god Tojil makes the day sign Muluc or Toj symbolic of the Sacred Ceremonial Fire.

The most fundamental of Mayan rituals is the Fire Ceremony. Tojil is the spirit of the sacred ceremonial fire and the deity who rules over the ritual flame. This is the fire of Ajaw; it is the Heart of Sky and the Heart of Earth. This fire is to be distinguished from the ordinary hearth fire that illuminates our homes and which is symbolized by the day sign Kan (K'iche': K'at). The flames of the Fire Ceremony are pure. Other elements, like earth and water and air, can become polluted by the unthinking actions of human beings, but fire always remains pure and is thus the perfect medium for burning away our misdeeds and our debts to the world.

Thus Muluc is the sign of offering. There are many offerings we can place in the sacred fire so that they be consumed. Candles, incense, tobacco, sugar, flowers, liqueur, and sweet-smelling herbs may all be cast into the flames. Some of these offerings honor our ancestors, or the four elements, or the spirits of sacred places, as well as the spirits of the day signs themselves. But most importantly, our offerings are a kind of payment, a debt we pay in order to correct our imbalances and bring us back into harmony. In terms of contemporary spirituality, one could say that this is the sign of paying our karmic debts. In the divination ritual, Muluc may sometimes represent these karmic debts and burdens, especially those related to misconduct with or mistreatment of our spouses and our children, the closest members of our family circle and those most deserving of respect.

When we pay our debts to the gods, we walk in balance once again. Hence Muluc is a sign of equilibrium. When we reach a point of equilibrium, we become truly free. Hence Muluc is a sign of liberty as well.

Though the Maya perform very few rituals on days with the number 13, the day Muluc is sometimes an exception to the rule. In the traditional community of Momostenango, 13 Muluc is regarded as a special day upon which we are able to pay back large karmic debts all at once.

Upon this day we humbly acknowledge our karmic debts and assert our intention to "pay it all back" by placing our lives in harmony. Make atonement for all disequilibrium and be thankful for all that is in balance. This is a day on which to give thanks for everything we have received in our life, the good and the bad.

Muluc Natives

Natives of Muluc have warm and magnetic personalities; they are also extremely sensitive. They are attached to their homes. They have natural protection from the Divine, as long as they remember to pay back all karmic debts and help others to do the same. Gifted with the spirit of our forefathers who chanted up the first sunrise of the Fourth World, they possess powerful solar energy and have the strength to deal with any situation, a strength that often grows stronger as they grow older.

This is the sign of "karmic payback." These people often have health issues as well as money issues, due to the fact that they are born with such a heavy load of karma. With effort, they can clear away their karmic debts in this very lifetime. They need to be kind to others, and devote themselves to service. Some of the most dedicated humanitarians and world-servers are born under the day sign Muluc. Caretaking is part of their destiny.

They may sometimes have to deal with ill health, but this is a clear signal that they need to focus on "burning away" their debts. If they are out of balance, if their debts remain unpaid, they are likely to suffer on the physical level.

Because of their mythic connection with the sacred fire, they often have an affinity with candles. Even for those who lead the most typically "modern" lifestyles, it is always beneficial for them to light a few candles every time a Muluc day occurs, and to remember their debts and their responsibilities as caretakers.

Muluc is associated with rain as well as with fire. Being near water is beneficial to them and helps them stay in balance. They should try to spend time near rivers and streams, or near the ocean. They were born to walk in the rain.

They have passionate relationships. Sometimes their romantic attachments lead them into dramatic scenarios filled with jealousy and fierce pride. They often need to learn to control their emotions, which are naturally impulsive and can lead them into infidelity. They can be ill-tempered and vain, and occasionally monopolistic; sometimes they seek attention and are inclined to get angry when people don't acknowledge every little thing they do. These selfish traits can cause real havoc in their home lives. As caretakers and servers, Muluc people have a special duty to avoid getting caught in these negative patterns, and to try always to see the best in all people and all situations.

Muluc natives are gifted in math and economics and make excellent bankers, especially those dealing with loans. If they are poverty-stricken or suffer from major prosperity problems, it means that they have not focused enough of their energy on clearing away their karmic debts. They make good helpers and intermediaries. They are freedom lovers and often very good with animals. Their animal totems are the shark and the puma. Many Muluc people have a talent for energy healing, especially if they use their left hand. They have the potential to become at peace with everything around them.

Oc
(Tz'i)
Law and Spiritual Authority

In many Mesoamerican Calendar systems, this is the day called "dog," and in fact it is related to all members of the "dog" family. The Mayan definition of "dog" is somewhat different than our own, for it includes raccoons, the jungle *tepezcuintle*, and so on—almost any hairy creature with four legs falls into the "dog" category in Mayan thinking.

In the *Pop Wuj*, the two Hero Twins disguise themselves as traveling magicians and take on "dog names," Jun Ajpu Wuch' (Possum Hunter) and Jun Ajpu Utiw (Coyote Hunter). They perform their tricks in front of the Lords of Death, with Xb'alanke sacrificing Junajpu and then restoring him to life. Fascinated by this magic, the Lords of Death want to learn all about it and offer themselves up for the sacrifice trick.

But this time the sacrifice is for real, and the Lords of the Dead stay dead. Junajpu and Xb'alanke have triumphed. The universe is once again in balance.

Cosmic balance is the foundation of all true law, and thus Oc is the sign of law, of the natural order. It is connected with all those who either enforce or practice the law; hence it is the symbol of the police as well as of lawyers and judges. In Oc, the cosmic balance is established upon earth through the enlightened creation and maintenance of law and order—in other words, of authentic spiritual justice.

It is also said that Oc, in its totemic aspect as a dog, a raccoon, or a coyote, is the animal guardian of hills and mountains. Oc is one of those day signs, like Manik' and Ix, that has a strong connection with primal nature and with the wilderness.

Like Eb, Oc has a connection with the Road of Life. For if Eb is the road itself, Oc is the means by which we walk the road. In the Yucatec tongue, Oc means a "foot" or a "footstep." According to a myth recorded in the Book of Chilam Balam of Chumayel,[23] four women began the first counting of the days by measuring the footsteps (*oc*) of a primal traveler upon the Road of Life. This traveler, it turns out, is none other than Time himself, for the ancient Maya conceived of the spirit of time as a man walking down an eternal road. The women fall into step with Time and begin walking down the Road of Life. Together, in a spirit of communion with distinctly sexual overtones, they all generate the twenty day signs together. From 13 Oc, mentioned in the myth, we imaginatively leap to 1 Chuen. From the end of the twenty-day count, we circle back to the beginning.

Thus, under the influence of the day sign Oc, we try to walk the road of life in a spirit of balance and harmony by placing ourselves in accordance with cosmic law.

The generation of the day signs from the union of Time and the four original mothers also demonstrates the sexual, procreative aspect of this day sign, for Oc can have its wilder side as well. The Maya often think of dogs in terms of their uninhibited sexual habits; in that sense, Oc is the principal *nawal* of sexuality. It is also a sign of vengeance, which is what happens when we take the law into our own hands.

Because lust and revenge can so often lead us away from the path of balance, Oc is one of the day signs most closely associated with the so-called Seven Shames (see Ix and Cib). Divine law leads us back into harmony. Oc is a day upon which we may usefully assess our lives in order to ascertain where we have lost the path of balance, and to begin the work of restoring that internal and external harmony. This day sign is a symbol of accuracy and precision, which are qualities that we would expect to find in a code of law.

Because this day has connections with law and its practice, on Oc days we pray that justice may be done to all people. It is a good day to address any legal issues of our own, as well as correcting the difficulties which may have arisen in our lives due to an excess of the passions.

Oc Natives

Oc people are faithful and kind, strong and long-suffering. At their best, they are very balanced individuals, and hence can be helpful in community matters, bringing clarity and good judgment to any situation. Their unquenchable idealism helps them to achieve things that others believe to be impossible. All the same, they may need to learn how to moderate their passionate ideals. They tend to be volatile, and their moods may swing with the phases of the moon.

This is a sign of judges and administrators, of lawyers and politicians. They are hard workers and make good scientists, researchers and investigators; they are also gifted and skilled in all areas of law and legal writing. They make excellent guardians and protectors; they command respect, authority and leadership.

Oc natives are frequently talented with communication and writing. They are warrior spirits who are constantly doing battle with negative forces in their environment. They are strong believers in social justice, but sometimes they want to make their own laws, and care little about others so long as they get what they want. This doesn't usually work out very well for them. As the sign associated with police, lawyers, and so on, there is also a strong connection with institutions such as jails, which is where Oc natives are likely to end up if they insist on making up their own rules in life and disregarding the needs of others. But even when they get into trouble, they usually get out again, for they have a natural fund of good luck.

Oc people are well known as pleasure seekers. They can be libidinous and are known for their sensuality. They have many relationships, primarily because so many people are magnetically attracted to the magical aura of sensuality that they exude. It is best if they choose partners who are at least as strong as they are—they don't do well with submissive types, and can easily become bored.

When they are bored, they are likely to.... well, indulge. All the same, they often tend to choose to live alone in their mature years.

They are often fruitful and have many children—or, on the contrary, none at all. They are equally passionate about their families and about history, and hence make extremely good genealogists. They are also prone to substance abuse problems, which is a by-product of their essentially sensual nature. They tend not to be very responsible with money, either. A good sense of direction is badly needed. They can be manipulative, and must frequently learn the lesson of allowing others to make their own way in life, without interference from Oc types who always believe that they are right! Sometimes they like to gossip. They may be overly ambitious, overly strict and authoritarian at home and with others; they can become corrupt officials, especially those who accept bribes. In Spanish-speaking countries, the term *mordida* can refer either to the bite of a dog, or to the bite of someone who tries to extract money from you. One ought to hope that a dishonest Oc type doesn't try to take a *mordida* out of you! If they can establish a clear and honest sense of direction, they may become genuine representatives of spiritual authority.

Oc people have an easier time of it if they are born on an even-numbered day. Otherwise, their ideals and well-intentioned social projects are likely to attract opposition and hostility rather than cooperation and gratitude. Sometimes their health can be a little bit fragile.

It is said that their senses are very finely tuned—their eyesight, hearing, and so on. In the human body, Oc represents the nose. They can have an extremely finely tuned sense of smell.

They tend to become more spiritual as they grow older, and may in time develop true inner vision.

Chapter 3

The Numbers

A great deal of individual thinking has characterized interpretations of the 13 numbers, especially by those who attempt to link Western numerological concepts with this Native American system. The numerology designed by Jose Arguelles, for example, is entirely Western in character and owes nothing to Mayan concepts. The numerological system propounded by Carl Calleman represents his own highly personal interpretation of material from the Aztec Borgia Codex.

Essentially, one should remember that all the numbers are feminine, and may be regarded as the "wives" of the 20 day signs (who are male).

Therefore, a union between day sign and number is in the nature of a "mystic marriage" that unites the essentially masculine and changeless nature of the day signs with the active, vibrant female principle of the numbers.

The Moon Goddess, known as Ix Chel or "Lady of the Rainbow" in the Yucatec language, is the patroness of divination and, some would say, of the *tzolk'in* itself. While there are twelve months in a solar year, the sidereal lunar month is somewhat shorter than a solar month, averaging 29 days rather than 30. Thus the year is comprised of 12 lunar months and a partial month, often known as the "thirteenth lunar month." This is one of the most fundamental meanings of the number 13.

Let us also remember that the Maya tend to perceive time in terms of lunar rather than solar months. Many Western scholars have described the *tzolk'in* as comprised of 8½ months, but I have never heard a Mayan Daykeeper employ such a description. It is universally said that the *tzolk'in* equals nine lunar months.

The Tz'utujil Maya of Santiago Atitlan recognize twelve Moon Goddesses or "Marias," all of whom are aspects or manifestations of the Great Goddess herself. These are the months of the year, with the thirteenth and incomplete lunar month regarded as sacred to the Goddess as Crone.[1] This is Ix Chel in her aspect as the waning moon, the very same Xmucane or First Grandmother of the *Pop Wuj* who uses *tz'ite* seeds representing the day signs to perform the first divination.

In order to understand the Mayan concept, we may have to start thinking of the "feminine principle" in a somewhat different way. In Hermetic philosophy and Chinese Taoism, the masculine principle is always active and in motion, while the feminine principle is quiescent and still. It is somewhat different among the Maya.

The Maya think of the mountains, in their changeless solitude and eternal strength, as the "masculine earth." They think of the Pacific coast, with its crashing waves, steaming jungles, chattering birds and burgeoning foliage, as the "feminine earth." In this sense, the Mayan understanding seems, at least to me, to be closer to Tantric Hinduism, wherein the masculine principle remains unchanging while the *shakti* or feminine principle creates activity.

The number 13 has other meanings as well. It is commonly said that there were thirteen heavens in the ancient Mayan Otherworld, arranged like a pyramid above the earth; thus 13 is the number of heaven. This may be true; some scholars are skeptical about this idea,[2] but I have known Daykeepers who arrange teaching diagrams in pyramidal structure based on the number 13 and appear to accept the notion that there were indeed 13 heavens in the ancient system.

The relationship between day signs and numbers can be usefully understood in the form of a diagram (see Figure 6).

But Daykeepers also insist upon the fact that 13 is a number which appears commonly in nature. Since the numbers are feminine and the earth is our mother, this makes perfect sense.

Figure 6. THE RELATIONSHIP BETWEEN
DAY SIGNS AND NUMBERS

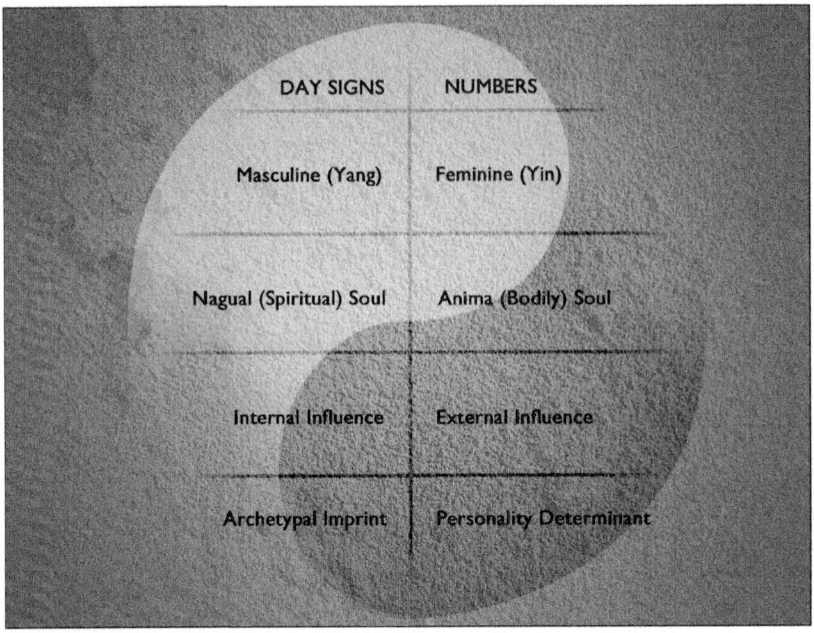

DAY SIGNS	NUMBERS
Masculine (Yang)	Feminine (Yin)
Nagual (Spiritual) Soul	Anima (Bodily) Soul
Internal Influence	External Influence
Archetypal Imprint	Personality Determinant

• Not counting various individual markings or protrusions, there are 13 rectangles on the shell of a turtle. Thus 13 is the number of Turtle Island, the North American continent (a paradigm known to the Maya as well as to indigenous peoples farther north).

• There are also 13 rattles on a rattlesnake's tail; there may perhaps be some connection here with the Pleiades, which are known as the "rattlesnake's tail" in Yucatan.

• Finally, the number 13 is strongly associated with the 13 major joints in the human body. These are the ankles, the knees, the hips, the wrists, the elbows, the shoulders, and the neck. Thus 13 is also a number of humanity. (see Figure 7)

But there is more to it than that, for the number 13's correspondence with the joints of the human body conceals a deep esoteric teaching.

The Power Within

In the previous chapter, we began to explore the internal energy known as *koyopa*, represented in contemporary Mayan thinking by the archetype of the Feathered Serpent. It is time to examine this concept a little further.

The existence of a powerful bio-psychological energy within the human body has been postulated by many civilizations. The best known example comes from Hinduism, where this energy is known as the *kundalini* or serpent power. The *kundalini* is in essence a goddess just as much as it is a form of energy. It travels through different energetic centers in the body, known as *chakras*, and can be manipulated through meditation and spiritual practice. The feminine power known to Kabbalists as the Shekinah, which also dwells in centers within the body, is an analogous concept.

Figure 7. THE THIRTEEN ENERGY CENTERS

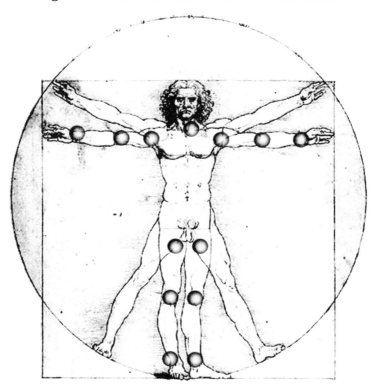

In K'iche' Maya, this powerful inner energy is called *koyopa*. The word literally means "sheet lightning." However, the Maya also think of a bolt of lightning as a "sky serpent," so in that sense the *koyopa* is a serpent power too.

Called the "body lightning" or "the lightning in the blood," the *koyopa* is the energy upon which shamans draw for important rituals, especially the divination ritual in which the day signs of the *tzolk'in* are represented by groups of seeds from the sacred *tz'ite* tree. A shaman's hand may literally shake with the power of *koyopa* as he holds it over the divining seeds. (I have actually seen this.) Sometimes the *koyopa* "awakens" as a pulsing in one's leg or other limb.

The *koyopa*, like the *kundalini*, is essentially feminine because it is associated with the 13 numbers. *Koyopa* collects in the 13 major joints of the human body, which thus form a Mayan analogy to the *chakras*. It is from one of these 13 points that the pulsing and hand-trembling will have their origin.

In the last chapter, we learned that the Maya believe that a human being has two souls. One of them is an immortal soul, the *nawal* that is represented by one's day sign. Yet there is another soul, one which is vested in the human body and which dissolves at the time of our death. This bodily soul is called the *uxlab* or, in Spanish, the *anima*. We may have a tendency to think of the bodily soul as a somewhat lesser entity than the *nawal*; after all, it remains within the human body and dissipates at death. But the *koyopa* dwells within the body and is thus connected with the bodily soul.

Here, then, we see a deeper esoteric significance at work. The day signs are a masculine energy that represents the immortal soul or *nawal*, while the numbers are a feminine energy that represents the in-dwelling power of the bodily soul and its *koyopa*.

The Wave of Time

The Mayan Calendar is a symphony of cycles within cycles. The 260-day *tzolk'in* is interwoven with the solar year, and may be divided into 20 periods of 13 days, commonly known by the Spanish term *trecenas*. Our pyramid of days reveals the inner meaning of these thirteen-day *trecena* cycles (see Figure 8).

Figure 8. THE PYRAMID OF TIME

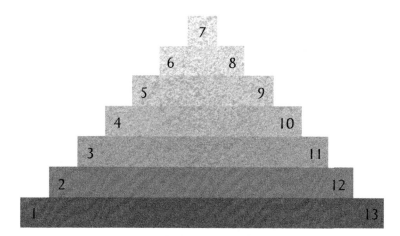

The *trecena* periods are essential to an understanding of the Calendar. The number cycle runs from 1 through 13, then returns to the number 1 again. Each time the number 1 recurs, it will do so on a different day sign.

The *trecenas* are the essential component of what we may call "living the Calendar." They set the clock for the major rituals of Mayan life. The Daykeepers of Guatemala say that low numbers are "weak" and lack strength, while the middle numbers—6, 7, 8, and 9—represent the days of balanced energy and power. The final days, 10 through 13, are "too strong," so powerful as to be potentially dangerous. Therefore, all major rituals are performed on the days of balanced power at the center of each *trecena*.

The cycle of the *trecena* can best be shown as a pyramid, equivalent to the pyramid of the Thirteen Heavens which was part of the cosmology of ancient Mexico.

The energy inherent in a particular *trecena* cycle is still tentative or weak in the beginning, not yet fully established in its own nature. As it climbs the pyramid, it begins to grow in power. It reaches the region of perfect balance on day 6, and it reaches the peak of the pyramid on day 7. As the current cycle begins its course down the pyramid, it will grow in power, just like a wave that has reached its crest and then begins to crash downward. This descent of power is still in a balanced condition on the eighth and ninth days; after that, the energy inherent in the current cycle of time becomes more and more intense—too intense to be safely dealt with in ritual terms.

If, for the moment, we leave behind the somewhat static or architectonic image of the pyramid, we may return to the metaphor of the wave as a concept that is closer both to the world of nature and the world of post-Einsteinian physics. Each *trecena* cycle may be regarded as a particular quantum of energy, an energy that travels in a wave-like motion. Precisely like a wave, it begins as an underground surge, symbolized by the sun's emergence from the Underworld on the first day of the cycle. This wave of energy grows in power until it crests. Then it begins to descend, discharging its quantum of energy in a thundering crash to the shore. As the energy inherent in the wave trickles away into the sand on the night of the thirteenth day, a new wave cycle has already begun farther out at sea. The power of the day sign that will begin the new *trecena* is already present. At sunset on the thirteenth day, the Daykeepers welcome the spirit of the coming day, the one who will begin the next *trecena* cycle. They think of the next day as a "guest" who is already entering the sacred space defined by their communal and family altars.

Interpreting the Numbers

In terms of astrological interpretations, it is much too simple merely to say that low numbers are weak, middle numbers balanced, and high numbers too strong. This may be true in a very general way, but the numbers all have their individual characteristics.

We may take some of the high numbers as a good example of this principle. While many people regard the numbers 10, 11, 12 and 13 as "too strong," there are some important ritual activities which require the power of the high numbers. For example, high-level shamans with special psychic or mystical gifts are often initiated on 10 or 12 Chicchan days—Chicchan being, of course, the day sign associated most strongly with the *koyopa* or "inner lightning." There is a ritual circuit of Momostenango's four sacred mountains which takes place on 11 Aj, 11 Ajpu, 11 Kame and 11 Kej. There are four days with the number 13 which are set aside for "special" rituals, especially 13 Toj for the repayment of karmic debts and 13 Iq' for our sacred altars. 13 B'atz' is regarded as an especially auspicious day for marriage and 13 Tz'ikin a day to pray for money; while these are not ritualistic in the same sense as 13 Toj or Iq', they are part of the tradition of the four special 13 days.[3]

Thus we should avoid making hasty judgments, especially when dealing with the lives of human beings.

Most of the following information regarding the qualities of each separate number was given to me by Rigoberto Itzep Chanchavac of Momostenango. Among the Maya, the astrological delineation of numbers is never as detailed as that of day signs. The day signs remain the essential characterization of the individual's soul, the personal archetype. The numbers, fluid and changeable, shape the archetype into the human personality we see before us.

There is sometimes said to be a correlation between specific numbers and specific day signs. This is common among some Maya teachers, but not all. I obtained that information not from Don Rigoberto but from an entirely different source.

The Astrological Significance of the Numbers

While the day signs represent essential archetypes, the numbers are personality factors that modify the nature of the day sign.

Although each number has its positive and challenging aspects, the even numbers find it easier to bring their positive qualities into manifestation. Odd numbers are regarded as more intense; it takes us a bit more work to help them manifest their positive qualities.

In the same way, middle numbers tend to manifest themselves in ways that are positive and balanced. Low numbers need help from other parts of the horoscope in order to boost their energy. High numbers can be difficult because of their intensity.

While these guidelines are useful, they should not be regarded as absolutes. There are exceptions to every rule, as we shall see when we examine each individual number.

Above all, it should be remembered that "every number is good for something."

●

One
(1)

The number One is the seed from which the cycles of time must grow. Not surprisingly, it symbolizes beginnings, unity, thought, firmness, solidity, stability, strength, resoluteness of character, and inspiration. One is the original energy of creation. It is the root of time itself. In the number One is embodied the concept of totality. It possesses great strength and power. It corresponds to the day sign Chuen, which most modern practitioners regard as the beginning of the *tzolk'in* cycle.

Even though One is both a low number and an odd number, it cannot be described as "weak" or "difficult." In fact, a person born on a One day is usually filled with strength and resolution under any and all circumstances. Thought, and by extension desire, lead to actions, movement and results. Thought and inspiration lead a person to act or create, construct things, make new things. So thought, desire and inspiration are the seed or source of many things.

Daykeepers often make offerings on a One day to welcome the arrival of the new time period. In Momostenango there is a special shrine dedicated to the number One.

●●

Two
(2)

The number Two is a symbol of duality. As we have seen, the Maya think in terms of cosmic polarities. This is embodied in their mythology: there are two Hero Twins, two principal Lords of the Underworld, as well as the two monkey twins who act as patrons of all the arts. There is the eternal dichotomy of this world and the Underworld, day and night, darkness and light. These themes run like a common thread through all of Mayan myth, especially in their sacred book the *Pop Wuj*. In human life, these polarities express themselves through birth and death, joy and suffering. Life is a struggle; it has its positive side and its negative side. Death is the spouse or partner of Birth; they both represent two important steps or stages in life.

The corresponding day sign is Akb'al, which symbolizes romance between two people and thereby embodies the energy polarities of male and female intertwined.

A person born on a Two day can have twice as much strength or power than an ordinary person because s/he can draw upon either side of the cosmic polarities. By the same token, one's status as an "in-betweener" can make one indecisive. The duality of existence also expresses itself through love and partnership; natives of a Two day are natural born lovers.

Three
(3)

At its best, the number Three stands for all the virtues that we associate with hearth and home. It is the power of reproduction, thus symbolizing one's descendants and one's disciples. In Mayan mythology, the world was created when the three original hearth stones were laid down by the Creator Gods. These three hearth stones established the principles of home and family which are fundamental to all Mayan thinking. In traditional homes, three hearth stones are still often placed upon the wood-burning stove to hold the *comal* or tortilla griddle. Thus the corresponding day sign is Ben, which governs matters related to the home.

Three is a cosmological number as well. There are three

worlds—Heaven, Earth, and the Underworld (sometimes referred to as Supramundo, Mundo, and Inframundo).

Despite all of this symbolic potential, Three is not without its difficulties. Carl Jung, objecting to the Christian notion of a Trinity, said that the number Three is incomplete. Jung wrote that it is the number Four which signifies completion and fullness, and as we shall soon see, the Maya would probably agree. This number implies doubt, risk, obstruction and uncertainty. On a Three day, one's intentions become muddled and things don't work out as planned. A Three day can bring energies which prevent or obstruct the realization of projects and activities, so it's best to wait for a better moment or a more appropriate time. Many traditional Daykeepers avoid initiating new projects on a Three day.

Because Three is both a low number and an odd number, it can be one of the most challenging birth numbers. A person born on a Three day can waver like a leaf in the wind and typically finds her or his real strength in other areas of the horoscope.

Four
(4)

The number Four symbolizes wholeness. This is why December 21, 2012, is a Four day. The number Four is associated with Ajaw, the Sun God as cosmic lord (the word *ajaw* literally means "lord"). Why is this a solar number? The word for day is the same as the word for sun; a day is a complete passage of the sun. The sun or the day has four stations: dawn, noon, sunset and midnight. These four components of each day, each "sun," can be conceptually expanded to include the solstices and equinoxes; thus the solar year may also be symbolized by the number Four. There is evidence that the Classic Maya also divided the universe into four sections marked by the two intersections of the Milky Way with the ecliptic.

As we have previously seen, Mayan spirituality asserts that we live in a fourfold universe. The symbol of the fourfold universe is sometimes called a "quatrefoil," though to us it may look like a cross, and it is commonly found in Classic Period hieroglyphs. But it is also a kind of Medicine Wheel. And the Maya still lay out their ritual altars in a fourfold pattern.

Four is symbolic of the Four Directions, as well as the four colors of corn which represent the four races of humanity. In Mayan myth there are four pillars which keep the Earth and Sky in their rightful places. In the number Four, all things reach a point of balance. The number Four also represents the four elements: Fire, Earth, Air, and Water; these compose nature and give us life. Since Manik' is the day sign representing the four quarters, it corresponds to the number Four.

A person born on a Four day has many powers, and can draw on her/his internal completeness or wholeness in order to manifest many strengths, abilities, and possibilities.

Five
(5)

The number Five represents the human hand with its five fingers, as well as the five senses. In the marketplace, the term *un manojo* or "a handful" indicates that you wish to buy five of some particular item. Some Maya teachers say that the five fingers and five senses are directly related to one another; each finger relates to one of the senses. In some ways of traditional Mayan thinking there are five stages of life as well: childhood, youth, adulthood, mature adult, and elder.

Our hands do our work for us. Hence Five may be regarded as the number of work, and of karma. In some Mayan traditions, the number Five is also related to the sacred fire of the Fire Ceremony, and hence to the idea of paying our karmic debts, for it is our karma and our misdoings that are burned away in the fire. Hence the corresponding day sign is Muluc.

Those who are born on a Five day often arrive early. They are the first to reach a goal, and may be ahead of their time. Sometimes their tendency to rush into things without forethought may lead them into awkward situations.

Six
(6)

The number Six is considered very positive in Mayan thinking. It is strong, stable, and enduring. Why should it not be? After all, it is an even number and a middle day in the *trecena*.

The number Six represents the vitality of the family: 1.) health; 2.) understanding; 3.) work/employment; 4.) friendship; 5.) property or possessions; 6.) positive and negative actions. Each one of these six affects the other; they are all closely related. If any one of these is lacking, the family suffers.

Six is the number of ultimate stability. In ancient Mayan mythology, the World Tree had certain symbolic associations with the number Six, and in contemporary Momostenango it is the "Place of Number Six," the sacred hill called Paklom, which represents the *axis mundi* or world center. In a sense, Six is both the center around which all things revolve and the road we take to reach it. Six is the Road of Life and corresponds to the day sign Eb.

People born on Six days are very realistic and practical; their actions have concrete reality and are based on an understanding of the practical aspects of life.

Seven
(7)

The number Seven may confuse some people, for it represents death or at least "endings." The reason for this may not be readily apparent. After all, isn't Seven the middle number? If we arrange the numbers on a pyramid, in accordance with the 13 Heavens of ancient myth, is Seven not the very apex of the pyramid?

Yes, but many Daykeepers see it from a different point of view. In order to illustrate this, return to the Calendar Board diagram in Chapter One of this book and examine the horizontal sequence of numbers for the day sign Caban. It will be like this:

1, 8, 2, 9, 3, 10, 4, 11, 5, 12, 6, 13, 7

Any day sign sequence beginning with one will end in a seven. This is why Seven is so often considered a symbol of endings. Even though it is the middle number between 1 and 13, and hence a day of balanced energy, major rituals are seldom performed on a Seven day—although rituals for an all-important Eight day may in fact begin on the evening of a Seven day, because that is when the energy of the new day sign first begins to make itself felt. In the *Pop Wuj*, the Hero Twins are named One Junajpu and Seven Junajpu, while the most important Underworld Lords are named One Death and Seven Death. When One and Seven are paired together in such a fashion, it is as if we were saying: "The beginning and end of the Hero Twins archetype," or "The alpha and omega of the Death archetype." The totality of the archetype, with all its attendant symbolism, is always implied when the *Pop Wuj* expresses itself in terms of "One and Seven."

But for those who were born upon a Seven day, the birth number has the significance of "middle" rather than "death." What can you see from the top of the pyramid? Everything!

With such clear, 360-degree vision, natives of this birth number will be able to see all sides of an issue and thus create new, harmonious solutions which resolve the seeming tension of the opposites. But because all points of view seem equally valid to them, they often avoid making decisions, thus appearing to withdraw from the scene just when their energy is needed most. It is part of the life path for many of the Sevens to learn to be decisive, to use one's "view from the top of the pyramid" for developing creative solutions rather than remaining in a state of indecisive neutrality.

At worst, the Sevens can be morally ambiguous. Let us not forget the "seven shames" described in the previous chapter. The day sign which corresponds to this number is Cib, which is likewise a symbol of the seven shames. Since all paths seem equal, why not take the path of least resistance? This is always a danger for the Sevens, who can manifest their energy in quite a destructive way if they allow their indecisiveness to turn into moral decline.

If the Sevens can use their meditative skills creatively, they can accomplish some of the finest work of any of the numbers. Mastering first things and last things, we master the material world. Seven is the beginning of magic.

Eight
(8)

If 1 and 7 are the beginning and the end, then 1 + 7 = 8, making Eight a number of completion or wholeness, much like the number Four. This is why there is some sort of ritual for almost every Eight day, and why some extremely traditional communities like Momostenango have a special local shrine dedicated to the number Eight. Of course, 4 + 4 = 8, so the wholeness implied in the number 4 is doubled here, as if the wholeness of the fourfold universe were seen from the viewpoint of both polarities: night and day, light and darkness, sun and moon, yin and yang.

The number Eight represents the weaving of life, the thread or cord of time, the sacred energy of birth. Eight represents the infinity of time or of the world. Time and life are depicted, symbolized by a ball of thread wound up or by yarn wrapped around the spindle of a spinning wheel; time and life unfold like a ball of thread unraveling or unrolling itself. The K'iche' believe that the umbilical cord is composed of eight threads.

The Mayan symbol for Eight, a bar with three dots over it, has meaning; the three dots on top represent man and day, the bar underneath represents Mother Earth. Eight is the male principle of the universe. Its day sign correspondence is Ahau, the symbol of the heroic, conquering solar force.

One might easily imagine that life is easy for those born on an Eight day, but this is not always the case. In reality, the Eights are surprisingly volatile. A person born on an Eight day can easily or quickly change his or her thoughts and feelings. Some are prone to become upset, disturbed, angry, and annoyed.

Nine
(9)

Though even numbers manifest their positive qualities more easily than odd ones, I have tried to stress that there are infinite variations within this general scheme. Nine is an excellent example, because even though it is an odd number, it is an extremely positive one, often used for ritual purposes. (Momostenango has community shrines for the numbers 1, 6, 8, and 9.) In modern Yucatan, the days are no longer kept (and probably have not been kept for more than a hundred years). But the sanctity of the number Nine is still remembered. The Cruzob Maya of Quintana Roo hold their

Ceremony of the Speaking Cross on the ninth day of each month—even though they are using the Gregorian Calendar, they still remember the special nature of Nine.

The number Nine is often called "the number of life". It represents the process of human gestation; there are nine months of pregnancy, nine months of human development prior to birth. Nine is associated with women, pregnancy, and the nine moon cycles of the 260-day ritual or sacred calendar. (9 x 29 = 261; nine moon cycles are a metaphor for a human pregnancy, which is a bit more than 261 days.) Thus Nine is the female principle of the universe and its corresponding day sign is the extremely feminine Ix, symbolic of Mother Nature.

As the number of life, Nine also symbolizes the struggle of life and its unfolding, its development. Life poses a struggle between light and darkness, between happiness, good fortune, opportunities and positive experiences or suffering, problems, challenges, difficulties and misfortunes. Nine represents the Underworld/Xib'alb'a (the Nine Lords of Xib'alb'a, the nine levels of Xib'alb'a or "Nine Hells" of Mayan, Toltec and Aztec mythology), but this is not necessarily the astrological significance of Nine, a number whose symbolism is overwhelmingly positive. The Maya say that there are nine steps to follow in the construction of a house. There are also nine steps or nine stages to growing and harvesting crops. One begins by clearing, cleaning and preparing the land, then plowing or digging to create furrows, then planting seeds, etc. until harvest time arrives. The harvest is the ninth step. There are nine steps or stages in the creation of a child; the first is the union of man and woman, the last stage is birth. The human being needs a house, a body to house the soul. A house or home needs souls to occupy and inhabit it.

A person born on a Nine day is very stable and balanced. Both men and women will seem to have very feminine personality traits.

Ten
(10)

The number Ten represents our two hands with their ten fingers. Therefore it also represents human cooperation, family, society, man and woman together as a couple. As such, it is a symbol of universal law, as embodied in principles such as Justice and Order and symbolized by the corresponding day sign Oc.

Ten symbolizes the bonds and relationships between people. It also symbolizes the ups and downs of life. One has moments of success, gain, advancement and improvement; sometimes we are capable of overcoming all our problems and obstacles. But life also presents moments of loss and failure. This is the duality inherent in all our actions, and hence in the number Ten.

A person born on a Ten day is very stable, as we would expect to find among the even numbers. But there is a certain fragile quality to the Tens. Underneath the surface, they are extremely vulnerable.

Eleven
(11)

As noted in our general remarks about the wave of time, high numbers are considered "too intense." Odd numbers are more difficult than even ones. Eleven is a high odd number, and its energy is neither positive nor negative but neutral. Eleven represents the past, present and future, everything that develops or unfolds over time. At its best, it is the balance of life. Some shamans make special visits to local sacred mountains on certain Eleven days. But for the most part, Eleven can be a very challenging number.

A person born on an Eleven day has great potential but tends to lack direction and a sense of location or "home." Such people tend to be drifters. Afflicted with indecision and insecurity, they are able to find their path and purpose only with great effort. However, all this turmoil has an unexpected benefit—creativity. With all of their existential dilemmas, Eleven natives can develop into some of the finest creative artists of all. The corresponding day sign is Kan.

Twelve
(12)

As the highest of the even numbers, Twelve represents reflection on life, an inner summing up of the meaning of one's experiences. With the number Twelve, we reach understanding about life and come to certain conclusions. We reflect upon and recollect all our actions and experiences, everything we have done and accomplished, weaving together all individual, family, societal and cultural thought. We create a record or file of our life and thoughts.

Thus Twelve represents the generality of thought. It is a gestalt, a wholeness. It embodies our entire life circle—family and community, teachers and students, and the "universal community" that is symbolized by its corresponding day sign Cauac.

People born on Twelve days have much energy, power and strength. They are often able to reach a high level of self-reliance and independence.

Thirteen
(13)

Thirteen has special qualities, some of which are of great value—despite the fact that Thirteen is both very high and an odd number. On Thirteen days, the spirit world is closer to our own world. Hence a Thirteen day is the best day upon which to meditate, seek visions, and cultivate potential psychic gifts.

The number Thirteen is the completion of life, the completion of all movement and process. As we have seen, it represents the thirteen major joints in the human body and therefore the overall ability of humans to move. In keeping with Mayan teachings regarding *koyopa* or psycho-spiritual energies in the human body, it is believed that energy is distributed in these thirteen major joints in the human body and in thirteen dimensions. (Perhaps this relates to the "Thirteen Heavens" of Toltec, Aztec and Mayan myth.)

The human being and the human body have many powers and abilities. There is not only the physical power and ability to move about and create things that are useful and practical as well as beautiful and aesthetic; there is also great potential to develop psychic and spiritual powers, to make contact and enter into communication with other worlds and dimensions. Thirteen relates to the development, acquisition and accumulation of such great powers; it relates to the ability to prophesy, to foretell the future, to predict trends, natural disasters and events, to forecast, to be skilled and accurate in many forms of divination and the related spiritual advice or counseling that goes with it (a skill developed by Daykeepers and Maya priests). Thirteen also relates to the refinement and greater sensitivity, enhanced perception and acute intuition that one can develop. This includes having premonitions. The K'iche' Maya consider Thirteen to be a great "source of consultations and/or divinations," meaning that it is favorable to consult shamans and diviners on Thirteen days, and that those born on such a day have innate talents in that direction. The number Thirteen symbolizes those activities and facilitates them; it enhances the accuracy and precision of divination readings/consultations and the related spiritual counseling involved. It facilitates forecasts, predictions and prophecy about the future. It enhances the ability to feel and perceive signs and signals in the blood (i.e. messages that come via pulsations and energy movements in different parts of the body). It enhances and symbolizes the ability to journey to other dimensions and realms. All these powers, abilities and skills would be increased and enhanced on a Thirteen day.

A person born on a Thirteen day will have great psychic and spiritual powers or be able to develop such powers easily. This potential always lies within those who are born on a day numbered Thirteen. In fact, such an individual may find life difficult if he or she neglects to explore this dimension of life.

The number Thirteen has no corresponding day sign, for it transcends the cycles of time.

Chapter 4

The Mayan Destiny Chart

Now we are ready to examine the way in which the basic day sign and number are woven together with other factors to create a simple form of Mayan horoscope. This horoscopic diagram, known by a number of names, including "Destiny Chart," "Mayan Cross," or "Tree of Life," has been popularized internationally by Don Alejandro Cirilo Perez Oxlaj beginning in the early 1990s.

The origins of the Mayan Destiny Chart are unclear. I have encountered Daykeepers who regard it as a fairly recent development, part of the ongoing spiritual renaissance of the Maya; they claim that they do not remember having seen it during childhood, only as adults. Others claim that it is an inheritance from the Four Fathers of humanity whose migrations are chronicled in the *Pop Wuj* and who, as we learned in Chapter 2, witnessed the first sunrise of this present World Age.

Whenever and wherever the Mayan Destiny Chart may have originated, it is based upon ancient principles. The symbol of the cross was not introduced to the Maya by the proponents of European Christianity; it can be found on the walls of Palenque and other Classic Mayan cities. To the Maya, the cross was the World Tree, the axis at the center of all things. The World Tree was the origin of the eternal wheel of the four directions. This is what the cross symbol actually means in Mayan spirituality: It is the center point of the fourfold universe.

This fourfold reality also serves as an axis for the way in which we human beings orient ourselves to the cosmos all around us. A simple mental exercise will illustrate this concept.

- *Stand facing East, your arms extended from your sides as in a cross. This is the traditional orientation of Mayan Daykeepers, just as it is with Hindu yogis and mystics from other world traditions. Imagine that your future lies before you in the East, along with your children, all your descendants, and all your lives to come. Behind you, in the West, are your ancestors and your own past existences. To your right, in the South, lie all your male qualities, as well as the men who cross your life's path. On your left, in the North, lie your female qualities, including the women you encounter in life.*

- *Now, imagine that your heart center, the very core of your inner World Tree, is occupied by the day sign upon which you were born.*

- *Ahead of you (East) lies a day sign that is symbolic of your children and your future.*

- *Behind you (West) is another day sign, symbolic of your past.*

- *On your right (South) is the Power of the Right Hand, a day sign symbolic of the masculine or yang energies of your psyche.*

- *On your left (North) is the Power of the Left Hand, a day sign representing your feminine or yin energies.*

Now let us see how to build a personal "Tree of Life," or Mayan Destiny Chart, based on the principles above.

1. Begin by using the Mayan Calendar Tables in Appendix B to find your basic day sign. For example, let us assume that you wish to find the day sign for an individual born August 18, 1961. Begin by finding the year 1961 in the Mayan Calendar Tables. Running your finger down the list of dates, you will note that August 9 was 1 Etznab, while August 22 was 1 Chuen.

2. Next, consult the Calendar Board diagram, also in Appendix B. Locate 1 Etznab and count forward: August 9 is 1 Etznab, August 10 is 2 Cauac, and so on until you reach August 18, which will be 10 Manik'. If you were born in late February or early March of an even-numbered year, be alert for leap year days! They can throw off your count. (Leap years are marked with an asterisk in the Mayan Calendar Tables.)

10 Manik' is the Mayan birth sign for any individual born on August 18, 1961. This is the single most important factor in the Mayan Destiny Chart, for each day sign imparts its *nawal* and its energies to all those born under its influence. The *tzolk'in* day upon which we are born determines the indwelling spirit that acts as our guardian. The *tzolk'in* day of our birth gives us its "face."

In other words, the day sign of your birth is the center point of your Mayan Destiny Chart (you can think of it as a cross, medicine wheel, or Tree of Life), which includes five signs total: one for each of the four directions and one for the center. Now let us discover which day signs form the branches of your personal Tree of Life.

The four directional day signs that accompany you and your basic birth sign through life are found by a magical-mathematical formula that makes use of the numbers 7 and 9. Let's continue with our example, that of an individual born on 10 Manik':

3. Use the Calendar Board diagram to count backwards nine days from the day sign 10 Manik' until you reach 2 Cauac, which is your Conception Sign.

4. Count forward nine days from 10 Manik'. This brings you to 5 Men, which is your Future Sign or Destiny Sign.

5. Now, count backward seven days from 10 Manik'. This will bring you to 4 Imix. This is the Power of the Right Hand, symbolic of your masculine or yang energies.

6. Count forward seven days from 10 Manik' to 3 Ben, the Power of the Left Hand, symbolic of feminine or yin energies. You now have a complete Mayan Destiny Chart (See Figure 9).

Figure 9. MAYAN DESTINY CHART FOR 10 MANIK'

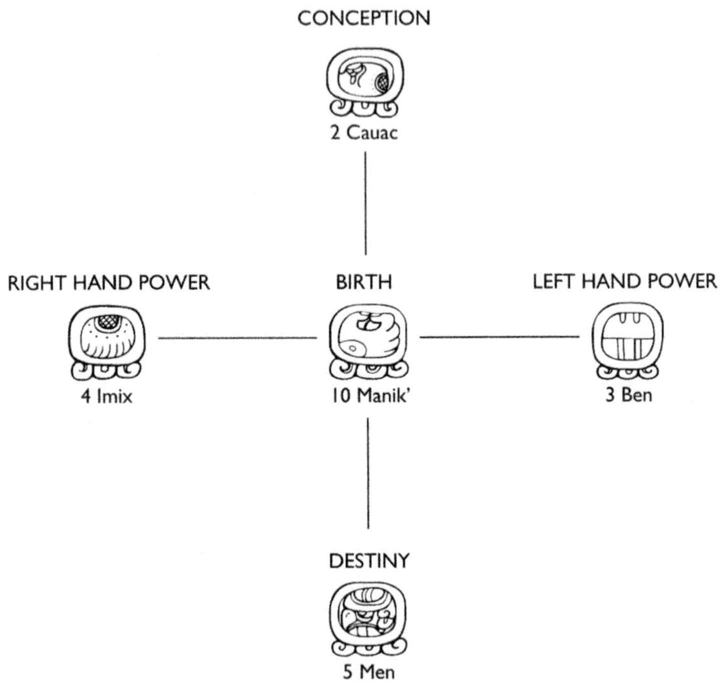

CONCEPTION

2 Cauac

RIGHT HAND POWER   BIRTH   LEFT HAND POWER

4 Imix   10 Manik'   3 Ben

DESTINY

5 Men

A few guidelines about how to interpret a Mayan Destiny Chart can now be established. As we learned in the previous two chapters, your birth sign and number establish your indwelling archetype and the way it manifests itself in terms of human personality. But what about the other signs? Let's explore what they mean:

The Conception Sign:

This is the second most important factor in the Mayan Destiny Chart, next only to the day sign and number of birth. The Conception Sign is symbolic of the months spent in the mother's womb. It represents your pre-conscious experiences before birth, and as such it serves as the template of your family karma, your immediate family of origin as well as your ancestral karma. The early experiences that shape you and provide you with an outlook on life—whether you turn out naturally trusting and friendly, or angry and uncertain—all depend, to a certain degree, on the nature of your birth family. And yet these individuals, these family members, are in turn conditioned by the experiences they had in their own families, and so on and so on, back to the very beginning of humankind. Since the Maya have a concept of reincarnation, it is by no means unusual to encounter Daykeepers who will say that the Conception Sign even represents your karma of incarnation, the fruits of your former lives—which, after all, condition the nature of the life and hence the family into which you were born in this lifetime.

Some will have already noted that the day sign of conception must mathematically be the same for everyone born upon a particular day sign. Just as anyone born upon Manik' will have Cauac as a Conception Sign, so anyone born upon Chuen will have Akb'al as a Conception Sign, while anyone born upon Ix will have Cimi, and so on. Does this mean that we should rely upon the number of the Conception Sign to give us more details about the native's family system?

Don Rigoberto told me not to bother much with the number of the Conception Sign. Numbers, as we have seen, are factors which modify our day sign and thus shape our outward personality. The meanings of the Conception Sign have to do with factors that are buried deep in the subconscious. Since they are not "personality indicators," the Conception Sign draws very little influence from its number. Instead, all those who incarnate with a particular day sign as their *nawal* will also bring with them a similar karmic inheritance, that symbolized by the Conception Sign.

Personally, I have found that the number of the Conception Sign does in fact play a role, if only a small one, especially if it is very low (1 to 3) or very high (11 to 13). If the number is low, the individual may have very little sense of attachment to the family system and may very well be functioning quite independently. If the number is high, the force of past karma may be quite turbulent and difficult to overcome.

The Destiny Sign or Future Sign

Together with the Birth Sign and Conception Sign, the Destiny Sign comprises the central column or "trunk" of your World Tree. To work with your Destiny Sign and realize its full potential in your life is a choice. For many, it will be enough simply to harness the full potential of their Birth Sign. To be able to look ahead, into the future, is a gift. The seed of things to come, the Destiny Sign symbolizes all those archetypal themes that are both rewarding and appropriate for natives of your day sign to cultivate.

If we make use of the qualities that are characteristic of this sign, we may usefully shape for ourselves a vision of the future that is in accordance with the flow of our basic life pattern as established by the Birth Sign. In terms of material world manifestation, I have also found that the Destiny Sign often rather accurately describes our children (or at least some of them), for they are part of the future that we create for ourselves and for the world at large.

The Power of the Right Hand

As in so many other metaphysical polarity paradigms around the globe, the right side symbolizes the masculine or yang polarity of your existence. Some have described this sign as our way of functioning in the material world. It governs the way we reason and think, as well as the way we take (or do not take) strong, bold actions to realize our dreams and our desires.

A forceful, positive day sign combined with a balanced number in this position indicates an individual who can easily take charge of her or his destiny, maneuvering through the ups and downs of the material world with grace and skill. A challenging day sign or difficult number here shows an individual for whom such skills do not come naturally and who must work in order to develop a useful way of functioning in the "real" world.

I have also found that whether you are female or male, this sign will often indicate the character of the men who impact your life.

The Power of the Left Hand

This is the feminine, or yin, polarity of your life. It symbolizes the quality of your intuition, your inner, mystical way of knowing. It governs the way you perceive emotionally and spiritually.

If the sign in this position is one that easily establishes a connection with the "otherworld" all around us, you will have an innate talent to navigate the deep waters of the unconscious; you can rely upon your intuition to guide you. Challenging combinations here can lead to impulsive emotions, as well as illusions or apprehensions that interfere with the clarity of your intuition.

I have also found that whether you are female or male, this sign will often indicate the character of the women in your life.

Let us take a look at an actual Tree of Life and see how this works. Since almost everyone on the planet has heard of Marilyn Monroe and knows at least a little bit about her, we shall use her Mayan Destiny chart as our example (see Figure 10).

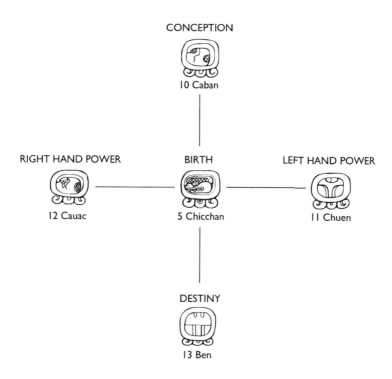

Figure 10. MAYAN DESTINY CHART FOR MARILYN MONROE

Marilyn Monroe was born on 5 Chicchan. As we have seen, the day sign of birth is the most important factor; it constitutes one's essential archetype. Chicchan is the sign of the Feathered Serpent; it is the destiny of these individuals to delve deeply into the mysteries of the universe, seeking for absolute knowledge and absolute truth. Quite apart from her status as a legendary sex symbol, Monroe was also something of an intellectual, a constant reader of books, a student of psychology and a lover of classical music.

Since Chicchan is the symbol of the "serpent power" within, its knowledge is never far removed from the physical body which houses it. Marilyn Monroe was not the only Chicchan native who was famous for physical sensuality. Mae West and Angelina Jolie were also born under the sign of the Feathered Serpent.

How does the number 5 modify the nature of the Chicchan archetype? A person born on a 5 day tends to be the first in line; these people are typically in a hurry. They may be ahead of their time, and sometimes their tendency to rush into things without forethought may lead them into awkward situations. At a time when psychology was regarded by most Americans as "head shrinking" and therapists as a species of "witch doctor," Monroe was one of its advocates. She made no secret of the fact that she was an exhibitionist. She was also open about her love for Russian literature—at a time when a bowl of borscht could place someone under fire from Senator Joe McCarthy's minions as a suspected Communist.

It's no wonder that the 5's are always in a hurry. These people are always surrounded by the four highest and most intense numbers, with 10 in their past, 11 to their left, 12 to their right and 13 in their future. With 10 Caban as the Conception Sign, we can see that Marilyn's interest in intellectual matters was something deep within her, an innate part of her karma. She was not by any means raised in a highly intellectual environment, but those who grew up with her remember her running down the hallways of junior high school loaded down with books, even as she went from one foster home to another.

11 Chuen to her left was a mixed bag. As a day sign, in and of itself, Chuen is altogether positive, and its position on her intuitive side may have been largely responsible for her artistic temperament.

The 11 is more difficult; though this number can be highly creative at its best, it also tends to spark controversy and a sense of aimlessness. Considered as a unit, 11 Chuen is a fair portrait of the artistic temperament haunted by inner conflict expressed through a variety of indulgences and addictions. It is also worth noting that the women in her life were a mixed bag as well, with some acting as staunch trusted friends and others as a source of betrayal.

12 Cauac on the right is also problematical. In essence, there is nothing wrong with it, but it would have worked better on the left rather than the right. The Power on our Right Hand is intended to guide our logical, rational decisions in the material world. With gentle, dreamlike Cauac in that position, there is very little logic or practicality to draw on. Her worldly life was a mess. She did, however, have the support of a number of strong but sensitive artistic men, embodying the 12 Cauac archetype. The most important man in her life was arguably her third husband, Pulitzer prize-winning playwright Arthur Miller.

Finally, there is 13 Ben, the sign of her destiny. Ben is the symbol of the resurrected corn, the promise of life eternal, and 13 is the highest, most mystical number. As remarked earlier, not everyone chooses to reach for the potential inherent in the Destiny Sign or Future Sign. She did. 13 Ben is the archetype. It represents the ultimate triumph of life over death.

In the pages that follow, I shall not give detailed expositions for every sign in every possible position. Instead, the reader is urged to use the following pages as workbook examples.

Collect all the people you know whose birth signs are available to you and map out their charts. As you ponder the meaning of their Conception Sign, Future Sign, and so on, return to Chapter 2 and re-read the descriptions of the relevant day signs.

Ask yourself: How does this day sign impact the person's rational side (Right Hand Power)? Is this person reaching toward her or his Destiny Sign? How does the day sign on the left relate to this person's intuition?

Then flip to Chapter 3. How do the numbers modify the day signs and turn archetypes into personalities?

It is only by practice that we learn. Treat these templates as a little astrological laboratory. Print out the page that serves as a template for the person you are studying, then fill in the numbers.

CHUEN
Master of All the Arts

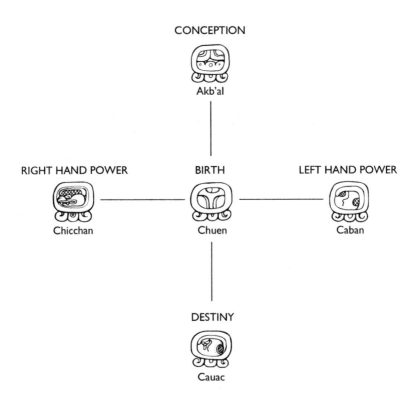

CONCEPTION

Akb'al

RIGHT HAND POWER   BIRTH   LEFT HAND POWER

Chicchan   Chuen   Caban

DESTINY

Cauac

EB
The Road of Life

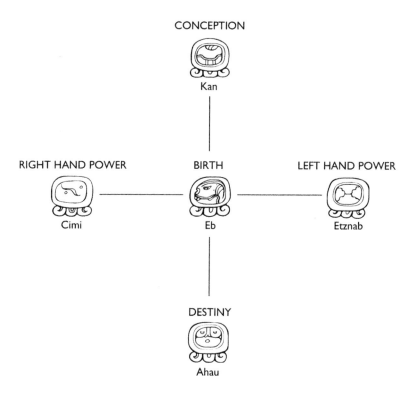

CONCEPTION
Kan

RIGHT HAND POWER   BIRTH   LEFT HAND POWER

Cimi   Eb   Etznab

DESTINY
Ahau

BEN
The Resurrection of the Corn

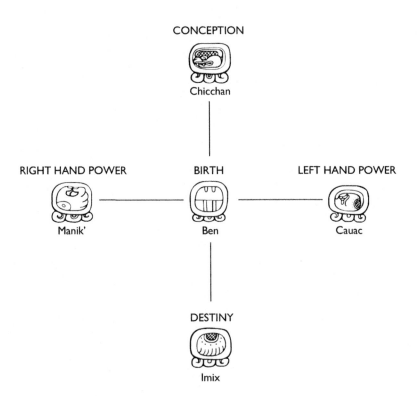

CONCEPTION

Chicchan

RIGHT HAND POWER   BIRTH   LEFT HAND POWER

Manik'   Ben   Cauac

DESTINY

Imix

IX
The Jaguar

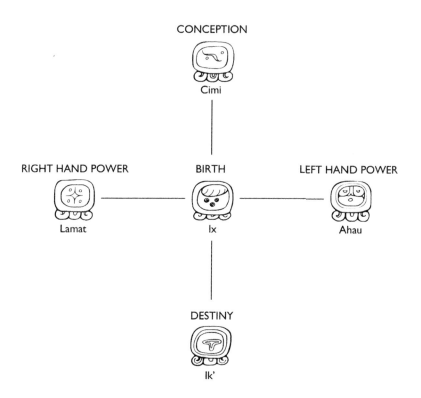

CONCEPTION

Cimi

RIGHT HAND POWER   BIRTH   LEFT HAND POWER

Lamat   Ix   Ahau

DESTINY

Ik'

MEN
The Vision of the Bird

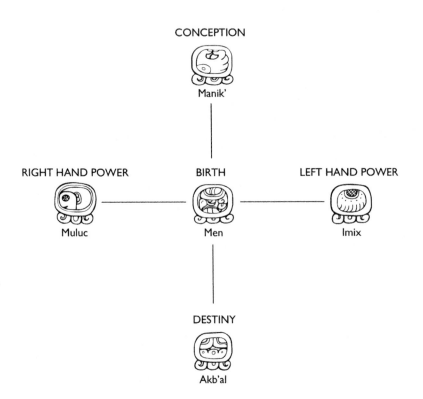

CONCEPTION

Manik'

RIGHT HAND POWER   BIRTH   LEFT HAND POWER

Muluc   Men   Imix

DESTINY

Akb'al

CIB
Forgiveness

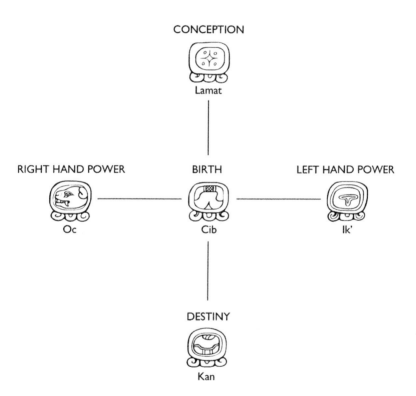

CONCEPTION

Lamat

RIGHT HAND POWER   BIRTH   LEFT HAND POWER

Oc   Cib   Ik'

DESTINY

Kan

CABAN
The Vision of the Cosmos

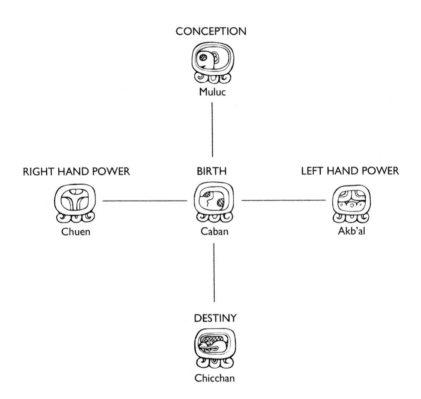

CONCEPTION

Muluc

RIGHT HAND POWER   BIRTH   LEFT HAND POWER

Chuen   Caban   Akb'al

DESTINY

Chicchan

ETZNAB
Obsidian Knife

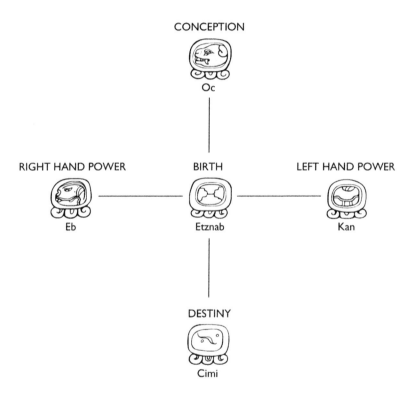

CONCEPTION
Oc

RIGHT HAND POWER   BIRTH   LEFT HAND POWER
Eb   Etznab   Kan

DESTINY
Cimi

CAUAC
The Universal Community

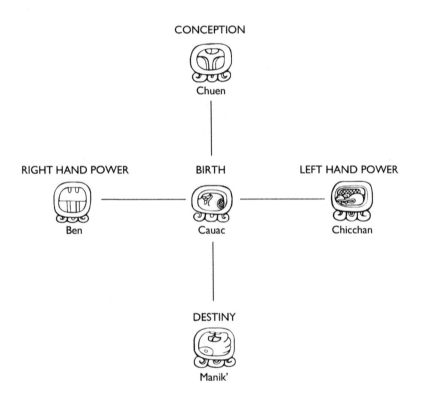

CONCEPTION

Chuen

RIGHT HAND POWER   BIRTH   LEFT HAND POWER

Ben   Cauac   Chicchan

DESTINY

Manik'

AHAU
The Hunter

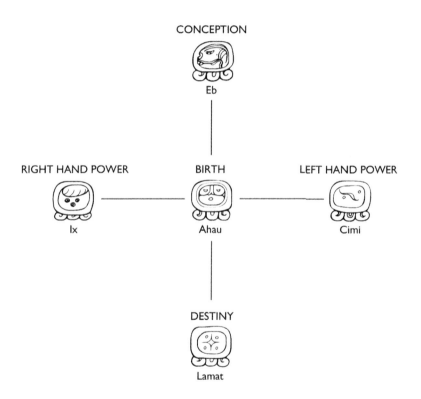

CONCEPTION

Eb

RIGHT HAND POWER   BIRTH   LEFT HAND POWER

Ix   Ahau   Cimi

DESTINY

Lamat

IMIX
The Left Hand

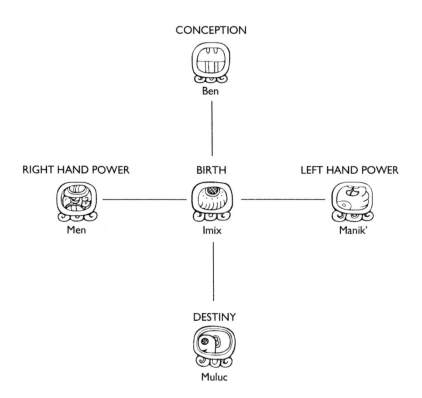

IK'
The Breath of Life

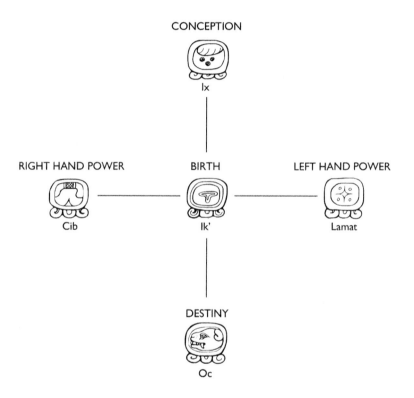

CONCEPTION

Ix

RIGHT HAND POWER   BIRTH   LEFT HAND POWER

Cib   Ik'   Lamat

DESTINY

Oc

AKB'AL
Dawn

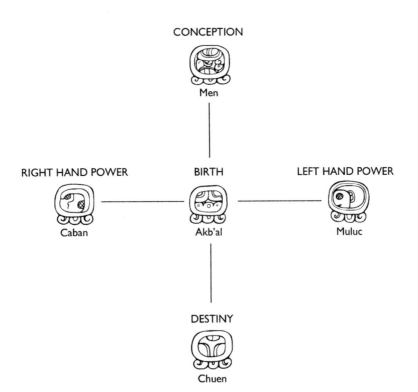

CONCEPTION
Men

RIGHT HAND POWER
Caban

BIRTH
Akb'al

LEFT HAND POWER
Muluc

DESTINY
Chuen

KAN
The Net

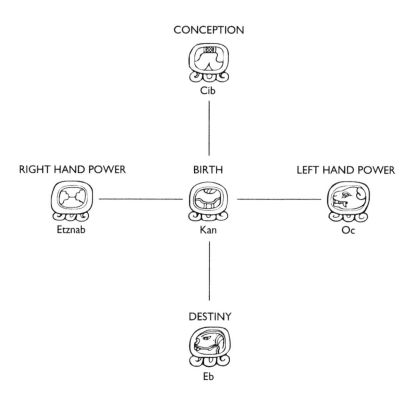

CONCEPTION

Cib

RIGHT HAND POWER   BIRTH   LEFT HAND POWER

Etznab   Kan   Oc

DESTINY

Eb

CHICCHAN
Feathered Serpent

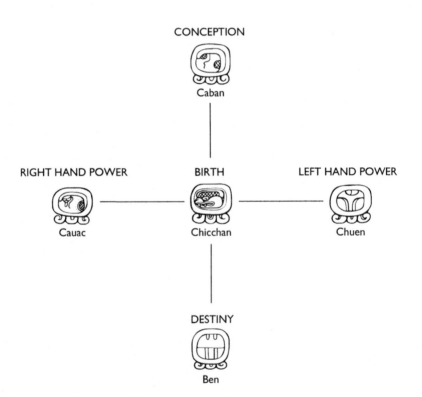

CONCEPTION
Caban

RIGHT HAND POWER   BIRTH   LEFT HAND POWER
Cauac   Chicchan   Chuen

DESTINY
Ben

CIMI
Death and Rebirth

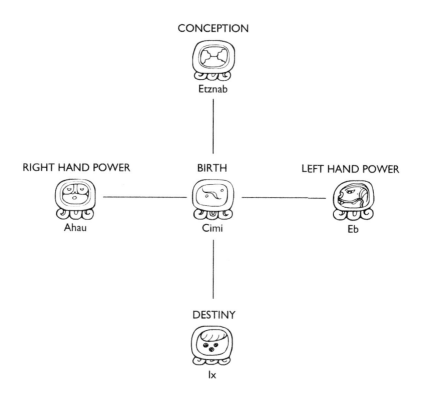

CONCEPTION

Etznab

RIGHT HAND POWER

Ahau

BIRTH

Cimi

LEFT HAND POWER

Eb

DESTINY

Ix

MANIK'
The Pillars of the Universe

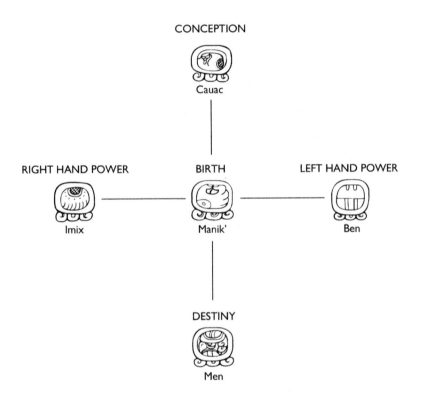

CONCEPTION

Cauac

RIGHT HAND POWER   BIRTH   LEFT HAND POWER

Imix   Manik'   Ben

DESTINY

Men

LAMAT
The Regeneration of the Earth

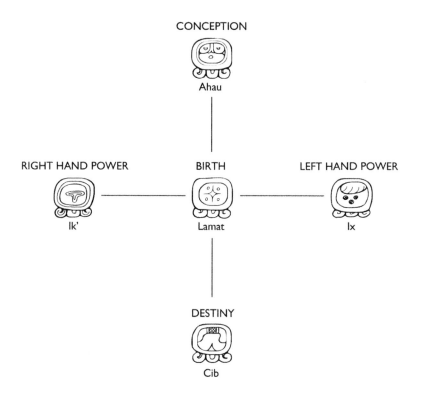

CONCEPTION

Ahau

RIGHT HAND POWER   BIRTH   LEFT HAND POWER

Ik'   Lamat   Ix

DESTINY

Cib

MULUC
Offering

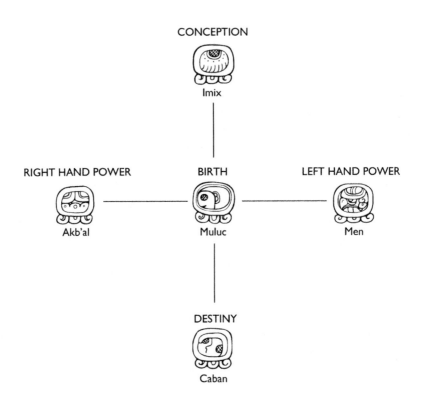

CONCEPTION

Imix

RIGHT HAND POWER   BIRTH   LEFT HAND POWER

Akb'al   Muluc   Men

DESTINY

Caban

OC
Law and Spiritual Authority

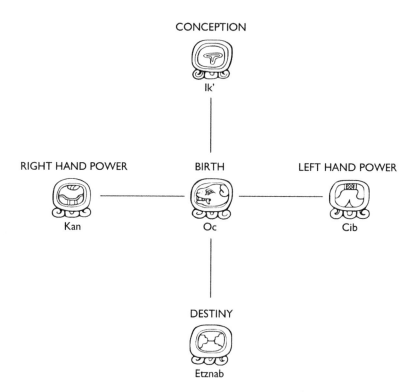

Chapter 5

The Year Lord

At this point, the astrologer trained in Western, Vedic, or Chinese systems of thought may very well raise a skeptical eyebrow, asking:

"Isn't this entire system a bit limited? In other systems, each horoscope is absolutely and completely unique, as individual as a snowflake, never replicated. That gives depth to these other systems of astrology, but in Mayan astrology there are still only 260 possible combinations, even if we use all the signs included in the Destiny Chart. Shouldn't there be something more to it?"

That's a very good question, and a valid objection.

In the next two chapters, we shall explore some of the factors used by contemporary Mayan astrologers to discover the individuality and uniqueness inherent in each Mayan horoscope.

The Solar Calendar

One element that is too often forgotten in the practice of Mayan Astrology is the Lord of the Year.

The Mayan solar calendar is called the *ab'* (Yucatec: *haab*). The Maya recognized the solar year of 365 days, just as we do. However, they divided it differently. We use a calendar of 12 months, each of approximately 30 days. The Maya divided the year into 18 months of 20 days each, followed by five extra days at the end of the year.

The days of the *haab* are not numbered from one through twenty. Instead, the first day of each month is called the "seating" of that month (i.e., the seating of Pop, the seating of Uo, and so on).

This terminology derives from the fact that each month was a kind of deity or spiritual entity unto itself, and, like a chieftain or lord, took its "seat" upon its throne. The first day of each month—the seating day—is numbered 0, then the days proceed from 1 through 19. At the end of 360 days come five final days, collectively called the *uayeb*. These five days were traditionally considered unlucky, especially by the Aztecs, who fasted, prayed, and quenched all fires throughout the *uayeb* period. I have spent the five *uayeb* days among traditional Daykeepers in Momostenango. No projects or important matters were initiated at that time. It was regarded as a time for reflection and meditation, a time to be spent quietly with the family rather than in the haste and hurry of the outside world.

Note that the *haab* equals 365 days, whereas the true solar year is a little longer than that. This is why our Gregorian Calendar includes an extra day every four years—to bring the 365-day calendar back into harmony with the actual cycle of the sun. The Maya were aware of the true duration of the year, but for reasons of ritual timing they made no attempt to reconcile the *haab* with the solar cycle; the *haab* kept moving ahead of the solar year. In 1553, the first day of the solar year, 0 Pop, occurred on July 26 (according to the most recent revision of the Gregorian Calendar), whereas the Calendar shamans of Guatemala now celebrate the arrival of 0 Pop near the end of February. In 2010, when I celebrated the arrival of the new year in Momostenango, Lord 11 Manik' (Kej) "arrived" on February 22.

The Year Lords

Now let us look at the way in which the *haab* and the *tzolk'in* combine. Each day has a position in both the secular and sacred calendars—a specific resonance in terms of both ordinary and sacred time. Consider the date March 2, 1977. This was the Mayan New Year's day, 0 Pop. In terms of the Sacred Calendar, the *tzolk'in*, it was also the day 4 Ik'. Because of the disparity between the number of days in these cycles, the *tzolk'in* completed an entire cycle of 260 days and returned to the day 4 Ik' on November 17, 1977, while the solar calendar had only reached the day 0 Kankin.

How long will it take before 4 Ik' and 0 Pop once again fall on the same day? How long a time must pass before the solar and sacred calendars once again coincide? The answer is 18,980 days—just a few days short of fifty-two years. On February 28, 2029, it will once again be 4 Ik' 0 Pop.

This cycle of fifty-two years is called the Calendar Round. It was recognized as a significant cycle by the Maya, and attained paramount importance among the Aztecs, who referred to it as a "bundle of years."

Due to the way in which the two calendars interpenetrate, the New Year's day of 0 Pop can only coincide with one of four *tzolk'in* day signs. These four New Year's days were called Year Bearers (Spanish: *cargadores*) by most Mesoamerican cultures, and different Native traditions used different sets of Year Bearers. For example, the Aztecs used Ben, Etznab, Akb'al, and Lamat as their Year Bearers, while the Yucatec Maya, during early Spanish colonial times, used Muluc, Ix, Cauac, and Kan. The great Mayan city of Tikal, as well as the central Mexican metropolis of Teotihuacan, celebrated the New Year on Ik', Manik', Eb, and Caban. The K'iche' Maya of today use these same Year Bearers. The Lord of the Year is called the *Mam*, a word which quite simply means "grandfather."

Although this may all seem a bit arbitrary and confusing, there is a kind of logic to it. As we have seen, each day sign of the *tzolk'in* is associated with one of the four cardinal directions. No matter which four days were designated as Year Bearers, there was always one day for each direction. Any given year had certain characteristics according to the directional attribute of the day that served as Year Bearer.

The years succeed each other in an orderly fashion. For example, as we have seen, 0 Pop fell on the day 4 Ik' in 1977. Thus the year received the name 4 Ik'. In 1978, 0 Pop fell on 5 Manik', in 1979 upon 6 Eb, and in 1980 upon 7 Caban—the number of the year increasing by one each time. By 1986, 13 Manik' had been reached; so 1987 received the name 1 Eb. How long will it take until our initial year 4 Ik' comes around again? The answer, of course, is fifty-two years (4 day signs x 13 numbers = 52). The year 2029 will be 4 Ik'. This progression of the Year Bearers played—and still plays—a major role in what we might call "political astrology," the prediction of future events through the study of the cycles of time. The Year Bearers were also important in the prediction of climatic and agricultural cycles, forming a kind of "farmer's almanac" for the Maya.

Figure 11. THE LORDS OF THE YEAR

THE LORDS OF THE YEAR				
I	II	III	IV	V
IMIX	CABAN	BEN	MULUC	CHICCHAN
CIMI	IK'	ETZNAB	IX	OC
CHUEN	MANIK'	AKB'AL	CAUAC	MEN
CIB	EB	LAMAT	KAN	AHAU

Before we proceed any farther with our study of the Year Lords, a few words of caution are necessary. Each civilization in Mesoamerica—the Olmecs, Toltecs, Maya, and Aztecs—had its own way of counting the solar year. Each culture had its own New Year's day, and its own Year Lords.

Who was right and who was wrong?

Looking for the answer can drive you crazy. Maybe no one was "right" or "wrong." Maybe they were all just different.

Even among the Maya of today, there are several different ways of counting the solar year. One method, which has recently become quite popular internationally, asserts that the year 2011 is 13 Eb, and that the "arrival of the Mam" occurs in April.

Not only were many of my own personal studies undertaken in Momostenango, but Maya traditionalists and anthropologists both agree that that the Momostecan count of the solar year is the most ancient, and that it has survived intact for many centuries.

According to the Daykeepers of Momostenango, 2011 is the year 12 Eb, and the Year Lord or "Mam" arrived on February 22.

It is the Momostecan count that we shall use in this book. Some Mayan astrologers find the whole issue of the correct counting of the solar year so controversial that they avoid it all together.

The Year Lord in Mayan Astrology

Much like the signs of the Chinese zodiac, the four Year Lords have an influence over everyone born during that particular year (see Figure 12.)

This establishes four basic "core personalities." No matter which of the 260 possible day sign and number combinations we may be, we are all under the influence of one of these four essential personality types, depending on the year we were born.

For the most part, the astrological significance of a day sign which functions as the Year Lord is identical or at least similar to its significance as a *nawal* or birth-sign. Some of the important points are reiterated below:

Manik': The Energizer. Year Lord of the East.

People born in a Manik' year have a strong masculine energy regardless of their own gender. They are strong, brave, but often very refined at the same time. The men make excellent leaders, bosses, and authority figures; they may also be gifted as spiritual guides and teachers. Manik' men can be bossy and domineering but sometimes hide their true strength and energy beneath a passive demeanor.

Both women and men are true romantics and are often bohemians, frequently with an artistic flair or talent. They have a tendency to become involved in very intense but obsessive relationships. Manik' women are agile and strong; they are able to assume great responsibilities and occupy important positions. They are affectionate and appreciative, but must often make sacrifices to achieve their goals. They tend to dominate their husbands; they often seek fame, and unless they are careful to remain in balance, they too can become overbearing and domineering.

In order to maintain their equanimity, those born in Manik' years need to be in nature, for they are the archetypal guardians of the wild.

Eb: The Path Walker. Year Lord of the West.

Those born in an Eb year have an innate curiosity about the world around them, which makes them perpetual students of life. The most common expression of their curiosity is through travel, and their wanderings and explorations frequently endow them with wisdom. This year's natives commonly enjoy a long, healthy life. They derive sincere satisfaction from helping others. They tend to have numerous relationships in life, for their restless spirit is seldom satisfied with a single love. Because of their intrinsic good nature, most of their relationships will be fortunate, though one could not exactly describe them as the most faithful of partners.

Without a goal in mind, these people can wander without a clear sense of direction. They may be as cheerful and enthusiastic as ever, but they have no destination in mind. Those born in an Eb year need to keep the end of the road in sight, and to have a goal towards which they strive. Perhaps their worst qualities arise when they invest themselves too strongly in their opinions, always needing to be right. They often flourish in foreign countries and make cheerful, successful expatriates.

Caban: The Thinker. Year Lord of the North.

Those born in a Caban year are creative and clever. They love to read, but should not be mistaken for dreamy intellectuals who accomplish nothing. Their ideas are eminently practical and their problem-solving techniques are workable; this gives them natural leadership ability, and they frequently become pillars of their communities. This is a very masculine sign, and its natives have a masculine tone regardless of their own gender. Because they prefer the realm of the mind, they tend to live lives of extreme simplicity.

They tend to have a good record for maintaining lasting partnerships and relationships; they usually make wise choices in love, and they are able to weather the challenges which relationships bring throughout the years. They may sometimes be tactless and hurtful, even though they seldom intend to be. Some can be overly proud of their clever ideas; vanity and self-importance are among their worst faults. In terms of the human body, Caban is associated with the brain. These people are the "thinkers" of the *tzolk'in*.

Ik': The Hurricane. Year Lord of the South.

Even though this is the sign of the breath of life, those who are born under Ik' can blow in all kinds of directions. They can shift from a "breath of life" personality to a "hurricane" personality in minutes. And when they begin to storm, it is best to stay out of their way. They bluster more than any other year sign and have a reputation for taking things to extremes, frequently leveling everything in their paths.

On the positive side, those born in an Ik' year are brimming with cosmic energy. Their best qualities include confidence and self-assurance. Some are truly spiritual. Ik' people rely on their brains, are often skilled in math and make excellent investors or stockholders. They are also very good with words. Natives of an Ik' year can tackle difficult topics or arts of all kinds and acquire solid proficiency in such things. Able to navigate through almost any situation, they are among the strongest, toughest, and most resilient of the day signs. Their powerful energy tends to insure that they will become successful at something.

Figure 12. THE FOUR K'ICHE' YEAR LORDS

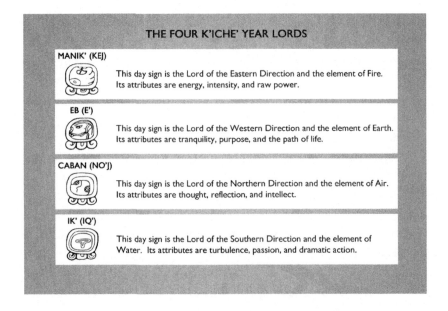

THE FOUR K'ICHE' YEAR LORDS	
MANIK' (KEJ)	This day sign is the Lord of the Eastern Direction and the element of Fire. Its attributes are energy, intensity, and raw power.
EB (E')	This day sign is the Lord of the Western Direction and the element of Earth. Its attributes are tranquility, purpose, and the path of life.
CABAN (NO'J)	This day sign is the Lord of the Northern Direction and the element of Air. Its attributes are thought, reflection, and intellect.
IK' (IQ')	This day sign is the Lord of the Southern Direction and the element of Water. Its attributes are turbulence, passion, and dramatic action.

Though the *tzolk'in* itself yields only 260 combinations, these 260 combinations must occur in a particular year ruled by a particular Year Lord. Since each of the four Year Lords will combine with all 13 numbers, this works out to 4 (Year Lords) x 13 (numbers) = 52 (which is called a Calendar Round). If 260 potential combinations doesn't seem that substantial to astrologers trained in the Western or Vedic systems, it should be recognized that each of the 260 days will recur at least once (sometimes more often) during every year. This brings us to 52 x 260 = 13,520 potential combinations. At this point Mayan astrology becomes genuinely complex!

We can use the Year Lords to add individuality and depth to any *tzolk'in* combination.

A good example lies with the two founders of modern psychology, Sigmund Freud and Carl Jung. Both men were born on 10 Ben. It is Ben's nature to act as an authority figure, both in the material and spiritual realms but especially in the spiritual. These natives are deep thinkers. Since 10 is both a high number and an even number, it easily manifests itself as both stability and power. Some Daykeepers have asserted that there is a certain "sensitivity" or "fragility" to the 10s as well.

Let's look at the Mayan birth chart for both men (see Figure 13.) The Conception Sign, representing the karmic past, is 2 Chicchan in both cases, and since the serpentine symbolism of this day sign is regarded among the Maya as very similar to the *kundalini* serpent symbolism among Tantric Hindus, we can see here the importance of human sexuality, which indeed became a part of the early phases of the field of psychology for which these men lay the foundation. Since Chicchan is just as much the scientist as the sexual mystic, it is also not surprising that both men were medical doctors at the outset of their careers.

Their Destiny Sign was 5 Imix, the sign of "the left hand of the Divine," which lends itself to mystical visions and the "deep waters" of the unconscious. Both men eagerly embraced their Destiny Sign of Imix, building upon its energy to explore the world of dreams and visions.

Their Right Hand Power, symbolizing the more rational or "masculine" aspect of consciousness, was 4 Manik', and their

Figure 13. THE FREUD–JUNG MAYAN CHART

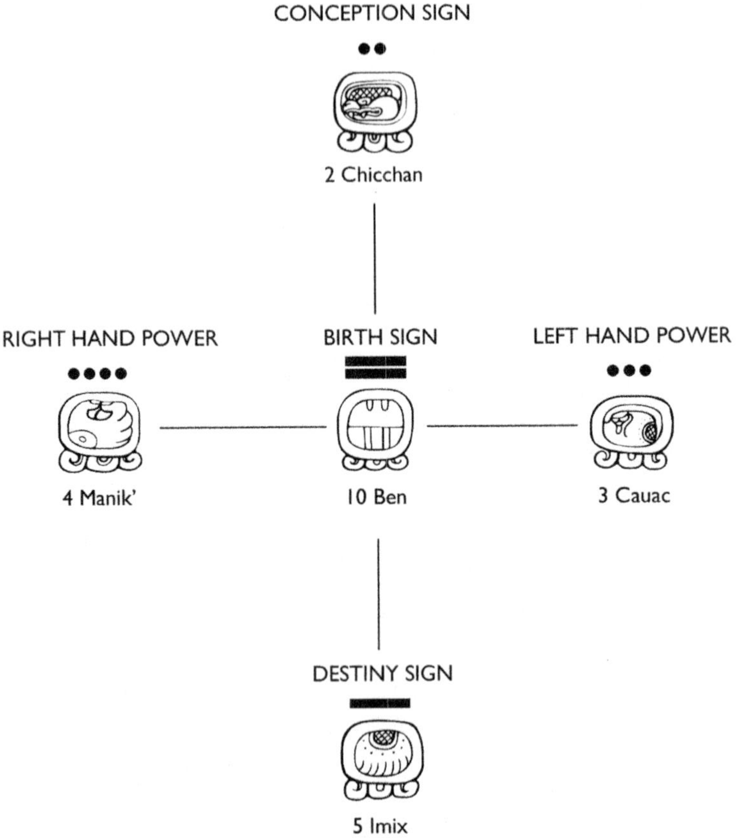

CONCEPTION SIGN

●●

2 Chicchan

RIGHT HAND POWER	BIRTH SIGN	LEFT HAND POWER
●●●●	▬▬	●●●

4 Manik'   10 Ben   3 Cauac

DESTINY SIGN

▬▬

5 Imix

Left Hand Power, the feminine or intuitive nature, was 3 Cauac. Manik' is always regarded as an especially masculine sign, and Cauac as quintessentially feminine. It is no wonder, then, that both men worked with the fine distinctions between male and female consciousness.

These are the similarities we can perceive in their lives and careers, given their sharing the same *tzolk'in* birth date. But there were abundant differences between them. Jung was large and athletic, jolly and gregarious, always a "hail fellow well met." Freud was of fragile health, nervous and introverted, difficult to get along with. How shall we explain such a difference in personality?

It is the Year Lord that makes all the difference. Freud and Jung may have been born on the same *tzolk'in* date, but they were born in different years: Freud in 13 Caban (1856) and Jung in 6 Eb (1875).

Freud was born in a Caban year, and Caban is the sign of the Thinker. Freud's philosophy was a product of deep thought; an introvert, he required plenty of solitude in order to do his work. Caban is regarded as a somewhat "tricky" year, in the sense that our thoughts may be either positive or negative. Freud's mental world shows signs of a dark and somewhat pessimistic outlook on human nature, and he certainly enjoyed upsetting others' vision of reality. The worldwide impact of his thinking lies partly in the fact that he was born in a 13 year. This highest of all the numbers lends itself to a deep connection with the mystical side of life; though Freud pretended to be a scientific rationalist, his insights into the human mind were more likely based upon pure intuition. His close relationship with the otherworldly side of life accentuated the "fragile" aspect of his 10 birth number; he was notorious for his nervous sensitivity. As we have noted, those who have a strong influence from the number 13 often need to access their mystical side in order to feel a sense of wholeness. A dedicated rationalist who fiercely rejected all things mystical, Freud developed the sense of nervous apprehension which so often results from that sort of neglect.

By contrast, Jung was born in the year 6 Eb. Of all the Year Lords, Eb is the mellowest. This day sign symbolizes the Road of Life. The outgoing Jung was an enthusiastic world traveler, literally walking the Road of Life by visiting many different nations and discoursing with wise men at every possible opportunity. Six is a middle number and an even number; there is stability here, and strength, lessening the potential "fragility" of his 10 birth number. Eb also walks the Road of Life in terms of a deep appreciation for the everyday challenges and joys of human existence. Though we think of Jung as the great proponent of the collective unconscious (his Future Sign Imix), he was deeply concerned with integrating the unconscious into the round of "ordinary" human existence, which he cherished.

This is in sharp contrast to Freud, whose Caban intellectualism was oriented entirely towards self-examination and self-discovery, with little concern for a larger society into which he himself did not fit. Some Daykeepers have written that the number 6 stands for the six life factors of health, understanding, vocation, property, and good or bad actions. All of these were important to Jung, for whom the exploration of the collective mind required harmonization with the demands of daily life.

Thus two men, both born on 10 Ben and both pioneers of modern psychology, had extremely different temperaments. It is the Year Lord which gives us an understanding of these differences, and it should never be neglected in the practice of Mayan astrology.

The Astrological Significance of the Year Lords

Year Lords establish four essential "core" personalities, corresponding to the structure of the fourfold universe in which we live.

The number of the year modifies the influence of the Year Lord in exactly the same way that numbers modify the influence of the day signs.

Year Lords have an influence over all those who were born during their rulership.

Year Lords help us to distinguish between character traits of individuals who were born on the same *tzolk'in* day.

Chapter 6

Sun and Moon

Diego de Landa, a bishop of Yucatan during the colonial period, records a ceremony that gives us a window into the Mayan concept of cyclic time. In terms of the Mayan vision of history, the most important cycle was that of the *k'atun*, a period which comprised approximately twenty years.[1]

Each *k'atun* was ruled or governed by a particular deity, and its energy was vested in a particular *lugar sagrado,* or sacred site. It was here that the statue of the ruling deity of each *k'atun* was kept. After ten years, at the very midpoint of the *k'atun*, another icon would be installed alongside the first one—the statue of the deity destined to rule over the next *k'atun*. Finally, at the end of the *k'atun* period, the first deity icon would be ritually set aside, his duty finished, and only the second one would remain, presumably to be transferred to the new center of geomantic power.

This ritual illustrates the Mayan conception of the flow of time; in fact, this rhythm is still perceptible today in Mayan astrological teachings regarding the influence of the Sun and Moon on a person's Mayan birth chart.

The lunar cycle is by far the more commonly used element of the two. As we have seen earlier, there is a great deal of debate as to whether one ought to use local time or Central American time when determining the day sign of one's birth. The cycle of the sun is based on local time; Daykeepers who work with Central American time simply don't use it.

On the other hand, many students may find it difficult to obtain information on the specific phase of the moon that was active at the time of someone's birth. Those with a background in some other form of astrology, such as Western or Vedic, will be able to do this immediately, but others may have to do a bit of research on the Internet. In order to determine the native's place within the cycle of a solar day, however, all you need is the time of birth. For the sake of ease of use, we shall use the solar cycle as an example.

In Mayan languages, the word for "day" and "sun" is usually the same. Let's take another look at what we said in Chapter 1:

> In order to understand the Mayan concept of the days, we need to understand a bit of the language as well. The word for "day" (k'in in Yucatec or q'ij in K'iche') is exactly the same as the word for "sun." If I am talking about "this day," I use the word q'ij. If I want to remark that the sun is hot today and point at that orb in the sky, I also use the word q'ij.
>
> The words are the same because, in Mayan thinking, a day is defined as the course of the sun through the four stations of midnight, dawn, noon, and sunset. Here again we see the essential Mayan world view of a fourfold universe coming into play. It should also be remembered that in Mayan thinking "north" is the same as "up," and "south" is the same as "down." Thus dawn = east, noon = north, sunset = west, and midnight = south. We live in a fourfold reality, which is not merely static but forever in motion.

Here, our model of the waxing and waning energy of each individual day sign also comes into play. When the sun goes down this evening, it will mark the moment at which the energy of the current day sign crosses into the Underworld. The deeper it travels into the Underworld, the more its energy shall wane. As soon as the sun is down, the energy of the next day will begin to make itself felt. The Daykeepers will light candles and burn incense in their shrine rooms to honor the advent of the day to come. As the sun travels farther into the Underworld, the energy of the current day becomes less and less powerful as its essence surrenders to the overwhelming forces of the darker half of the eternal polarity. Somewhere around midnight, the growing energy of the new day will become stronger and more powerful than that of the waning day. By the time the dawn arrives, the old day will have disappeared completely and the new one will rule the day alone until sunset, when it too shall pass into the Underworld, and the energy of yet another day will begin to make itself felt.

Now we can also understand what Bishop de Landa was talking about in relation to the twenty-year *k'atun* cycles:

When a *k'atun* began and an icon stood alone in its sacred place, it was equivalent to the dawning of a new day.

When the second icon, representing the next *k'atun*, was installed alongside the first, it was equivalent to sunset.

When the first icon was removed and the second one ruled alone, it was equivalent to the dawning of the next day.

This cyclic paradigm is almost all we need to understand the significance of the solar cycle. But in order to interpret its meaning in an individual horoscope, we should also remember that in Mesoamerican thinking, these four stations of the day are equivalent to the four stages of human life, as outlined by the Kaqchikel Maya philosopher Jose Lem Batz:[2]

> The moment of midnight, when the energy of a new day triumphs over that of the old, corresponds to the time of birth, when a new individuality emerges into the world.

> The moment of dawn, when the new day shines forth in all its glory, corresponds to the time of youth, when we are filled with confidence and enthusiasm.

> The moment of noon, when the sun is at its brightest, corresponds to our strong, vital maturity, when we accomplish our greatest achievements.

> The moment of sunset, when the sun crosses the threshold of night and merges with the world of the ancestors, corresponds to the time in life when we begin to grow old.

Figure 14. CYCLE OF THE SOLAR DAY (Q'IJ)
Daylight / Yang
Ruled by the Sun

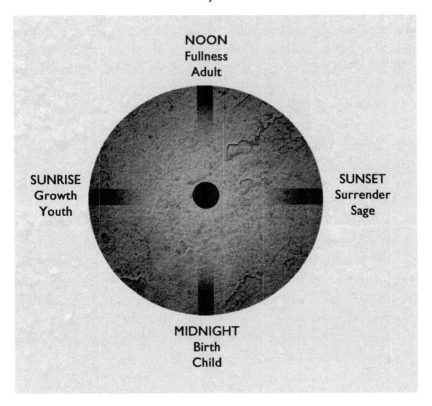

NOON
Fullness
Adult

SUNRISE
Growth
Youth

SUNSET
Surrender
Sage

MIDNIGHT
Birth
Child

Keeping in mind that everything in Mesoamerican thought is perceived in terms of polarities such as day and night, male and female, summer and winter, let us also remember that the solar or masculine polarity governs our logic, our reason, our sense of activity and achievement in the material world. The influence of the sun (see Figure 14) encompasses this dimension of human life. Now we can usefully interpret the meaning of a person's hour of birth:

Those born between midnight and dawn have an intellect that is still at least partly hidden in the darkness of intuition; they may find their feelings a better guide to life

than their reason and they may sometimes be more than a bit confused about "how the system works," but they also have the wide-eyed innocence and open minds of very small children.

Those born between dawn and noon are forever youthful, filled with enthusiasm. Their minds "rush in where angels fear to tread." This can make them fabulous and highly original thinkers and entrepreneurs, but it can also cause them to stumble and fall in the complexities of a world they still only partly understand.

Those born between noon and sunset are clear in their thinking, confident, able to navigate the waters of the real world with ease. These are the achievers.

Those born between sunset and midnight have the wisdom of age. Even as children, there is something of the sage about these people. This is commonly considered the most difficult phase in which to be born. Just as the sun surrenders to darkness, the sage must surrender her or his wisdom to our ultimate mortality. Surrender is never easy... and neither is wisdom.

The lunar cycle is based on the same principles. Among Maya Daykeepers, it is somewhat more widely used than the solar cycle, although it may be more difficult for some students of Mayan astrology to obtain information on the lunar phase active at the time of a person's birth.

Almost every culture that has developed a form of astrology has charted the monthly course of the moon, including its waxing and waning cycles. In most cases, the power and energy of the lunar force is measured by its brightness, from new moon to full and back again. This was true among the astrologers of medieval Europe; it is true among astrologers in India to this day. The lunar energy grid in Figure 15, adapted from the work of Don Roberto Poz, illustrates this concept.

Figure 15. THE LUNAR ENERGY GRID

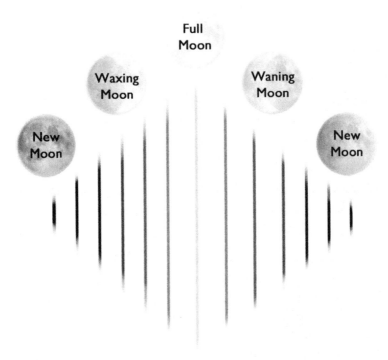

The lunar cycle (see Figure 16) works on the same principle as the solar one, but it governs our feelings, emotions, and our intuition rather than our reason, logic, and active life:

> Those born at the time of the new moon have powerful feelings and intuitions; but like children, they have not yet developed a "hard shell" to shield their tender emotions from the harsh realities of life, and may often be somewhat overly sensitive or easily hurt.

> Those born during the cycle of the waxing moon are filled with emotional enthusiasm. They wear their hearts on their sleeve. This can make them very warm and therefore very popular individuals, but it can also cause them to suffer

from too much uncontrolled passion.

Figure 16. CYCLE OF THE LUNAR MONTH (IQ')
Darkness / Yin

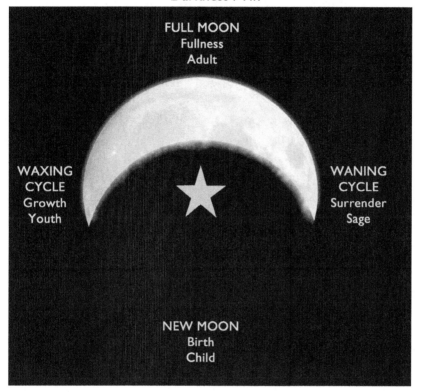

Ruled by the Moon

Those born at the time of the full moon are strong of heart and clear in their intuitions. These are the people whom everyone else turns to in time of need.

Those born during the cycle of the waning moon possess an inner wisdom of the heart. As with the solar cycle, this is commonly considered the most difficult phase in which to be born. These people, the most highly intuitive of all, are eternally aware of the darkness to which we all must surrender in time—sometimes painfully aware. Wisdom is a beautiful but sensitive thing.

The Astrological Significance of the Solar and Lunar Cycles

In Mayan spirituality, all things are part of an ever-changing dance of polarities, embodied as day and night, masculine and feminine, mountain and seashore, etc.

The solar cycle defines the way in which our masculine or rational polarity functions.

The lunar cycle defines the way our feminine or intuitive polarity functions.

As with the Year Lord, both may be used to add individuality and depth to a horoscope.

Chapter 7

Compatibility

Every system of astrology has a method of comparing the way in which human beings interact with each other. These methods of establishing compatibility (or the lack thereof) are used to assess the potential of our relationships with others. If two signs are compatible, the path to friendship, business, and love is easily traveled. An underlying affinity helps us reach out and truly relate to others with a compatible astrological temperament. If they are incompatible, we have to work harder in order to establish a deep and lasting connection.

It is no different in the Mayan Calendar system. Persons born with certain day signs have an easy time getting along with each other and are said to form bonds of friendship or romantic affection more easily.

In Western astrology, for example, signs that are of the same element (Fire, Earth, Air, or Water) are said to have a natural affinity, as do individuals whose Sun and Moon or Mars and Venus positions harmonize with each other. In the Chinese astrological system, there are certain animals on the zodiacal wheel that are compatible or incompatible with others.

Directional Compatibility
Among the Maya Daykeeepers, I have encountered several systems of defining compatibility. The most common one closely resembles the Western system: people whose day signs are of the same cardinal

direction are said to be compatible with each other in much the same way that Western astrology asserts compatibility between those who share the same element (Fire, Earth, Air or Water). Here again, as so often in Mayan cosmovision, it is the philosophy of a fourfold reality or fourfold universe that proves essential.

Human temperament isn't commonly defined in terms of directions or elements. In Western astrology, for example, water signs are said to be highly emotional while air signs are said to be more mental in their approach to life. In Mayan astrology, such generalizations are uncommon; it is, however, part of the common tradition that the directional or elemental attributes are important in determining compatibility.

The directional families are commonly acknowledged as a compatibility factor by most Mayan astrologers. In fact, this is the best known type of compatibility and is used throughout Guatemala. The type of compatible relationship experienced by those who share the same cardinal direction is very broadly based. Compatibility between directional families can be either friendly or romantic. They are also said to be good for business relationships.

Note that the central column of your Mayan Destiny Chart or Tree of Life will always be made up of signs that partake of the same cardinal direction. If you make a list of people who are close to you, you will probably find that your own Conception and Destiny signs appear as the birth signs of those whom you know best.

Here are the four directional "families":

EAST

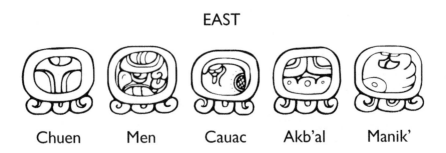

Chuen   Men   Cauac   Akb'al   Manik'

WEST

Eb Cib Ahau Kan Lamat

NORTH

Ben Caban Imix Chicchan Muluc

SOUTH

Ix Etznab Ik' Cimi Oc

Year Lord Compatibility

But that is not the beginning or the end of it. Well-known Mayan astrological writer Carlos Barrios distinguishes between compatibility based on the directional families and that based on the groups of Year Lords (see Chapter 5).

After studying relationships based on groups of Year Lords as opposed to those based on shared directions, I feel that the Year Lord groups are extremely significant and represent a higher level of compatibility, sometimes reaching a deep, abiding spiritual affinity. The Year Lord connections are the ones that are most likely to produce life-long friendships and loves that can never be forgotten.

When we examined the Year Lords in Chapter 5, we learned that each set contains one sign from each of the four directions. The Year Lords represent a compatibility that binds the four elements or directions one to another.

The Year Lord families are as follows:

YEAR LORD GROUP I

Chuen   Cib   Imix   Cimi

YEAR LORD GROUP II

Eb   Caban   Ik'   Manik'

YEAR LORD GROUP III

Ben   Etznab   Akb'al   Lamat

YEAR LORD GROUP IV

| Ix | Cauac | Kan | Muluc |

YEAR LORD GROUP V

| Men | Ahau | Chicchan | Oc |

It should be pointed out that one's own day sign is, of course, included in both the directional and Year Lord groups of compatible signs. In other words, if you are comparing two people of the same day sign, they are compatible in both the directional and the Year Lord systems.

Does this mean that one's own day sign is the best of all when it comes to partnership, and that the compatibility goes twice as deep? Not necessarily. While it is generally agreed that individuals of the same day sign possess a great deal of natural compatibility and are strongly drawn to one another, the level of compatibility doesn't necessarily go "deeper" than any other combination.

The nature of compatibility between those of the same day sign is based upon similarity. Other day signs from the same directional group or Year Lord group may share certain similarities but also create shades of difference simply because, after all, we are talking about different signs. Some may find a blend of "same but different" to be more stimulating and dynamic than the similarity that tends to occur between those of the same sign.

Composite Charts

These are the common systems used to determine compatibility in Mayan astrology. But we all know that human relationships are too complex and unpredictable to be described by any purely formal system. Compatibility factors such as the directional group or the Year Lord group are merely guidelines. Real human beings will always surprise you and "break the mold."

Practitioners of any astrological system throughout the world understand that one needs methods of comparing human relationships that go beyond mere numerical groupings. One common method in the highlands of Guatemala is the "composite chart," which creates a whole new Tree of Life or Mayan Destiny Chart to describe the relationship between any two people.

First, we assign numerical equivalents to the day signs of the *tzolk'in*, as follows:

1 – Chuen	11 – Imix
2 – Eb	12 – Ik'
3 – Ben	13 – Akb'al
4 – Ix	14 – Kan
5 – Men	15 – Chicchan
6 – Cib	16 – Cimi
7 – Caban	17 – Manik'
8 – Etznab	18 – Lamat
9 – Cauac	19 – Muluc
10 – Ahau	20 – Oc

To compose a sample composite chart, let us return to one of our previous sample horoscopes, that of Marilyn Monroe, born on 5 Chicchan. She was "famously married" to baseball legend Joe DiMaggio, born on 11 Cauac (November 25, 1914).

We then add the numerical equivalent of Monroe's day sign (15) to that of DiMaggio's (9). 15 + 9 = 24. Of course, we only have 20 day signs, so if the total is more than 20, we must subtract 20, which in this case leaves us with a remainder of 4, and that's the numerical equivalent of Ix.

Now let's do the same with their birth numbers. Monroe was born on a 5 day, while DiMaggio was born on an 11 day. 11 + 5 = 16. Since we are dealing now with the 13 numbers and not the 20 day signs, the limit is 13, and since 16 is higher than 13, we need to subtract 13, leaving us with a difference of 3.

Their composite chart, therefore, is 3 Ix (see Figure 17).

While 10 Lamat on the Right Hand and 9 Ahau on the Left Hand have a fair amount of potential, the basic birth chart itself is not strong. 3 is one of the weakest numbers, and lacks a sense of direction and clarity. Combined with the symbolism of Ix as one of the indicators of the Seven Shames, we can see that this relationship may stand upon a rather uncertain foundation.

Notice that their Destiny Sign is 11 Ik'. This day sign and number combination has a fairly difficult reputation. With Ik' as the most anger-prone of all the day signs and 11 as the most inherently unbalanced of the high numbers, the already shaky foundation of the entire relationship makes the Destiny Sign or Future Sign of 11 Ik' all the more ominous. DiMaggio's world view was fairly less progressive or open-minded than that of his spouse. On the night of the well-known "subway grate" incident, 11 Ik' came to the forefront. DiMaggio flew into a rage over her very public stunt and beat Monroe so badly that the make-up department was hard pressed to cover her bruises and welts for the next week of filming.

Now let us take a look at another one of her spouses, Pulitzer Prize-winning dramatist Arthur Miller, born on 4 Cib (November 17, 1915).

Replicating our process for finding the composite chart, we add Chicchan (15) to Cib (6). 15 + 6 = 21, so once again we subtract 20, to produce a result of 1 (the numerical equivalent of Chuen). When we add the numbers together (4 + 5), we get 9, so the Monroe–Miller composite chart is 9 Chuen (see Figure 18).

There are several factors here that demand our attention. Chuen is one of the most positive day signs, and 9, unique among the odd numbers, is regarded as inherently favorable and balanced. Also, as we have seen, 9 is a quintessentially feminine number. Can we guess, from the very beginning, that Miller's artistic sensibilities enabled him to support Monroe's unique feminine persona much more than the more conventional DiMaggio?

Figure 17. COMPOSITE CHART
Marilyn Monroe and Joe DiMaggio

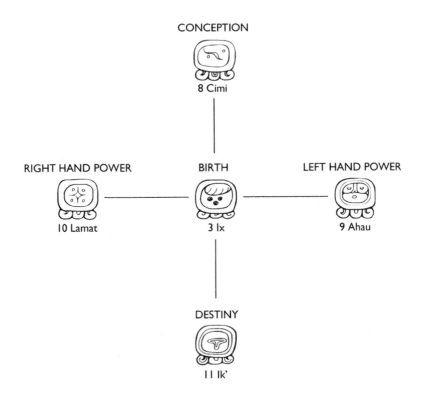

CONCEPTION

8 Cimi

RIGHT HAND POWER   BIRTH   LEFT HAND POWER

10 Lamat   3 Ix   9 Ahau

DESTINY

11 Ik'

Beyond that, notice how many of the day signs in this composite chart are also present in Monroe's personal Destiny Chart. Chuen, Caban, Chicchan, and Cauac are all part of her essential "tapestry of life." This also implies that this relationship, unlike her marriage with DiMaggio, would be more productive in helping her to realize her own potential.

At a time in American history when Monroe's passion for Russian literature and music sparked the ire of the McCarthy Commission, Miller was bold enough to cry out against the excesses of Senator Joe McCarthy and his cohorts with his still-famous play *The Crucible*. Even after he and Monroe were no longer living together (Monroe was not the easiest person in the world to get along with), Miller continued to support her. Monroe had always longed to do "serious

Figure 18. COMPOSITE CHART
Marilyn Monroe and Arthur Miller

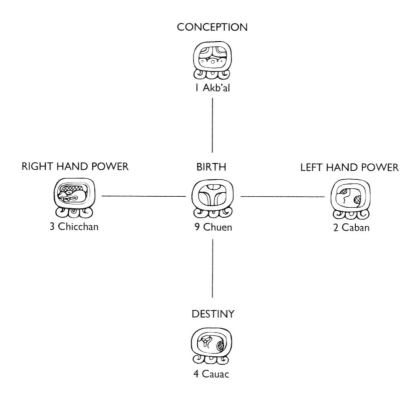

CONCEPTION

1 Akb'al

RIGHT HAND POWER   BIRTH   LEFT HAND POWER

3 Chicchan   9 Chuen   2 Caban

DESTINY

4 Cauac

acting," and was chronically disappointed with the "kitty fluff" parts she always played. It was Arthur Miller who wrote the script for director John Huston's astonishing (but largely forgotten) film *The Misfits*, in which Miller gave Monroe what was arguably her greatest role as a good-natured but hopelessly confused divorcée adrift in the clubs and casinos of modern Nevada.

As you begin to work more and more deeply with the Mayan system, you will of course encounter many relationships that are not based on the essential compatibility factors of cardinal direction or Year Lord. Does this mean that the individuals in question are destined to have a rocky relationship road?

Not at all. The complexities of human love can never be reduced to a mere formal system. The best way to approach relationships in

Mayan astrology is to start with the people, not the signs. In every day sign combination, there is an infinite amount of potential. Look for the essence and not the form.

Chapter 8

The Path of Feathered Serpent

The five-sign Mayan Destiny Chart or Tree of Life that we introduced earlier is the basic, fundamental document of what we call "day sign astrology." But this relatively simple diagram can be expanded into a chart comprising nine signs, often known as "the Path of Feathered Serpent." While the five-sign chart is perfectly adequate for basic readings, this nine-sign horoscope represents Mayan astrology on its most highly developed level.

In this chapter we shall explore the depths of the nine-sign Path of Feathered Serpent chart. Using Figure 19 as reference, this is how we construct the diagram:

1. Let us return to the example chart we used in Chapter 4, that of Marilyn Monroe, born on 5 Chicchan. Beginning with the central column, we counted seven signs forward from the birth sign to arrive at the Left Hand Power, and seven signs backwards to arrive at the Right Hand Power.

2. Now, let us do the same with the Conception Sign, 10 Caban. Counting seven signs forward, we reach 3 Akb'al, which serves as a guardian on the Left Hand for the Conception Sign.

   Counting seven signs backward, we reach 4 Chuen, guardian on the Right Hand.

3. We already have our left and right hand guardians for the birth sign, so let us skip over the birth sign and continue to the Destiny Sign or Future Sign—13 Ben. Counting seven signs forward, we reach 6 Cauac, which serves as the guardian on the Left Hand for the Destiny Sign.

   Counting seven signs back, we reach 7 Manik', guardian on the Right Hand.

   We now have a nine-sign horoscope that looks like this:

Figure 19. PATH OF FEATHERED SERPENT
Marilyn Monroe

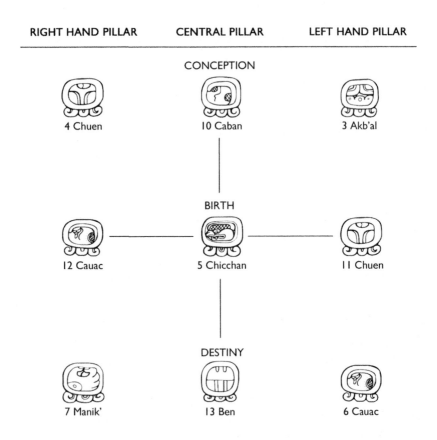

RIGHT HAND PILLAR	CENTRAL PILLAR	LEFT HAND PILLAR
	CONCEPTION	
4 Chuen	10 Caban	3 Akb'al
	BIRTH	
12 Cauac	5 Chicchan	11 Chuen
	DESTINY	
7 Manik'	13 Ben	6 Cauac

These nine signs form three columns or "pillars," one on the right, one on the left, and one in the middle. This is the path traveled by Feathered Serpent, the inner power that moves like lightning between the three pillars of our reality.

Some may wonder whether the choice of sevens and nines as our building blocks to construct the chart is accidental. It isn't. As Don Roberto Poz explained to me:

"Nine is the number of life. Seven is the number of death. By weaving a tapestry of life and death, we define the totality of a human being."[1]

The Feathered Serpent horoscope can be read from four different vantage points: the three columns, the road of life, timing, and the inner lightning.

The Three Columns

The three columns or pillars of the Path of Feathered Serpent chart represent our orientation and the different energies we use in our experience of life.

The central pillar is the most important. Composed of the Birth Sign, Conception Sign, and Destiny Sign, this pillar symbolizes the very core of our individuality and our purpose in life. This is our essential nature, our archetypal imprint.

Note that all three signs are always of the same cardinal direction—in the case of Marilyn Monroe's chart, the central pillar displays all northern signs. This establishes a fundamental orientation in terms of our affinities with energy (East), spirit (West), intellect (North), or emotion (South).

The pillars on the right and left hand establish yet another basic orientation: the two primal yin-yang polarities that underlie Mesoamerican cosmovision and psychology. The Right Hand Pillar symbolizes our way of functioning within the masculine polarity, the "real" world of logic and reason, the so-called material world. The Left Hand Pillar symbolizes our way of functioning within the feminine polarity, the inner world of feelings and intuition, the world of images and dreams.

Just as the Right Hand and Left Power support the unfolding and development of the Birth Sign, so these additional signs within the Right and Left Hand Pillars form rational and intuitive factors of support, respectively, for the Conception and Destiny Signs.

Note that in our example chart, both the Right and Left Hand Pillars are made up of signs from the Eastern direction. The East always serves as support to the North.

The Road of Life

The Feathered Serpent chart can be read horizontally as well as vertically—in other words, by rows rather than columns. From this perspective, the chart represents a timeline, a map of our own individual road of life, with each row equaling 26 years of life. Note that 26 is 2 (polarity) x 13 (the numbers of the days), and 4 x 13 brings us to 52, the number of years in a Calendar Round. When we reach our original position in the Calendar Round, we are "reborn" as an elder in our society.

In our example chart, the top row defines the first 26 years of Monroe's life. These years are defined primarily by 10 Caban, with 3 Akb'al and 4 Chuen playing supporting roles.

The middle row defines the next 26 years, until the age of 52—or at least it would have done so had Monroe lived long enough. Here, the Birth Sign 5 Chicchan comes into full play, with 11 Chuen and 12 Cauac supporting it intuitively and rationally.

The bottom row defines the years between 52 and 78. The Destiny Sign is the "ruler" of this time period, with its right and left hand signs playing the supporting roles.

As we explained in Chapter 5, it takes 52 years for the solar calendar and the *tzolk'in* to come back into synchronization with each other, and that this cycle is called a "Calendar Round." When a person reached this special "Mayan Calendar birthday," in ancient times it was regarded as a kind of "new birth," a transition, a personal initiation into the world of the elders. The time period ruled by the Destiny Sign begins with this event.

When we reach the age of 78, we return to the beginning, i.e., the top row of the nine-sign horoscope.

Timing

The practitioner of Western or Vedic astrology may wonder about such a rudimentary form of "time-keeping"—twenty-six years for each row, then a repeat of the "same old song." Where are the Mayan equivalents for transits, progressions, and solar returns?

In fact, there aren't any. The Maya never assume that one's destiny is etched in stone. We have an archetypal template—our birth day sign and number, and the supporting signs derived therefrom. What we do with it is entirely up to us. The three signs which form the key factors for each of these twenty-six year cycles are tools that we can use, or, alternatively, problems that we can fix.

And herein lies the point—Mayan astrology, as a whole, is much more shamanic and much less deterministic than anything in the Western astrologer's arsenal.

An example: As we have seen, people born on an Ik' day are likely to "blow like a hurricane," with energies, passions, and personality traits that are completely out of control. If a child born on an Ik' day should happen to show early signs of being "wild" or "mischievous," a traditional Maya family is likely to call upon a Daykeeper or an herbalist for help. There is a certain herb, in fact (and I have forgotten the name), which is believed to help an individual develop a gentler, more equitable temperament. One common way to "calm the hurricane" is to treat the overly energetic Ik' child with teas or poultices made from this herb. Rather than predict that the child *will* cause trouble, the Maya immediately set to work ensuring that he doesn't. The horoscope, therefore, is a map, not a script. You can use the map to get anywhere you want to go, but you don't have to follow the script word for word.

The modern Western astrologer will assert that words like "fate" or "destiny" belong to the repertoire of ancient and medieval astrology, and that "predictive" techniques like transits and progressions are used to assess the development of psychological trends, likewise with a view to shaping one's own destiny with available materials. Three day signs in a row, covering twenty-six years of life, doesn't seem to make for a great many "available materials."

And in fact the Maya do employ other methods to assess what the Western astrologer might call "developing psychological trends."

These methods fall largely into the category of divination. A Maya Daykeeper has a *vara* or "medicine bag" filled with seeds from the *tz'ite* tree. These seeds are laid out in patterns, and counted, usually several times, as if they were the days of the Calendar itself, so that a divination series might come to a conclusion such as (for example) 3 Manik and 7 Eb. The diviner then reads these day sign and number combinations as the answer to the client's question about future events.

All the same, such a divination is still less oriented toward prediction, per se, than most Tarot or I Ching readings in the Western world. I have received several such consultations from the Maya; the diviner always used recommendations rather than absolute statements, for example, "Well, things seem to be moving in this direction, so if you want to avoid such-and-such series of events, here is what you should do."

The diviner will then proceed to give advice (often shamanic in nature and involving rituals of one type or another) about how to shape one's own future.

I gave a brief description of such techniques in *Jaguar Wisdom*. I will not repeat them here. To many Western students, Mayan divination seems cumbersome and time-consuming in comparison to our own better known methods. Besides that, you're not allowed to possess a medicine bag or divine with *tz'ite* seeds unless you are a fully initiated shaman (not to mention the fact that the FDA will probably swoop down upon you like a team of vultures if they catch you trying to bring these "botanical products" back to the United States). Just as importantly, handling the *tz'ite* seeds raises the *koyopa* in a big hurry (unlike the slower method of the Feathered Serpent meditations, described below). This is not for beginners!

There is nothing wrong with combining Mayan astrology with Western or Vedic forms of the art. As a matter of fact, the 18th-century Maya of Yucatan were cheerfully mixing Western astrology with day sign astrology in some of their sacred books, notably the Chilam Balam of Kaua.[2] And if you feel the need, you can always use any methods of divination with which you feel comfortable.

The Inner Lightning

Let us now look at the basic Calendar Board diagram (Figure 20). First, locate the nine signs from our sample chart on the Calendar Board. Then, connect them in the order in which they actually occur in the *tzolk'in*.

Figure 20. THE CALENDAR BOARD

Chuen / B'atz'	8	2	9	3	10	4	11	5	12	6	13	7	1
Eb / E'	9	3	10	4	11	5	12	6	13	7	1	8	2
Ben / Aj	10	4	11	5	12	6	13	7	1	8	2	9	3
Ix / I'x	11	5	12	6	13	7	1	8	2	9	3	10	4
Men / Tz'ikin	12	6	13	7	1	8	2	9	3	10	4	11	5
Cib / Ajmaq	13	7	1	8	2	9	3	10	4	11	5	12	6
Caban / No'j	1	8	2	9	3	10	4	11	5	12	6	13	7
Etznab / Tijax	2	9	3	10	4	11	5	12	6	13	7	1	8
Cauac / Kawoq	3	10	4	11	5	12	6	13	7	1	8	2	9
Ahau / Ajpu	4	11	5	12	6	13	7	1	8	2	9	3	10
Imix / Imox	5	12	6	13	7	1	8	2	9	3	10	4	11
Ik' / Iq'	6	13	7	1	8	2	9	3	10	4	11	5	12
Akb'al/Aq'ab'al	7	1	8	2	9	3	10	4	11	5	12	6	13
Kan / K'at	8	2	9	3	10	4	11	5	12	6	13	7	1
Chicchan / Kan	9	3	10	4	11	5	12	6	13	7	1	8	2
Cimi / Kame	10	4	11	5	12	6	13	7	1	8	2	9	3
Manik' / Kej	11	5	12	6	13	7	1	8	2	9	3	10	4
Lamat / Q'anil	12	6	13	7	1	8	2	9	3	10	4	11	5
Muluc / Toj	13	7	1	8	2	9	3	10	4	11	5	12	6
Oc / Tz'i	1	8	2	9	3	10	4	11	5	12	6	13	7

Using our example chart, the order in which the day signs occur is as follows: 4 Chuen, 10 Caban, 12 Cauac, 3 Akb'al, 5 Chicchan, 7 Manik', 11 Chuen, 13 Ben, 6 Cauac.

If we connect all these signs, one after another, on the Feathered Serpent diagram, we will create a pattern which resembles a series of lightning bolts, flashing from one sign to the next. This lightning

Figure 21. PATH OF FEATHERED SERPENT
FOR MARILYN MONROE

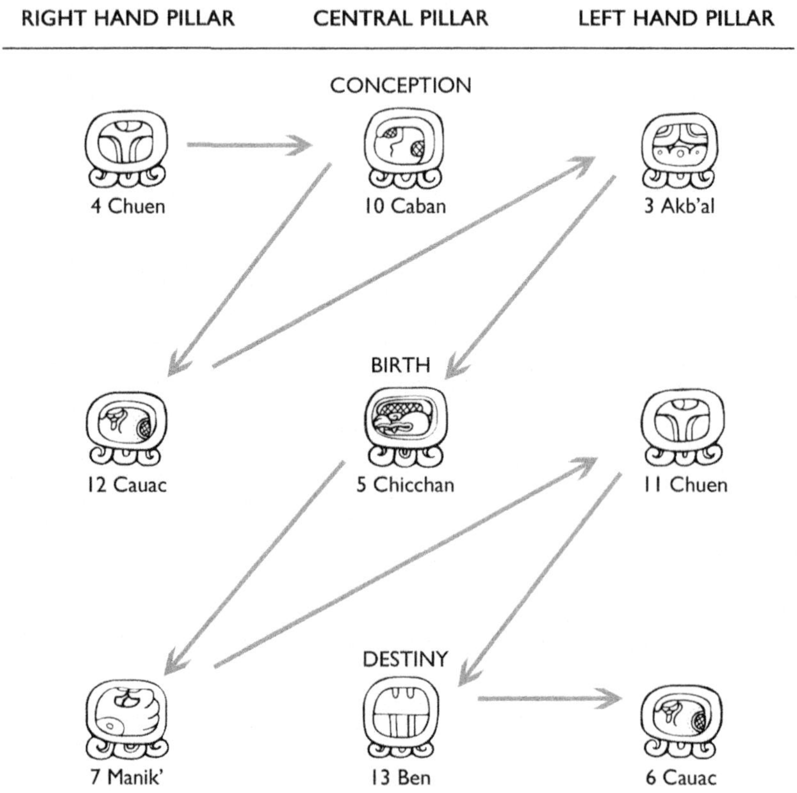

RIGHT HAND PILLAR	CENTRAL PILLAR	LEFT HAND PILLAR

CONCEPTION

4 Chuen   10 Caban   3 Akb'al

BIRTH

12 Cauac   5 Chicchan   11 Chuen

DESTINY

7 Manik'   13 Ben   6 Cauac

pattern is what we call the Path of Feathered Serpent. It defines the flow of the *koyopa* or "inner lightning" within us, as described under the day sign Chicchan in Chapter 2, and in the general discussion of numbers in Chapter 3. The path of the inner lightning allows us to make intuitive leaps in the interpretation of a chart. These implicit connections between day signs reveal archetypal links that would otherwise remain hidden (see Figure 21).

For example, notice that Monroe's quintessentially mental Conception Sign, 10 Caban, receives a *koyopa* connection from 4 Chuen. The number 4, representing completeness and wholeness, is a balanced number, sufficient unto itself. Since Chuen is the day sign of "the mastery of all the arts," the connection between Chuen and Caban helps us to understand why, in Monroe's case, the intellect (Caban) expressed itself through the performing arts (Chuen), especially when we remember that 4 Chuen appears on the right hand pillar, the "masculine" or "yang" side of a person's being that manifests itself through action in the world.

Another highly significant connection in this chart can be found between 11 Chuen as the Power of the Left Hand and 13 Ben as the Destiny or Future Sign. As we have seen, it is the powerful energy of 13 Ben that speaks eloquently of Monroe's archetypal quality. This archetype is "fed" energetically by 11 Chuen, an auspicious sign but a very difficult number, as well as one which addresses the intuitive or emotional side of the personality. It is the somewhat "shaky" nature of 11 Chuen—the gifted but emotionally damaged performer who could never remember her lines or show up on set on time—which, through a myriad of problems, created the Destiny archetype.

Finally, note that the Destiny Sign, 13 Ben, also connects energetically with 6 Cauac in the Left Hand Pillar. Six is a powerful, balanced number, and Cauac is the sign of the Divine Feminine—a fitting day sign for one who became the archetypal Aphrodite of an entire generation.

The possibilities inherent in these "energy connections" are almost limitless for the astrologer who is capable of developing her or his intuition to the point of perceiving, interpreting, and linking these patterns to the unique personality of a specific individual.

And that brings up another important point—the Path of Feathered Serpent is indeed a path. It is a road that may be consciously traveled. As a series of rituals and meditations, it is said to constitute our "personal lunar month." Once every nine lunar months, we may set aside twenty-nine days, upon nine of which we meditate.

Let us take the example of an individual born on 10 Imix (April 21, 1952). The chart of this person's Path of Feathered Serpent can be seen in Figure 22. Beginning on 9 Manik', which occurred on August 21 of 2010, this person undertook the Path of Feathered Serpent, just as he had done nine lunar months earlier and as he

Figure 22.   PATH OF FEATHERED SERPENT
PERSON BORN ON 10 IMIX

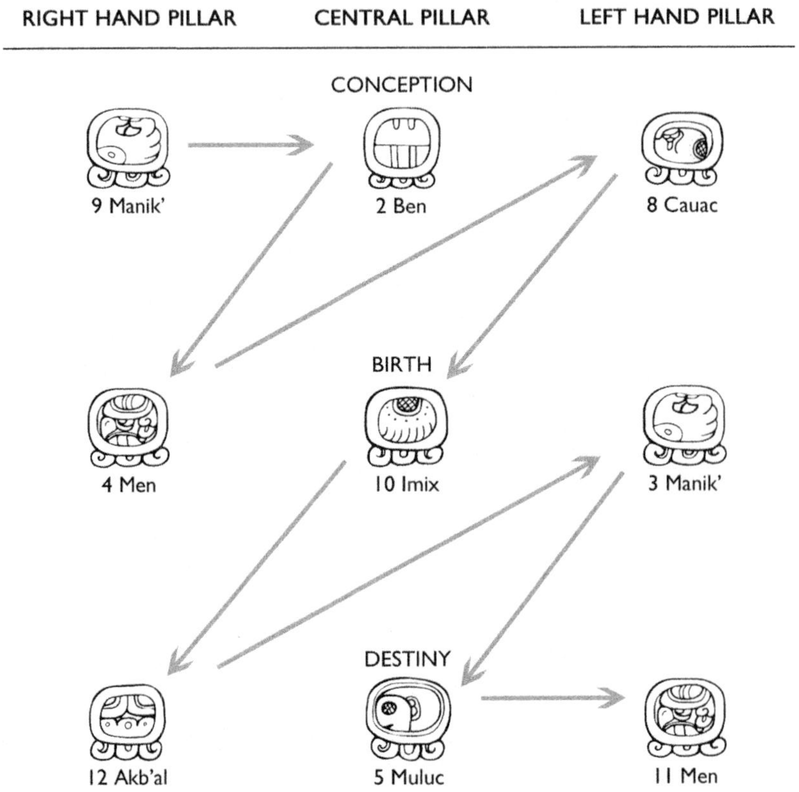

RIGHT HAND PILLAR	CENTRAL PILLAR	LEFT HAND PILLAR

CONCEPTION

9 Manik'   2 Ben   8 Cauac

BIRTH

4 Men   10 Imix   3 Manik'

DESTINY

12 Akb'al   5 Muluc   11 Men

would nine lunar months hence. You might ask, so how exactly does the system work?

Anyone can "keep the days," but if you were to attempt a traditional Mayan ceremony of "offering" in your own home, your landlord would probably call the fire marshal and have you arrested. Simple practices may suffice. Try to set aside a shrine or "sacred space" in your house, no matter how small. To honor the days, burn candles and light incense. Small candles are probably best. All candles and incense should be allowed to burn down to the end; after all, an "offering" means that something is given up or surrendered, fully and completely.

Prayer is the most important element of all. The Mayan sacred text, the *Pop Wuj*, asserts that it is the gift of speech which sets human beings apart from their animal brethren. The appropriate use of speech is to employ all of our innate eloquence and poetry to praise the beauty of the Blossoming World. This is the meaning of prayer to the Maya.

For one born upon 10 Imix, his "personal lunar month" in 2010, including the appropriate day sign meditations, would be as follows:

August 21, 9 Manik'
Upon this day, we pray for harmony among one and all.
This extends to the forces of the natural world around us
as well as to other human beings; one gains great power
and energy if one is able to spend this day in nature
or in the wilderness.

August 27, 2 Ben
We give thanks for the home in which we live, for this day
is connected with the nourishment and flourishing of all
things related to the home, whether human, animal, or
plant. It symbolizes the energy and vitality of life itself.
This is the day to give thanks for our children.

August 29, 4 Men
Unlike those who follow other spiritual traditions,
the Maya do not feel that material prosperity is
undesirable or "non-spiritual." Upon this day, we may
thank the universe for whatever prosperity we currently
enjoy while sincerely expressing the intention that more
prosperity may attend our lives. This day is as fortunate
for love as it is for money; we should therefore pay
attention to relationship issues. We should also pay
attention to our dreams, for on this day they may bring
powerful and important revelations.

September 2, 8 Cauac
Upon this day, we pray that there may always be harmony
in our home lives and among our friends. This day is
auspicious for all matters regarding health and healing.
It also has a special connection with women and with
feminine energy. This is sometimes said to be the day of
the Divine Feminine.

September 4, 10 Imix
This is a day associated with powerful psychic forces.
The world is filled with psychological perils and stresses.
Upon this day we pray for good mental health, both
for ourselves and for all those around us. This day has a
strong connection with water; to be close to a flowing
river or stream or the ocean is beneficial upon this day.
This is yet another day to pay attention to potential
wisdom from our dreams.

September 6, 12 Akb'al
This day symbolizes both darkness and dawn; hence it is
a day of new beginnings. Upon this day, we express our
intention always to think and act with perfect clarity. It
is also a favorable day for love, marriage, or finding a job.
This is the quintessential day for all things romantic.

September 10, 3 Manik'
Upon this day, we pray once again for harmony among
one and all. This extends to the forces of the natural world
around us as well as to other human beings; one gains
great power and energy if one is able to spend this day in
nature or in the wilderness.

September 12, 5 Muluc
Upon this day we humbly acknowledge our karmic debts
and assert our intention to "pay it all back" by placing
our lives in harmony. We should make atonement for all
disequilibrium and be thankful for all that is in balance.

September 18, 11 Men

Upon this day, we once again thank the universe for
whatever prosperity we currently enjoy while sincerely
expressing the intention that more prosperity may attend
our lives. And we should once again pay attention to
relationship issues and dreams.

As you perform the prayers and meditations pertinent to your
own Path of Feathered Serpent, giving thanks for the spiritual gifts
represented by the day signs in your chart, you should also meditate
upon the questions: *How do the gifts of the various day signs work
in my life? When and how do I experience the illumination and love
represented by the presence of 12 Akb'al (for example) in my horoscope?
How does the Otherworldly quality of Imix help or harm me, and how
could it work to my advantage? In what way do my actions in the
material world exemplify the energies of 4 Men, and how could they be
made to do so in an even more positive way?*

It is said that the practice of the Path of Feathered Serpent
awakens the energy of the *koyopa*, bringing the lightning bolt that
links your day signs into real-time manifestation. But despite the
fact that the *koyopa* seems to be identical to the energy known in
other traditions as *kundalini,* I want to make it very clear that **the
awakening of the koyopa is not the same thing as a full awakening
of the "serpent power."**

Those who have experienced a complete activation of the
kundalini have described it as so overwhelming that they nearly
died. The activation of the "inner lightning" which is part of the
Path of Feathered Serpent will enhance one's awareness and even
one's psychic abilities, but is not as life-threatening as the sort of
kundalini experience chronicled by Eastern mystics.

All the same, if unpleasant physical symptoms result from the
practice of this series of meditations, I would recommend to bring it
to a halt and consult an energy worker. Those who do not have access
to Mayan shamans may wish to seek out an Hispanic *curandera* or
other individual who works within the same energy paradigms.

Reading the Mayan Horoscope

It is time now to take everything we have learned and study how the various elements of Mayan astrology can be integrated in an actual life reading. Let us swim for a bit longer in the dreamlike ocean of Imix as we study the Mayan horoscope of Orson Welles.

Orson Welles (born May 6, 1915, at 7:00 a.m.) was one of the most phenomenal performers of his time, with a career encompassing writing, acting, and directing in stage, radio, and film. He was also one of the most controversial figures of the era.

Welles was a child prodigy. Born in a small Wisconsin town, he could read Shakespeare as a small child and was giving lectures by the time he was ten. At the tender age of sixteen, he made his stage debut in Dublin, Ireland. Always a physically massive character, he gave every appearance of being an adult by that time.

Welles' early achievements can be explained by several factors in his Mayan horoscope. In the first place, his Conception Sign, symbolizing the inheritance from his karmic past, was 9 Ben, and this is the sign that was in control of his life path until the age of 26. As we saw in the case of Monroe, who had Ben as her Future or Destiny Sign, this *nawal* has an authoritative and archetypal quality that produces individuals who, when Ben appears as a Conception Sign, have a fund of past karma that is powerful and motivated. Of course, these individuals are born under the day sign Imix, which has quite a different energetic nature—sometimes lazy and typically "spaced out." Nine is an important and masterful number, symbolizing "life" itself. The Conception Sign of 9 Ben was extremely helpful in the development of a child prodigy, but all the same, we must look for other factors to explain the sheer power of Welles' rise to fame so early in life.

First of all, we must never neglect the Year Lord. Orson Welles was born in the year 7 Eb. This was a factor in the ease with which he went from one achievement to another. Let us reiterate what we learned earlier about Eb as a Year Lord: "Those born in an Eb year have an innate curiosity about the world around them which makes them perpetual students of life. The most common expression of their curiosity is through travel, and their wanderings and explorations frequently endow them with wisdom. This year's natives commonly

Figure 23.   PATH OF FEATHERED SERPENT
ORSON WELLES, born MAY 6, 1915

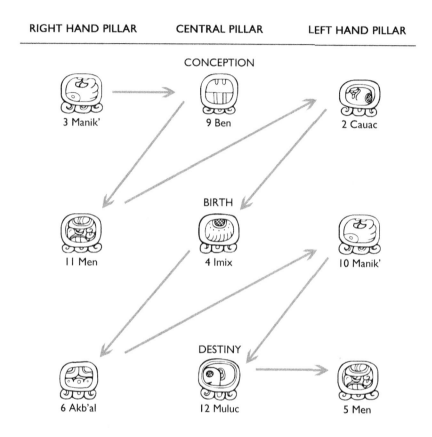

RIGHT HAND PILLAR	CENTRAL PILLAR	LEFT HAND PILLAR
	CONCEPTION	
3 Manik'	9 Ben	2 Cauac
	BIRTH	
11 Men	4 Imix	10 Manik'
	DESTINY	
6 Akb'al	12 Muluc	5 Men

enjoy a long, healthy life. They derive sincere satisfaction from helping others. They tend to have numerous relationships in life, for their restless spirit is seldom satisfied with a single love. Because of their intrinsic good nature, most of their relationships will be fortunate, though one could not exactly describe them as the most faithful of partners. Without a goal in mind, these people can wander without a clear sense of direction. They may be as cheerful and enthusiastic as ever, but they have no destination in mind.

"Those born in an Eb year need to keep the end of the road in sight, and to have a goal towards which they strive. Perhaps their worst qualities arise when they invest themselves too strongly in their opinions, always needing to be right. They often flourish in foreign countries and make cheerful, successful expatriates."

As we shall see, the uncertainty attached to the number 7 played a role in Welles' life path as well. Despite the good fortune he received from having been born in an Eb year, his "need to be right" led him to an uncompromising position that was to negatively impact his career.

Orson Welles was born right after sunrise. His solar cycle, governing activity and the masculine polarity, was passionate, youthful, and enthusiastic. Since this phase of the solar day also symbolizes the physical period of one's youth, it is little wonder that it helped impel him to full manifestation of the archetypal qualities inherent in his Conception Sign of 9 Ben. His lunar cycle was a participant in the same phase; on the day of his birth, the moon was just reaching its first quarter phase. Thus an equally enthusiastic and highly motivated lunar cycle was activating his intuition at the same time of life.

And there is no question that Welles exemplified all the intuition and talent for otherworldly fantasy that is symbolized by his *nawal*, Imix. He loved performing magic tricks and was rumored to be extremely clairvoyant. In Chapter 2, we learned that Imix people have a hypnotic quality to them. This aspect of his *nawal* also surfaced early in life. He was only twenty when his majestic voice became one of the most recognizable in all of public radio as the spokesman for the popular radio show, "The Shadow." If we remember that it is the eagle who "cries out" to express his vision, and that Welles' Conception Sign "feeds" the powerful 11 Men on the Path of Feathered Serpent, we should not be surprised that it was his voice that created so much of his performance persona. In true Imix fashion, there was an aura of mystery about it as well. "Who knows what evil lurks in the hearts of men? The Shadow knows!"

And he was still in the youthful, 9 Ben phase of his life when he achieved his greatest and most controversial feat of magic, manipulating the dream world of fantasy projection with as much power as two other Imix "magicians," Walt Disney and Federico Fellini. In 1938, Welles produced a radio version of the science fiction novel, *War of the Worlds*. His radio production was so convincing that the U.S. went into a panic. Believing that aliens had landed, people fled cities, jumped out of buildings to their deaths, and in general experienced a kind of mass hysteria that remains unique in American history.

Welles crossed into his adult years, ruled by Imix itself, while he was in the midst of his most celebrated achievement. *Citizen Kane* was released in 1941, the very year that Welles turned twenty-six. The American Film Institute has voted this piece the single greatest film ever made by anyone.

It was also an unmitigated financial disaster. Always uncompromising and convinced of his own "rightness," the native of 7 Eb had walked right into a personal "Underworld" from which his career never recovered. Welles' thinly disguised portrait of newspaper magnate William Randolph Hearst was a searing criticism of Hearst's life. Hearst, born on the tempestuous day 11 Ik, could come on like a hurricane when he was in the mood— and this time he was. Most of the nation's newspapers—the ones controlled by Hearst—refused to advertise or even mention Welles' extraordinary masterpiece.

It was the beginning of Orson's plunge into the darker side of the ocean of Imix. His career never quite recovered. In the adult phase of his life, the Powers on the Right Hand and the Left Hand came into full manifestation. The Power on the Right Hand governs the way we accomplish action in the material world. Welles' 11 Men day sign on the Right Hand made him long to express his vision and "cry out" against the darkness and corruption of rampant American capitalism. But, as we have seen, 11 is one of the more difficult numbers. Many people perceived his bold outcry as an unpleasant screech, a noise to be ignored.

Of course, he kept on working. But after the debacle caused when "Citizen Hearst" destroyed Welles' greatest achievement, he was never the same again. He drifted from one movie to another as if drifting through the dark subterranean waters of Imix, his day sign as well as the ruler of the years between 26 and 52. Some of his work was excellent; he also appeared in a few films that were perfectly awful. He remained an outspoken critic of the Hollywood system—a practice which certainly did not help his career. At one point, as we might expect from someone born in an Eb year, he left the United States altogether and lived as an expatriate in Europe.

He also experienced a number of relationships, marrying no fewer than three times. For the Imix-born, the Power on the Left Hand is Manik'. One would expect the women in his life to be powerful, like Manik'. One would also expect them to be somewhat masculine, which in fact they were not. Here, we should remember that his Left Hand Power was "fed" by 6 Akb'al on the Path of Feathered Serpent, and that Akb'al is one of the most feminine of all signs. Many of the women in Welles' life were celebrated and thus "powerful" because of their femininity.

The relationships in Orson's life demonstrate how uncannily accurate Mayan astrology can be. One of his most famous partnerships, second wife Rita Hayworth, was also Imix-born, in this case 3 (October 17, 1918). When we combine 3 Imix and 4 Imix as detailed in our chapter on relationships, we arrive at a composite of 7 Eb. This, of course, is Welles' own Year Lord! Hayworth was born in the year 10 Manik'. Welles' Left Hand Power, symbolizing his feminine side as well as the essential character of the women in his life, was precisely the same!

Another well known flame was the black songstress Lena Horne. Born on June 30, 1917, her *nawal* was none other than 10 Manik'. Lena Horne embodied Welles' "inner woman," what Jungians would describe as the *anima*, the feminine soul of a man. He never married her. Their composite *nawal* was 1 Etznab, "the origin (1) of conflict (Etznab)." The intensity of their relationship expressed itself better as lovers than it ever could have as marriage partners.

Welles entered the Muluc phase of his life at the age of 52, the "new birth" of the Calendar Round. It is said that high-numbered Muluc days imply "karmic payback" of a very intense order indeed. These were the years in which Orson plunged farther into an introverted funk. By this time regarded as an outcast or pariah because of his outspoken criticisms, no producer would even read the film scripts he wrote in those days—despite the fact that his writing continued to be excellent, as I can attest as his proofreader at that time. He survived on TV commercials for California wine. Always a large man, he seemed to collect his karma on his very body, becoming so seriously obese that he even had difficulty walking more than a few steps.

He died at the age of 70, sitting in front of his typewriter, working on a script that would remain forever unfinished.

In the pages that follow, I have provided templates for the nine-sign horoscopes of every day sign. You may regard these as a series of worksheets, to be copied, printed out, or used in whatever way works best for you. I have not drawn the lightning flash of Feathered Serpent; I recommend that students print out the template/s applicable for the specific individual/s whose chart/s they are working on, as in Chapter 4. Then, you can fill in the numbers and the lightning pattern/s yourself to obtain an actual sense for "how it works."

CHUEN
Master of All the Arts

RIGHT HAND PILLAR	CENTRAL PILLAR	LEFT HAND PILLAR

CONCEPTION

Caban

Akb'al

Muluc

BIRTH

Chicchan

Chuen

Caban

DESTINY

Ben

Cauac

Chicchan

EB
The Road of Life

RIGHT HAND PILLAR	CENTRAL PILLAR	LEFT HAND PILLAR
	CONCEPTION	
Etznab	Kan	Oc
	BIRTH	
Cimi	Eb	Etznab
	DESTINY	
Ix	Ahau	Cimi

BEN
The Resurrection of the Corn

RIGHT HAND PILLAR	CENTRAL PILLAR	LEFT HAND PILLAR
	CONCEPTION	
Cauac	Chicchan	Chuen
	BIRTH	
Manik'	Ben	Cauac
	DESTINY	
Men	Imix	Manik'

IX
The Jaguar

RIGHT HAND PILLAR	CENTRAL PILLAR	LEFT HAND PILLAR

CONCEPTION

Ahau	Cimi	Eb

BIRTH

Lamat	Ix	Ahau

DESTINY

Cib	Ik'	Lamat

MEN
The Vision of the Bird

RIGHT HAND PILLAR	CENTRAL PILLAR	LEFT HAND PILLAR

CONCEPTION

Imix	Manik'	Ben

BIRTH

Muluc	Men	Imix

DESTINY

Caban	Akb'al	Muluc

CIB
Forgiveness

RIGHT HAND PILLAR	CENTRAL PILLAR	LEFT HAND PILLAR

CONCEPTION

Ik'

Lamat

Ix

BIRTH

Oc

Cib

Ik'

DESTINY

Etznab

Kan

Oc

CABAN
The Vision of the Cosmos

RIGHT HAND PILLAR	CENTRAL PILLAR	LEFT HAND PILLAR

CONCEPTION

| Akb'al | Muluc | Men |

BIRTH

| Chuen | Caban | Akb'al |

DESTINY

| Cauac | Chicchan | Chuen |

ETZNAB
Obsidian Knife

RIGHT HAND PILLAR	CENTRAL PILLAR	LEFT HAND PILLAR

CONCEPTION

Kan	Oc	Cib

BIRTH

Eb	Etznab	Kan

DESTINY

Ahau	Cimi	Eb

CAUAC
The Universal Community

RIGHT HAND PILLAR	CENTRAL PILLAR	LEFT HAND PILLAR

CONCEPTION

Chicchan	Chuen	Caban

BIRTH

Ben	Cauac	Chicchan

DESTINY

Imix	Manik'	Ben

AHAU
The Hunter

RIGHT HAND PILLAR	CENTRAL PILLAR	LEFT HAND PILLAR
	CONCEPTION	
Cimi	Eb	Etznab
	BIRTH	
Ix	Ahau	Cimi
	DESTINY	
Ik'	Lamat	Ix

IMIX
The Left Hand

RIGHT HAND PILLAR	CENTRAL PILLAR	LEFT HAND PILLAR

CONCEPTION

Manik'	Ben	Cauac

BIRTH

Men	Imix	Manik'

DESTINY

Akb'al	Muluc	Men

IK'
The Breath of Life

RIGHT HAND PILLAR	CENTRAL PILLAR	LEFT HAND PILLAR

CONCEPTION

Lamat	Ix	Ahau

BIRTH

Cib	Ik'	Lamat

DESTINY

Kan	Oc	Cib

AKB'AL
Dawn

RIGHT HAND PILLAR	CENTRAL PILLAR	LEFT HAND PILLAR

CONCEPTION

Muluc	Men	Imix

BIRTH

Caban	Akb'al	Muluc

DESTINY

Chicchan	Chuen	Caban

KAN
The Net

RIGHT HAND PILLAR	CENTRAL PILLAR	LEFT HAND PILLAR
	CONCEPTION	
Oc	Cib	Ik'
	BIRTH	
Etznab	Kan	Oc
	DESTINY	
Cimi	Eb	Etznab

CHICCHAN
Feathered Serpent

RIGHT HAND PILLAR	CENTRAL PILLAR	LEFT HAND PILLAR

CONCEPTION

Chuen	Caban	Akb'al

BIRTH

Cauac	Chicchan	Chuen

DESTINY

Manik'	Ben	Cauac

CIMI
Death and Rebirth

RIGHT HAND PILLAR	CENTRAL PILLAR	LEFT HAND PILLAR

CONCEPTION

Eb

Etznab

Kan

BIRTH

Ahau

Cimi

Eb

DESTINY

Lamat

Ix

Ahau

MANIK'
The Pillars of the Universe

RIGHT HAND PILLAR	CENTRAL PILLAR	LEFT HAND PILLAR

CONCEPTION

Ben	Cauac	Chicchan

BIRTH

Imix	Manik'	Ben

DESTINY

Muluc	Men	Imix

LAMAT
The Regeneration of the Earth

RIGHT HAND PILLAR	CENTRAL PILLAR	LEFT HAND PILLAR
	CONCEPTION	

	CONCEPTION	
Ix	Ahau	Cimi

	BIRTH	
Ik'	Lamat	Ix

	DESTINY	
Oc	Cib	Ik'

MULUC
Offering

RIGHT HAND PILLAR	CENTRAL PILLAR	LEFT HAND PILLAR

CONCEPTION

Men

Imix

Manik'

BIRTH

Akb'al

Muluc

Men

DESTINY

Chuen

Caban

Akb'al

OC
Law and Spiritual Authority

RIGHT HAND PILLAR	CENTRAL PILLAR	LEFT HAND PILLAR

CONCEPTION

Cib	Ik'	Lamat

BIRTH

Kan	Oc	Cib

DESTINY

Eb	Etznab	Kan

Appendix A

The Pop Wuj

The *Pop Wuj*, more commonly known as the *Popol Vuh*, the "Book of the Mat," or "Book of Good Counsel," was written in the Western alphabet but in the Ki'che' language, probably in the middle of the 16th century. It was likely first recorded by elders who were working from a hieroglyphic text, now lost. Between 1701 and 1703, the priest Francisco Ximenez of Chichicastenango copied down the Ki'che' text and added a Spanish translation. Although the oldest copy we have of the *Pop Wuj* is the one transcribed by Ximenez, it is clear that the book records some of the most ancient and primal myths of Mayan civilization. Certain stories from the *Pop Wuj* can be found carved on monuments from the "proto-Mayan" site of Izapa, dating from the first few centuries before Christ; recently discovered murals at the pre-Classic site of San Bartolo and dated to c. 400 BCE appear to contain themes from the same mythic cycle.

The Maya describe creation as an interplay of positive and negative polarities not dissimilar to the Chinese concept of yin and yang. At its most fundamental level, the Divine is called Tz'aqol B'itol, the Architect and Maker, an energy which embodies the eternal polarities. This was the power that created Earth and Sky. This duality of creation can also be expressed as "Heart of Sky, Heart of Earth." Heart of Sky is also the god known as Hun Rakan— or, to use one of the few Mayan words that has been adopted into English, "Hurricane." This deity is the primal spirit of the wind and the air, and is an aspect of the day sign Iq' (Yucatec: Ik') as god of the wind. Lord Feathered Serpent (Tepeu Q'ucumatz in the K'iche' language) is also connected with the day sign Iq' as the power of the wind, and thus emerges as part of the creative energy of the universe itself

The primal creative entity known as Heart of Sky is said to have three aspects, one of which is called Nim Kaqulja', which could perhaps best be translated as "Great Thunderbolt." This particular aspect of Hun Rakan or Heart of Sky is also said to be associated with the day sign Iq' (Yucatec: Ik'). It may be said to symbolize "the power of nature" and has a certain relationship to the *koyopa* or "lightning in the blood."

According to the *Pop Wuj,* the gods resolved to create a race of beings who would praise them and sing out their names, who would keep the days of the Sacred Calendar and walk in the path of truth. And so they made the animals, the deer and the turkeys, the peccaries and the tapirs. And they said, "Sing out to us now, and worship us!" But the animals could only howl and roar and make strange noises.

Disappointed, the gods resolved to make a second creation. They fashioned a man of mud. He looked like a man should look, but he could not speak plainly, nor turn his head, nor act of his own mindful volition. When the rain came, he began to dissolve. And so the gods let him dissolve with the rain.

Next, Feathered Serpent and Hurricane resolved to create a man made out of wood. They approached the primal couple, the grandfather and the grandmother, Xpiyacoc and Xmucane. They asked them to divine with the sacred *tz'ite* seeds, reading the oracle of the days of the Sacred Calendar. And the grandfather and grandmother said, "It is good that you should make men out of wood."

So they fashioned men of wood, and there were many of them. They could speak like men, walk like men, and multiply like men, but they did not remember the gods. They did not call out to the gods in songs of praise. They did not keep the days of the Sacred Calendar. And so Feathered Serpent and Hurricane were once again disappointed. Hurricane sent a great storm which destroyed that creation, the creation of the wooden men. Their dogs and turkeys, even their household utensils, rose up against them, attacked them and killed them while the great storm raged. The few who survived were those who climbed into the trees and became the monkeys that we see today.

Once upon a time, perhaps in the days of these men of wood, Grandfather Xpiyacoc and Grandmother Xmucane had two twin sons, One Junajpu and Seven Junajpu. The brothers were great adepts of the Mesoamerican handball game; their ball court lay upon the edge of the earth at a place called the Great Abyss. In time their vigorous playing became so noisy that it annoyed the Lords of the Underworld, One Death and Seven Death, who sent brooding owls as messengers to challenge the twins to a game of handball in the very depths of Xib'alb'a, the Underworld. The twins left One Junajpu's sons, One Monkey and One Artisan, to care for their grandmother Xmucane. As musicians and poets, they could be relied upon to keep her entertained.

The Hero Twins then set forth to challenge the Lords of the Underworld. They traveled the path of the Milky Way or road of souls, following it through the sky until they reached the Crossroads, and then they took the dark or black road that leads to Xib'alb'a. This Crossroads is the place where the ecliptic and the Milky Way cross at the Galactic Center. The starry path of the Milky Way is the White Road, or *saq b'e*; a yellow (sometimes said to be green) road follows the ecliptic eastward while a red road follows it westward. The dark swathe of sky which we call the Great Rift in the Milky Way and which marks the Galactic Center is known among the Maya to this very day as the black road or the Road to Xib'alb'a, and it is this road that the Hero Twins chose.

In the Underworld, they were subjected to magical tests by One Death and Seven Death. In one such test, they had to pass the night in a House of Darkness and keep their cigars lit all night. They failed to do so; consequently, the Underworld Lords sacrificed them before they even had a chance to play handball. The head of One Junajpu was left hanging in a tree.

In time, a young maiden called Blood Woman, daughter of one of the Xilb'alb'a Lords, came to the tree and saw the head of One Junajpu. It spit into her right hand, thus impregnating her. When her father discovered that she was pregnant, she protested her innocence, claiming, truthfully enough, that she had not known a man sexually. When she realized that her father didn't believe her and intended to sacrifice her, she made her way to the upper world and to the very house of Xmucane.

She told Xmucane that she was about to give birth to twins who were the sons of her own son, One Junajpu. But Xmucane didn't believe her either. She gave her a magical test, telling her to go and bring back a net full of corn from a garden which she knew to contain only a single plant. But Blood Woman pulled the silk out of a single ear of corn, which was magically transformed into an abundant harvest.

Amazed, Xmucane went to the garden, poked around, and saw the imprint of Blood Woman's magical net. Knowing that her sons, the first pair of Hero Twins, were also the planet Venus, and knowing that Venus would return from the Underworld on a day called K'at in K'iche' (*k'at* means "net"), she realized that Blood Woman was telling the truth. Now she knew that Blood Woman's children were her own grandchildren.

Thus a new set of Hero Twins was born. Their names were Junajpu and Xb'alanke, and they grew up in their grandmother's house. Their twin half-brothers, One Monkey and One Artisan, teased them mercilessly. Being magicians of a high order, Junajpu and Xb'alanke coaxed their artistic, musical half-brothers into a tree, where they were magically transformed into monkeys. They tried to make their way back to Xmucane's house, but their grandmother laughed uproariously at their comical appearance as monkeys, so they went away again. This explains why the day sign Chuen, commonly symbolized by a monkey, is associated with the arts.

Junajpu and Xb'alanke grew up as heroes and magicians; they performed many miraculous exploits. At that time most "human beings" were made of wood. Failing to worship the gods properly, they instead worshiped a pretender, a false god called Seven Macaw who exemplified the Seven Shames. The macaw bird was perched on top of the tree which stood at the center of the universe, the world tree that forms the axis of all being. From his lofty vantage point, looking down upon the world below him, he began to assume that he was God. But he was mistaken. Only Ajaw is God. The macaw was deluded by pride, ambition, and ignorance. The gods sent the Hero Twins to dislodge him from his perch, causing him to see that, in reality, he was only a silly bird. Shooting him with a blowgun, they toppled Seven Macaw from the sky. They even disfigured him so that he now resembles the peculiar countenance of the scarlet macaw.

Then they defeated his two sons, who were primordial beasts, one named Zipacna who is in the form of a crocodile and the other one known as Earthquake.

Xmucane and Blood Woman had carefully hidden the ballgame gear which once belonged to One and Seven Junajpu, father and uncle of the Hero Twins. They didn't want the two twins to meet the same fate as their elders. But a cunning rat revealed to them that the ball-playing equipment was hidden in the rafters of Xmucane's house. Having discovered the equipment, the Hero Twins could not help but start playing handball. Once again, the Lords of Xib'alb'a heard the resounding noise, and once again they were annoyed, summoning the twins to play ball with them in the Underworld.

As the Hero Twins, Junajpu and Xb'alanke, were about to journey into the Underworld to challenge the Lords of Death in a game of handball, they each planted an ear of corn in their grandmother's patio. They told her that if the corn withered, it would mean that they were dead, but if it sprouted again, they were once more alive.

The two new Hero Twins took the ancient road to Xib'alb'a, but they were more clever than their predecessors. They endured many tests and challenges during their sojourn in the dark Underworld of Xib'alb'a. They were forced to spend the night in a number of different "houses," all of which were controlled by the Lords of the Underworld and all of which were fraught with peril. One of the most difficult such houses was called Chaim Ha or Razor House, a dark cave where sharp knives flew through the air. They played a trick on the Lords of Xib'alb'a, making them think they had kept their cigars lit all night in the House of Darkness. They met the Death Lords upon the handball court; the games went on, with many magical happenings, and with a new test for the Hero Twins in a new House of Darkness every night.

Finally Junajpu's head got bitten off by a bat, and it seemed as if all was lost. But Xb'alanke replaced his brother's head with a squash and chose to continue the game. Triumphantly, the Death Lords used Junajpu's severed head for a handball, but Xb'alanke knocked it into the trees. The Death Lords set off in pursuit, but ended up mistakenly following a rabbit instead. This gave Xb'alanke a chance to recover his brother's head and replace it upon his body, so that the Hero Twins were at full strength again.

All the same, the Hero Twins knew that the game was stacked against them, and that the Death Lords intended to sacrifice them in the fire, no matter what the game's outcome might be. The Hero Twins tricked the Lords of Death by instructing two shamans: "Tell the Lords of Death to grind up our bones and pour the dust into a river, for that shall surely rid them of us for good."

The Hero Twins leapt willingly into the fires of sacrifice; the Lords of Xib'alb'a followed the shamanic advice, grinding their bones into dust and pouring it into a river.

But it was all a ruse, for this was the formula that brought the Hero Twins back from the dead, first as a pair of catfish and then as men. The Hero Twins disguised themselves as traveling magicians and took on "dog names," Jun Ajpu Wuch' (Possum Hunter) and Jun Ajpu Utiw (Coyote Hunter). They performed their tricks in front of the Lords of Death, with Xb'alanke sacrificing Junajpu and then restoring him to life. Fascinated by this magic, the Lords of Death wanted to learn all about it and offered themselves up for the sacrifice trick.

But this time the sacrifice was for real, and the Lords of the Dead stayed dead. Junajpu and Xb'alanke had triumphed. The universe was once again in balance. Before leaving the Underworld, they visited the grave of their uncle Seven Junajpu. Thus began the Mayan custom (which still continues) of visiting the graves of one's ancestors on Ajpu (Ahau) days.

Now the gods transformed the world. The great god Hurricane sent storm and flood to destroy the world of the wooden men. The Hero Twins were transformed into the Sun and Moon of a new world, a world of true human beings who knew how to worship the gods properly.

The rest of the *Pop Wuj* details the migrations of these "true human beings" until they became the Ki'che' people. The animals came to the gods and told them of how they had discovered a mountain filled with white and yellow corn. Grandmother Xmucane ground the corn into fine cornmeal and combined it with water to fashion a new race of men. She made four men and four women who were the ancestors of all of today's clans and lineages.

And the gods were amazed, for the new creation was perfect; the new women and men had perfect knowledge, perfect vision. They kept the days of the Sacred Calendar and they praised the gods. In fact, the gods became afraid of them, of how powerful they were, and they sent a fog to cloud their perfect vision.

Meanwhile the first human beings still wandered in darkness, for the sun had not yet risen, and there was only the vague hint of the beginning of dawn. So they wandered to a place called Tulan Zuyua, the Place of the Seven Caves. And here gathered the ancestors of all the peoples, and here they began to speak different languages. The original people were led by four men, the first Four Fathers of humanity, the B'alameb' or Jaguar Men. These first forefathers were created directly by the gods, who also created their four wives. Thus the four is doubled in terms of yin and yang to equal the number eight, and it is upon days numbered eight that the most important rituals are performed by contemporary Daykeepers. It was the first Four Fathers who guided the people in ancient, primordial times, and led them upon their migrations or journeys in search of the light. The Morning Star, Venus, cast a faint glow, but it was the light that precedes the sun, the early pre-dawn light, for as of yet there was no sun. These leaders were in constant communication with their guardian deities, the most important of whom was Tohil or Tojil, the patron deity of the forefather named B'alam K'itze'.

The *Pop Wuj* tells us that they gathered upon the mountain called Hacavitz, where they wept to see the light of the Morning Star. The Four Jaguar Fathers made an offering, burning so much copal that great clouds rose into the sky. At last, the sun rose upon the Fourth World. Birds and animals cried out for joy, and so did the people, laughing and weeping at the same time. This the spirit in which we make sacrificial offerings, the spirit of resolution and reconciliation which blesses us and nourishes us when we surrender. It is the altar or table upon which those offerings are made. When the sun first rose upon the Fourth World, the gods of the forefathers were changed into stone. To this day, Mayan altars and sacred places in the wilderness are places of stone.

Appendix B

Mayan Calendar Tables

The following Calendar Tables list the beginning of each *trecena* (13-day period) from the beginning of *k'atun* 10 Ahau (February 1934) until the Gregorian year 2020, and can be used to find any Mayan Calendar date within that period.

How to Use the Calendar Tables
Let us say you want to find the Mayan equivalent for the Gregorian date of June 26, 1995. First, find the year 1995 in the Calendar Tables. Running your finger down the column, you will note that the *trecena* that began immediately before that date was 1 Imix, which began on June 15.

Now turn to the Calendar Board in this appendix. Find the day 1 Imix. Then count down to the appropriate day in the following manner:

June 15 = 1 Imix
June 16 = 2 Ik'
June 17 = 3 Akb'al
June 18 = 4 Kan
June 19 = 5 Chicchan
June 20 = 6 Cimi
June 21 = 7 Manik'
June 22 = 8 Lamat
June 23 = 9 Muluc
June 24 = 10 Oc
June 25 = 11 Chuen
June 26 = 12 Eb

It really is that simple. (If you're feeling creative, you can count backwards, if it's quicker, from the "1" Mayan date following the Gregorian date you're looking for.) However, be aware of leap years, as they can throw off your count. Leap years are important in another respect. Note that in each column listing the Mayan dates, a Mayan New Year's day is listed along with the name of the year. The actual New Year date changes every four years. This is because the Maya did not honor the custom of leap years (though they were aware of the astronomical factors that have caused Westerners to develop the concept). In these tables, leap years have been marked with an asterisk.

Below, you will see the Calendar Board diagram, which you can print out and keep by your desk as a handy reference for all your Mayan Calendar Astrology work.

THE CALENDAR BOARD

Chuen / B'atz'	8	2	9	3	10	4	11	5	12	6	13	7	1
Eb / E'	9	3	10	4	11	5	12	6	13	7	1	8	2
Ben / Aj	10	4	11	5	12	6	13	7	1	8	2	9	3
Ix / I'x	11	5	12	6	13	7	1	8	2	9	3	10	4
Men / Tz'lk'in	12	6	13	7	1	8	2	9	3	10	4	11	5
Cib / Ajmaq	13	7	1	8	2	9	3	10	4	11	5	12	6
Caban / No'j	1	8	2	9	3	10	4	11	5	12	6	13	7
Etznab / Tijax	2	9	3	10	4	11	5	12	6	13	7	1	8
Cauac / Kawoq	3	10	4	11	5	12	6	13	7	1	8	2	9
Ahau / Ajpu	4	11	5	12	6	13	7	1	8	2	9	3	10
Imix / Imox	5	12	6	13	7	1	8	2	9	3	10	4	11
Ik' / Iq'	6	13	7	1	8	2	9	3	10	4	11	5	12
Akb'al/Aq'ab'al	7	1	8	2	9	3	10	4	11	5	12	6	13
Kan / K'at	8	2	9	3	10	4	11	5	12	6	13	7	1
Chicchan / Kan	9	3	10	4	11	5	12	6	13	7	1	8	2
Cimi / Kame	10	4	11	5	12	6	13	7	1	8	2	9	3
Manik' / Kej	11	5	12	6	13	7	1	8	2	9	3	10	4
Lamat / Q'anil	12	6	13	7	1	8	2	9	3	10	4	11	5
Muluc / Toj	13	7	1	8	2	9	3	10	4	11	5	12	6
Oc / Tz'i	1	8	2	9	3	10	4	11	5	12	6	13	7

GREGORIAN DATE	MAYAN DATE	GREGORIAN DATE	MAYAN DATE
1934		Mar 13	1 Eb
Feb 16	1 Ik'	**Mar 13–Mayan Year 1 Eb**	
Mar 1	1 Men	Mar 26	1 Chicchan
Mar 13–Mayan Year 13 Manik'		Apr 8	1 Etznab
Mar 14	1 Lamat	Apr 21	1 Chuen
Mar 27	1 Imix	May 4	1 Kan
Apr 9	1 Ix	May 17	1 Caban
Apr 22	1 Manik'	May 30	1 Oc
May 5	1 Ahau	Jun 12	1 Akb'al
May 18	1 Ben	Jun 25	1 Cib
May 31	1 Cimi	Jul 8	1 Muluc
Jun 13	1 Cauac	Jul 21	1 Ik'
Jun 26	1 Eb	Aug 3	1 Men
Jul 9	1 Chicchan	Aug 16	1 Lamat
Jul 22	1 Etznab	Aug 29	1 Imix
Aug 4	1 Chuen	Sep 11	1 Ix
Aug 17	1 Kan	Sep 24	1 Manik'
Aug 30	1 Caban	Oct 7	1 Ahau
Sep 12	1 Oc	Oct 20	1 Ben
Sep 25	1 Akb'al	Nov 2	1 Cimi
Oct 8	1 Cib	Nov 15	1 Cauac
Oct 21	1 Muluc	Nov 28	1 Eb
Nov 3	1 Ik'	Dec 11	1 Chicchan
Nov 16	1 Men	Dec 24	1 Etznab
Nov 29	1 Lamat		
Dec 12	1 Imix	***1936**	
Dec 25	1 Ix	Jan 6	1 Chuen
		Jan 19	1 Kan
1935		Feb 1	1 Caban
Jan 7	1 Manik'	Feb 14	1 Oc
Jan 20	1 Ahau	Feb 27	1 Akb'al
Feb 2	1 Ben	Mar 11	1 Cib
Feb 15	1 Cimi	**Mar 12–Mayan Year 2 Caban**	
Feb 28	1 Cauac	Mar 24	1 Muluc

GREGORIAN DATE	MAYAN DATE	GREGORIAN DATE	MAYAN DATE
Apr 6	1 Ik'	May 14	1 Chicchan
Apr 19	1 Men	May 27	1 Etznab
May 2	1 Lamat	Jun 9	1 Chuen
May 15	1 Imix	Jun 22	1 Kan
May 28	1 Ix	Jul 5	1 Caban
Jun 10	1 Manik'	Jul 18	1 Oc
Jun 23	1 Ahau	Jul 31	1 Akb'al
Jul 6	1 Ben	Aug 13	1 Cib
Jul 19	1 Cimi	Aug 26	1 Muluc
Aug 1	1 Cauac	Sep 8	1 Ik'
Aug 14	1 Eb	Sep 21	1 Men
Aug 27	1 Chicchan	Oct 4	1 Lamat
Sep 9	1 Etznab	Oct 17	1 Imix
Sep 22	1 Chuen	Oct 30	1 Ix
Oct 5	1 Kan	Nov 12	1 Manik'
Oct 18	1 Caban	Nov 25	1 Ahau
Oct 31	1 Oc	Dec 8	1 Ben
Nov 13	1 Akb'al	Dec 21	1 Cimi
Nov 26	1 Cib		
Dec 9	1 Muluc	**1938**	
Dec 22	1 Ik'	Jan 3	1 Cauac
		Jan 16	1 Eb
1937		Jan 29	1 Chicchan
Jan 4	1 Men	Feb 11	1 Etznab
Jan 17	1 Lamat	Feb 24	1 Chuen
Jan 30	1 Imix	Mar 9	1 Kan
Feb 12	1 Ix	**Mar 12–Mayan Year 4 Manik'**	
Feb 25	1 Manik'	Mar 22	1 Caban
Mar 10	1 Ahau	Apr 4	1 Oc
Mar 12–Mayan Year 3 Ik'		Apr 17	1 Akb'al
Mar 23	1 Ben	Apr 30	1 Cib
Apr 5	1 Cimi	May 13	1 Muluc
Apr 18	1 Cauac	May 26	1 Ik'
May 1	1 Eb	Jun 8	1 Men

GREGORIAN DATE	MAYAN DATE	GREGORIAN DATE	MAYAN DATE
Jun 21	1 Lamat	Jul 29	1 Chuen
Jul 4	1 Imix	Aug 11	1 Kan
Jul 17	1 Ix	Aug 24	1 Caban
Jul 30	1 Manik'	Sep 6	1 Oc
Aug 12	1 Ahau	Sep 19	1 Akb'al
Aug 25	1 Ben	Oct 2	1 Cib
Sep 7	1 Cimi	Oct 15	1 Muluc
Sep 20	1 Cauac	Oct 28	1 Ik'
Oct 3	1 Eb	Nov 10	1 Men
Oct 16	1 Chicchan	Nov 23	1 Lamat
Oct 29	1 Etznab	Dec 6	1 Imix
Nov 11	1 Chuen	Dec 19	1 Ix
Nov 24	1 Kan		
Dec 7	1 Caban		
Dec 20	1 Oc	***1940**	
		Jan 1	1 Manik'
		Jan 14	1 Ahau
1939		Jan 27	1 Ben
Jan 2	1 Akb'al	Feb 9	1 Cimi
Jan 15	1 Cib	Feb 22	1 Cauac
Jan 28	1 Muluc	Mar 6	1 Eb
Feb 10	1 Ik'	**Mar 12–Mayan Year 6 Caban**	
Feb 23	1 Men	Mar 19	1 Chicchan
Mar 8	1 Lamat	Apr 1	1 Etznab
Mar 12–Mayan Year 5 Eb		Apr 14	1 Chuen
Mar 21	1 Imix	Apr 27	1 Kan
Apr 3	1 Ix	May 10	1 Caban
Apr 16	1 Manik'	May 23	1 Oc
Apr 29	1 Ahau	Jun 5	1 Akb'al
May 12	1 Ben	Jun 18	1 Cib
May 25	1 Cimi	Jul 1	1 Muluc
Jun 7	1 Cauac	Jul 14	1 Ik'
Jun 20	1 Eb	Jul 27	1 Men
Jul 3	1 Chicchan	Aug 9	1 Lamat
Jul 16	1 Etznab	Aug 22	1 Imix

GREGORIAN DATE	MAYAN DATE	GREGORIAN DATE	MAYAN DATE
Sep 4	1 Ix	Oct 12	1 Caban
Sep 17	1 Manik'	Oct 25	1 Oc
Sep 30	1 Ahau	Nov 7	1 Akb'al
Oct 13	1 Ben	Nov 20	1 Cib
Oct 26	1 Cimi	Dec 3	1 Muluc
Nov 8	1 Cauac	Dec 16	1 Ik'
Nov 21	1 Eb	Dec 29	1 Men
Dec 4	1 Chicchan		
Dec 17	1 Etznab	**1942**	
Dec 30	1 Chuen	Jan 11	1 Lamat
		Jan 24	1 Imix
1941		Feb 6	1 Ix
Jan 12	1 Kan	Feb 19	1 Manik'
Jan 25	1 Caban	Mar 4	1 Ahau
Feb 7	1 Oc	**Mar 11–Mayan Year 8 Manik'**	
Feb 20	1 Akb'al	Mar 17	1 Ben
Mar 5	1 Cib	Mar 30	1 Cimi
Mar 11–Mayan Year 7 Ik'		Apr 12	1 Cauac
Mar 18	1 Muluc	Apr 25	1 Eb
Mar 31	1 Ik'	May 8	1 Chicchan
Apr 13	1 Men	May 21	1 Etznab
Apr 26	1 Lamat	Jun 3	1 Chuen
May 9	1 Imix	Jun 16	1 Kan
May 22	1 Ix	Jun 29	1 Caban
Jun 4	1 Manik'	Jul 12	1 Oc
Jun 17	1 Ahau	Jul 25	1 Akb'al
Jun 30	1 Ben	Aug 7	1 Cib
Jul 13	1 Cimi	Aug 20	1 Muluc
Jul 26	1 Cauac	Sep 2	1 Ik'
Aug 8	1 Eb	Sep 15	1 Men
Aug 21	1 Chicchan	Sep 28	1 Lamat
Sep 3	1 Etznab	Oct 11	1 Imix
Sep 16	1 Chuen	Oct 24	1 Ix
Sep 29	1 Kan	Nov 6	1 Manik'

GREGORIAN DATE	MAYAN DATE	GREGORIAN DATE	MAYAN DATE
Nov 19	1 Ahau	*1944	
Dec 2	1 Ben	Jan 9	1 Cib
Dec 15	1 Cimi	Jan 22	1 Muluc
Dec 28	1 Cauac	Feb 4	1 Ik'
		Feb 17	1 Men
1943		Mar 1	1 Lamat
Jan 10	1 Eb	Mar 10–Mayan Year 10 Caban	
Jan 23	1 Chicchan	Mar 14	1 Imix
Feb 5	1 Etznab	Mar 27	1 Ix
Feb 18	1 Chuen	Apr 9	1 Manik'
Mar 3	1 Kan	Apr 22	1 Ahau
Mar 11–Mayan Year 9 Eb		May 5	1 Ben
Mar 16	1 Caban	May 18	1 Cimi
Mar 29	1 Oc	May 31	1 Cauac
Apr 11	1 Akb'al	Jun 13	1 Eb
Apr 24	1 Cib	Jun 26	1 Chicchan
May 7	1 Muluc	Jul 9	1 Etznab
May 20	1 Ik'	Jul 22	1 Chuen
Jun 2	1 Men	Aug 4	1 Kan
Jun 15	1 Lamat	Aug 17	1 Caban
Jun 28	1 Imix	Aug 30	1 Oc
Jul 11	1 Ix	Sep 12	1 Akb'al
Jul 24	1 Manik'	Sep 25	1 Cib
Aug 6	1 Ahau	Oct 8	1 Muluc
Aug 19	1 Ben	Oct 21	1 Ik'
Sep 1	1 Cimi	Nov 3	1 Men
Sep 14	1 Cauac	Nov 16	1 Lamat
Sep 27	1 Eb	Nov 29	1 Imix
Oct 10	1 Chicchan	Dec 12	1 Ix
Oct 23	1 Etznab	Dec 25	1 Manik'
Nov 5	1 Chuen		
Nov 18	1 Kan	1945	
Dec 1	1 Caban	Jan 7	1 Ahau
Dec 14	1 Oc	Jan 20	1 Ben
Dec 27	1 Akb'al	Feb 2	1 Cimi

GREGORIAN DATE	MAYAN DATE	GREGORIAN DATE	MAYAN DATE
Feb 15	1 Cauac	Mar 25	1 Ik'
Feb 28	1 Eb	Apr 7	1 Men
Mar 10–Mayan Year 11 Ik'		Apr 20	1 Lamat
Mar 13	1 Chicchan	May 3	1 Imix
Mar 26	1 Etznab	May 16	1 Ix
Apr 8	1 Chuen	May 29	1 Manik'
Apr 21	1 Kan	Jun 11	1 Ahau
May 4	1 Caban	Jun 24	1 Ben
May 17	1 Oc	Jul 7	1 Cimi
May 30	1 Akb'al	Jul 20	1 Cauac
Jun 12	1 Cib	Aug 2	1 Eb
Jun 25	1 Muluc	Aug 15	1 Chicchan
Jul 8	1 Ik'	Aug 28	1 Etznab
Jul 21	1 Men	Sep 10	1 Chuen
Aug 3	1 Lamat	Sep 23	1 Kan
Aug 16	1 Imix	Oct 6	1 Caban
Aug 29	1 Ix	Oct 19	1 Oc
Sep 11	1 Manik'	Nov 1	1 Akb'al
Sep 24	1 Ahau	Nov 14	1 Cib
Oct 7	1 Ben	Nov 27	1 Muluc
Oct 20	1 Cimi	Dec 10	1 Ik'
Nov 2	1 Cauac	Dec 23	1 Men
Nov 15	1 Eb		
Nov 28	1 Chicchan	**1947**	
Dec 11	1 Etznab	Jan 5	1 Lamat
Dec 24	1 Chuen	Jan 18	1 Imix
		Jan 31	1 Ix
1946		Feb 13	1 Manik'
Jan 6	1 Kan	Feb 26	1 Ahau
Jan 19	1 Caban	**Mar 10–Mayan Year 13 Eb**	
Feb 1	1 Oc	Mar 11	1 Ben
Feb 14	1 Akb'al	Mar 24	1 Cimi
Feb 27	1 Cib	Apr 6	1 Cauac
Mar 10–Mayan Year 12 Manik'		Apr 19	1 Eb
Mar 12	1 Muluc		

GREGORIAN DATE	MAYAN DATE	GREGORIAN DATE	MAYAN DATE
May 2	1 Chicchan	Jun 8	1 Lamat
May 15	1 Etznab	Jun 21	1 Imix
May 28	1 Chuen	Jul 4	1 Ix
Jun 10	1 Kan	Jul 17	1 Manik'
Jun 23	1 Caban	Jul 30	1 Ahau
Jul 6	1 Oc	Aug 12	1 Ben
Jul 19	1 Akb'al	Aug 25	1 Cimi
Aug 1	1 Cib	Sep 7	1 Cauac
Aug 14	1 Muluc	Sep 20	1 Eb
Aug 27	1 Ik'	Oct 3	1 Chicchan
Sep 9	1 Men	Oct 16	1 Etznab
Sep 22	1 Lamat	Oct 29	1 Chuen
Oct 5	1 Imix	Nov 11	1 Kan
Oct 18	1 Ix	Nov 24	1 Caban
Oct 31	1 Manik'	Dec 7	1 Oc
Nov 13	1 Ahau	Dec 20	1 Akb'al
Nov 26	1 Ben		
Dec 9	1 Cimi	**1949**	
Dec 22	1 Cauac	Jan 2	1 Cib
		Jan 15	1 Muluc
*1948		Jan 28	1 Ik'
Jan 4	1 Eb	Feb 10	1 Men
Jan 17	1 Chicchan	Feb 23	1 Lamat
Jan 30	1 Etznab	Mar 8	1 Imix
Feb 12	1 Chuen	**Mar 9–Mayan Year 2 Ik'**	
Feb 25	1 Kan	Mar 21	1 Ix
Mar 9–Mayan Year 1 Caban		Apr 3	1 Manik'
Mar 9	1 Caban	Apr 16	1 Ahau
Mar 22	1 Oc	Apr 29	1 Ben
Apr 4	1 Akb'al	May 12	1 Cimi
Apr 17	1 Cib	May 25	1 Cauac
Apr 30	1 Muluc	Jun 7	1 Eb
May 13	1 Ik'	Jun 20	1 Chicchan
May 26	1 Men	Jul 3	1 Etznab

GREGORIAN DATE	MAYAN DATE	GREGORIAN DATE	MAYAN DATE
Jul 16	1 Chuen	Aug 23	1 Ix
Jul 29	1 Kan	Sep 5	1 Manik'
Aug 11	1 Caban	Sep 18	1 Ahau
Aug 24	1 Oc	Oct 1	1 Ben
Sep 6	1 Akb'al	Oct 14	1 Cimi
Sep 19	1 Cib	Oct 27	1 Cauac
Oct 2	1 Muluc	Nov 9	1 Eb
Oct 15	1 Ik'	Nov 22	1 Chicchan
Oct 28	1 Men	Dec 5	1 Etznab
Nov 10	1 Lamat	Dec 18	1 Chuen
Nov 23	1 Imix	Dec 31	1 Kan
Dec 6	1 Ix		
Dec 19	1 Manik'		

1951

		Jan 13	1 Caban
1950		Jan 26	1 Oc
Jan 1	1 Ahau	Feb 8	1 Akb'al
Jan 14	1 Ben	Feb 21	1 Cib
Jan 27	1 Cimi	Mar 6	1 Muluc
Feb 9	1 Cauac		
Feb 22	1 Eb	**Mar 9–Mayan Year 4 Eb**	
Mar 7	1 Chicchan	Mar 19	1 Ik'
Mar 9–Mayan Year 3 Manik'		Apr 1	1 Men
Mar 20	1 Etznab	Apr 14	1 Lamat
Apr 2	1 Chuen	Apr 27	1 Imix
Apr 15	1 Kan	May 10	1 Ix
Apr 28	1 Caban	May 23	1 Manik'
May 11	1 Oc	Jun 5	1 Ahau
May 24	1 Akb'al	Jun 18	1 Ben
Jun 6	1 Cib	Jul 1	1 Cimi
Jun 19	1 Muluc	Jul 14	1 Cauac
Jul 2	1 Ik'	Jul 27	1 Eb
Jul 15	1 Men	Aug 9	1 Chicchan
Jul 28	1 Lamat	Aug 22	1 Etznab
Aug 10	1 Imix	Sep 4	1 Chuen
		Sep 17	1 Kan

GREGORIAN DATE	MAYAN DATE	GREGORIAN DATE	MAYAN DATE
Sep 30	1 Caban	Nov 19	1 Ben
Oct 13	1 Oc	Dec 2	1 Cimi
Oct 26	1 Akb'al	Dec 15	1 Cauac
Nov 8	1 Cib	Dec 28	1 Eb
Nov 21	1 Muluc		
Dec 4	1 Ik'	**1953**	
Dec 17	1 Men	Jan 10	1 Chicchan
Dec 30	1 Lamat	Jan 23	1 Etznab
		Feb 5	1 Chuen
*1952		Feb 18	1 Kan
Jan 12	1 Imix	Mar 3	1 Caban
Jan 25	1 Ix	**Mar 8–Mayan Year 6 Ik'**	
Feb 7	1 Manik'	Mar 16	1 Oc
Feb 20	1 Ahau	Mar 29	1 Akb'al
Mar 4	1 Ben	Apr 11	1 Cib
Mar 8–Mayan Year 5 Caban		Apr 24	1 Muluc
Mar 17	1 Cimi	May 7	1 Ik'
Mar 30	1 Cauac	May 20	1 Men
Apr 12	1 Eb	Jun 2	1 Lamat
Apr 25	1 Chicchan	Jun 15	1 Imix
May 8	1 Etznab	Jun 28	1 Ix
May 21	1 Chuen	Jul 11	1 Manik'
Jun 3	1 Kan	Jul 24	1 Ahau
Jun 16	1 Caban	Aug 6	1 Ben
Jun 29	1 Oc	Aug 19	1 Cimi
Jul 12	1 Akb'al	Sep 1	1 Cauac
Jul 25	1 Cib	Sep 14	1 Eb
Aug 7	1 Muluc	Sep 27	1 Chicchan
Aug 20	1 Ik'	Oct 10	1 Etznab
Sep 2	1 Men	Oct 23	1 Chuen
Sep 15	1 Lamat	Nov 5	1 Kan
Sep 28	1 Imix	Nov 18	1 Caban
Oct 11	1 Ix	Dec 1	1 Oc
Oct 24	1 Manik'	Dec 14	1 Akb'al
Nov 6	1 Ahau	Dec 27	1 Cib

GREGORIAN DATE	MAYAN DATE	GREGORIAN DATE	MAYAN DATE
		Feb 16	1 Eb
1954		Feb 3	1 Cauac
Jan 9	1 Muluc	**Mar 8–Mayan Year 8 Eb**	
Jan 22	1 Ik'	Mar 14	1 Etznab
Feb 4	1 Men	Mar 27	1 Chuen
Feb 17	1 Lamat	Apr 9	1 Kan
Mar 2	1 Imix	Apr 22	1 Caban
Mar 8–Mayan Year 7 Manik'		May 5	1 Oc
Mar 15	1 Ix	May 18	1 Akb'al
Mar 28	1 Manik'	May 31	1 Cib
Apr 10	1 Ahau	Jun 13	1 Muluc
Apr 23	1 Ben	Jun 26	1 Ik'
May 6	1 Cimi	Jul 9	1 Men
May 19	1 Cauac	Jul 22	1 Lamat
Jun 1	1 Eb	Aug 4	1 Imix
Jun 14	1 Chicchan	Aug 17	1 Ix
Jun 27	1 Etznab	Aug 30	1 Manik'
Jul 10	1 Chuen	Sep 12	1 Ahau
Jul 23	1 Kan	Sep 25	1 Ben
Aug 5	1 Caban	Oct 8	1 Cimi
Aug 18	1 Oc	Oct 21	1 Cauac
Aug 31	1 Akb'al	Nov 3	1 Eb
Sep 13	1 Cib	Nov 16	1 Chicchan
Sep 26	1 Muluc	Nov 29	1 Etznab
Oct 22	1 Men	Dec 12	1 Chuen
Nov 4	1 Lamat	Dec 25	1 Kan
Nov 17	1 Imix		
Nov 30	1 Ix	***1956**	
Dec 13	1 Manik'	Jan 7	1 Caban
Dec 26	1 Ahau	Jan 20	1 Oc
		Feb 2	1 Akb'al
1955		Feb 15	1 Cib
Jan 8	1 Ben	Feb 28	1 Muluc
Jan 21	1 Cimi	**Mar 7–Mayan Year 9 Caban**	
Mar 1	1 Chicchan		

GREGORIAN DATE	MAYAN DATE	GREGORIAN DATE	MAYAN DATE
Mar 12	1 Ik'	Apr 19	1 Chicchan
Mar 25	1 Men	May 2	1 Etznab
Apr 7	1 Lamat	May 15	1 Chuen
Apr 20	1 Imix	May 28	1 Kan
May 3	1 Ix	Jun 10	1 Caban
May 16	1 Manik'	Jun 23	1 Oc
May 29	1 Ahau	Jul 6	1 Akb'al
Jun 11	1 Ben	Jul 19	1 Cib
Jun 24	1 Cimi	Aug 1	1 Muluc
Jul 7	1 Cauac	Aug 14	1 Ik'
Jul 20	1 Eb	Aug 27	1 Men
Aug 2	1 Chicchan	Sep 9	1 Lamat
Aug 15	1 Etznab	Sep 22	1 Imix
Aug 28	1 Chuen	Oct 5	1 Ix
Sep 10	1 Kan	Oct 18	1 Manik'
Sep 23	1 Caban	Oct 31	1 Ahau
Oct 6	1 Oc	Nov 13	1 Ben
Oct 19	1 Akb'al	Nov 26	1 Cimi
Nov 1	1 Cib	Dec 9	1 Cauac
Nov 14	1 Muluc	Dec 22	1 Eb
Nov 27	1 Ik'		
Dec 10	1 Men	**1958**	
Dec 23	1 Lamat	Jan 4	1 Chicchan
		Jan 17	1 Etznab
1957		Jan 30	1 Chuen
Jan 5	1 Imix	Feb 12	1 Kan
Jan 18	1 Ix	Feb 25	1 Caban
Jan 31	1 Manik'	**Mar 7–Mayan Year 11 Manik'**	
Feb 13	1 Ahau	Mar 10	1 Oc
Feb 26	1 Ben	Mar 23	1 Akb'al
Mar 7–Mayan Year 10 Ik'		Apr 5	1 Cib
Mar 11	1 Cimi	Apr 18	1 Muluc
Mar 24	1 Cauac	May 1	1 Ik'
Apr 6	1 Eb	May 14	1 Men

GREGORIAN DATE	MAYAN DATE	GREGORIAN DATE	MAYAN DATE
May 27	1 Lamat	Jul 4	1 Chuen
Jun 9	1 Imix	Jul 17	1 Kan
Jun 22	1 Ix	Jul 30	1 Caban
Jul 5	1 Manik'	Aug 12	1 Oc
Jul 18	1 Ahau	Aug 25	1 Akb'al
Jul 31	1 Ben	Sep 7	1 Cib
Aug 13	1 Cimi	Sep 20	1 Muluc
Aug 26	1 Cauac	Oct 3	1 Ik'
Sep 8	1 Eb	Oct 16	1 Men
Sep 21	1 Chicchan	Oct 29	1 Lamat
Oct 4	1 Etznab	Nov 11	1 Imix
Oct 17	1 Chuen	Nov 24	1 Ix
Oct 30	1 Kan	Dec 7	1 Manik'
Nov 12	1 Caban	Dec 20	1 Ahau
Nov 25	1 Oc		
Dec 8	1 Akb'al	***1960**	
Dec 21	1 Cib	Jan 2	1 Ben
		Jan 15	1 Cimi
1959		Jan 28	1 Cauac
Jan 3	1 Muluc	Feb 10	1 Eb
Jan 16	1 Ik'	Feb 23	1 Chicchan
Jan 29	1 Men	**Mar 6–Mayan Year 13 Caban**	
Feb 11	1 Lamat	Mar 7	1 Etznab
Feb 24	1 Imix	Mar 20	1 Chuen
Mar 7–Mayan Year 12 Eb		Apr 2	1 Kan
Mar 9	1 Ix	Apr 15	1 Caban
Mar 22	1 Manik'	Apr 28	1 Oc
Apr 4	1 Ahau	May 11	1 Akb'al
Apr 17	1 Ben	May 24	1 Cib
Apr 30	1 Cimi	Jun 6	1 Muluc
May 13	1 Cauac	Jun 19	1 Ik'
May 26	1 Eb	Jul 2	1 Men
Jun 8	1 Chicchan	Jul 15	1 Lamat
Jun 21	1 Etznab	Jul 28	1 Imix

GREGORIAN DATE	MAYAN DATE	GREGORIAN DATE	MAYAN DATE
Aug 10	1 Ix	Sep 17	1 Caban
Aug 23	1 Manik'	Sep 30	1 Oc
Sep 5	1 Ahau	Oct 13	1 Akb'al
Sep 18	1 Ben	Oct 26	1 Cib
Oct 1	1 Cimi	Nov 8	1 Muluc
Oct 14	1 Cauac	Nov 21	1 Ik'
Oct 27	1 Eb	Dec 4	1 Men
Nov 9	1 Chicchan	Dec 17	1 Lamat
Nov 22	1 Etznab	Dec 30	1 Imix
Dec 5	1 Chuen		
Dec 18	1 Kan		
Dec 31	1 Caban	**1962**	
		Jan 12	1 Ix
		Jan 25	1 Manik'
1961		Feb 7	1 Ahau
Jan 13	1 Oc	Feb 20	1 Ben
Jan 26	1 Akb'al	Mar 5	1 Cimi
Feb 8	1 Cib	**Mar 6–Mayan Year 2 Manik'**	
Feb 21	1 Muluc	Mar 18	1 Cauac
Mar 6	1 Ik'	Mar 31	1 Eb
Mar 6–Mayan Year I Ik'		Apr 13	1 Chicchan
Mar 19	1 Men	Apr 26	1 Etznab
Apr 1	1 Lamat	May 9	1 Chuen
Apr 14	1 Imix	May 22	1 Kan
Apr 27	1 Ix	Jun 4	1 Caban
May 10	1 Manik'	Jun 17	1 Oc
May 23	1 Ahau	Jun 30	1 Akb'al
Jun 5	1 Ben	Jul 13	1 Cib
Jun 18	1 Cimi	Jul 26	1 Muluc
Jul 1	1 Cauac	Aug 8	1 Ik'
Jul 14	1 Eb	Aug 21	1 Men
Jul 27	1 Chicchan	Sep 3	1 Lamat
Aug 9	1 Etznab	Sep 16	1 Imix
Aug 22	1 Chuen	Sep 29	1 Ix
Sep 4	1 Kan	Oct 12	1 Manik'

GREGORIAN DATE	MAYAN DATE	GREGORIAN DATE	MAYAN DATE
Oct 25	1 Ahau	Dec 2	1 Akb'al
Nov 7	1 Ben	Dec 15	1 Cib
Nov 20	1 Cimi	Dec 28	1 Muluc
Dec 3	1 Cauac		
Dec 16	1 Eb	***1964**	
Dec 29	1 Chicchan	Jan 10	1 Ik'
		Jan 23	1 Men
1963		Feb 5	1 Lamat
Jan 11	1 Etznab	Feb 18	1 Imix
Jan 24	1 Chuen	Mar 2	1 Ix
Feb 6	1 Kan	**Mar 5–Mayan Year 4 Caban**	
Feb 19	1 Caban	Mar 15	1 Manik'
Mar 4	1 Oc	Mar 28	1 Ahau
Mar 6–Mayan Year 3 Eb		Apr 10	1 Ben
Mar 17	1 Akb'al	Apr 23	1 Cimi
Mar 30	1 Cib	May 6	1 Cauac
Apr 12	1 Muluc	May 19	1 Eb
Apr 25	1 Ik'	Jun 1	1 Chicchan
May 8	1 Men	Jun 14	1 Etznab
May 21	1 Lamat	Jun 27	1 Chuen
June 3	1 Imix	Jul 10	1 Kan
Jun 16	1 Ix	Jul 23	1 Caban
Jun 29	1 Manik'	Aug 5	1 Oc
Jul 12	1 Ahau	Aug 18	1 Akb'al
Jul 25	1 Ben	Aug 31	1 Cib
Aug 7	1 Cimi	Sep 13	1 Muluc
Aug 20	1 Cauac	Sep 26	1 Ik'
Sep 2	1 Eb	Oct 9	1 Men
Sep 15	1 Chicchan	Oct 22	1 Lamat
Sep 28	1 Etznab	Nov 4	1 Imix
Oct 11	1 Chuen	Nov 17	1 Ix
Oct 24	1 Kan	Nov 30	1 Manik'
Nov 6	1 Caban	Dec 13	1 Ahau
Nov 19	1 Oc	Dec 26	1 Ben

GREGORIAN DATE	MAYAN DATE	GREGORIAN DATE	MAYAN DATE
1965		Feb 2	1 Cib
Jan 8	1 Cimi	Feb 15	1 Muluc
Jan 21	1 Cauac	Feb 28	1 Ik'
Feb 3	1 Eb	**Mar 5–Mayan Year 6 Manik'**	
Feb 16	1 Chicchan	Mar 13	1 Men
Mar 1	1 Etznab	Mar 26	1 Lamat
Mar 5–Mayan Year 5 Ik'		Apr 8	1 Imix
Mar 14	1 Chuen	Apr 21	1 Ix
Mar 27	1 Kan	May 4	1 Manik'
Apr 9	1 Caban	May 17	1 Ahau
Apr 22	1 Oc	May 30	1 Ben
May 5	1 Akb'al	Jun 12	1 Cimi
May 18	1 Cib	Jun 25	1 Cauac
May 31	1 Muluc	Jul 8	1 Eb
Jun 13	1 Ik'	Jul 21	1 Chicchan
Jun 26	1 Men	Aug 3	1 Etznab
Jul 9	1 Lamat	Aug 16	1 Chuen
Jul 22	1 Imix	Aug 29	1 Kan
Aug 4	1 Ix	Sep 11	1 Caban
Aug 17	1 Manik'	Sep 24	1 Oc
Aug 30	1 Ahau	Oct 7	1 Akb'al
Sep 12	1 Ben	Oct 20	1 Cib
Sep 25	1 Cimi	Nov 2	1 Muluc
Oct 8	1 Cauac	Nov 15	1 Ik'
Oct 21	1 Eb	Nov 28	1 Men
Nov 3	1 Chicchan	Dec 11	1 Lamat
Nov 16	1 Etznab	Dec 24	1 Imix
Nov 29	1 Chuen		
Dec 12	1 Kan	**1967**	
Dec 25	1 Caban	Jan 6	1 Ix
		Jan 19	1 Manik'
1966		Feb 1	1 Ahau
Jan 7	1 Oc	Feb 14	1 Ben
Jan 20	1 Akb'al	Feb 27	1 Cimi

GREGORIAN DATE	MAYAN DATE	GREGORIAN DATE	MAYAN DATE
Mar 5–Mayan Year 7 Eb		Apr 5	1 Muluc
Mar 12	1 Cauac	Apr 18	1 Ik'
Mar 25	1 Eb	May 1	1 Men
Apr 7	1 Chicchan	May 14	1 Lamat
Apr 20	1 Etznab	May 27	1 Imix
May 3	1 Chuen	Jun 9	1 Ix
May 16	1 Kan	Jun 22	1 Manik'
May 29	1 Caban	Jul 5	1 Ahau
Jun 11	1 Oc	Jul 18	1 Ben
Jun 24	1 Akb'al	Jul 31	1 Cimi
Jul 7	1 Cib	Aug 13	1 Cauac
Jul 20	1 Muluc	Aug 26	1 Eb
Aug 2	1 Ik'	Sep 8	1 Chicchan
Aug 15	1 Men	Sep 21	1 Etznab
Aug 28	1 Lamat	Oct 4	1 Chuen
Sep 10	1 Imix	Oct 17	1 Kan
Sep 23	1 Ix	Oct 30	1 Caban
Oct 6	1 Manik'	Nov 12	1 Oc
Oct 19	1 Ahau	Nov 25	1 Akb'al
Nov 1	1 Ben	Dec 8	1 Cib
Nov 14	1 Cimi	Dec 21	1 Muluc
Nov 27	1 Cauac		
Dec 10	1 Eb	**1969**	
Dec 23	1 Chicchan	Jan 3	1 Ik'
		Jan 16	1 Men
*1968		Jan 29	1 Lamat
Jan 5	1 Etznab	Feb 11	1 Imix
Jan 18	1 Chuen	Feb 24	1 Ix
Jan 31	1 Kan	**Mar 4–Mayan Year 9 Ik'**	
Feb 13	1 Caban	Mar 9	1 Manik'
Feb 26	1 Oc	Mar 22	1 Ahau
Mar 4–Mayan Year 8 Caban		Apr 4	1 Ben
Mar 10	1 Akb'al	Apr 17	1 Cimi
Mar 23	1 Cib	Apr 30	1 Cauac

GREGORIAN DATE	MAYAN DATE	GREGORIAN DATE	MAYAN DATE
May 13	1 Eb	Jun 20	1 Men
May 26	1 Chicchan	Jul 3	1 Lamat
Jun 8	1 Etznab	Jul 16	1 Imix
Jun 21	1 Chuen	Jul 29	1 Ix
Jul 4	1 Kan	Aug 11	1 Manik'
Jul 17	1 Caban	Aug 24	1 Ahau
Jul 30	1 Oc	Sep 6	1 Ben
Aug 12	1 Akb'al	Sep 19	1 Cimi
Aug 25	1 Cib	Oct 2	1 Cauac
Sep 7	1 Muluc	Oct 15	1 Eb
Sep 20	1 Ik'	Oct 28	1 Chicchan
Oct 3	1 Men	Nov 10	1 Etznab
Oct 16	1 Lamat	Nov 23	1 Chuen
Oct 29	1 Imix	Dec 6	1 Kan
Nov 11	1 Ix	Dec 19	1 Caban
Nov 24	1 Manik'		
Dec 7	1 Ahau	**1971**	
Dec 20	1 Ben	Jan 1	1 Oc
		Jan 14	1 Akb'al
1970		Jan 27	1 Cib
Jan 2	1 Cimi	Feb 9	1 Muluc
Jan 15	1 Cauac	Feb 22	1 Ik'
Jan 28	1 Eb	**Mar 4–Mayan Year 11 Eb**	
Feb 10	1 Chicchan	Mar 7	1 Men
Feb 23	1 Etznab	Mar 20	1 Lamat
Mar 4–Mayan Year 10 Manik'		Apr 2	1 Imix
Mar 8	1 Chuen	Apr 15	1 Ix
Mar 21	1 Kan	Apr 28	1 Manik'
Apr 3	1 Caban	May 11	1 Ahau
Apr 16	1 Oc	May 24	1 Ben
Apr 29	1 Akb'al	Jun 6	1 Cimi
May 12	1 Cib	Jun 19	1 Cauac
May 25	1 Muluc	Jul 2	1 Eb
Jun 7	1 Ik'	Jul 15	1 Chicchan

GREGORIAN DATE	MAYAN DATE	GREGORIAN DATE	MAYAN DATE
Jul 28	1 Etznab	Sep 3	1 Imix
Aug 10	1 Chuen	Sep 16	1 Ix
Aug 23	1 Kan	Sep 29	1 Manik'
Sep 5	1 Caban	Oct 12	1 Ahau
Sep 18	1 Oc	Oct 25	1 Ben
Oct 1	1 Akb'al	Nov 7	1 Cimi
Oct 14	1 Cib	Nov 20	1 Cauac
Oct 27	1 Muluc	Dec 3	1 Eb
Nov 9	1 Ik'	Dec 16	1 Chicchan
Nov 22	1 Men	Dec 29	1 Etznab
Dec 5	1 Lamat		
Dec 18	1 Imix	**1973**	
Dec 31	1 Ix	Jan 11	1 Chuen
		Jan 24	1 Kan
*1972		Feb 6	1 Caban
Jan 13	1 Manik'	Feb 19	1 Oc
Jan 26	1 Ahau	**Mar 3–Mayan Year 13 Ik'**	
Feb 8	1 Ben	Mar 4	1 Akb'al
Feb 21	1 Cimi	Mar 17	1 Cib
Mar 3–Mayan Year 12 Caban		Mar 30	1 Muluc
Mar 5	1 Cauac	Apr 12	1 Ik'
Mar 18	1 Eb	Apr 25	1 Men
Mar 31	1 Chicchan	May 8	1 Lamat
Apr 13	1 Etznab	May 21	1 Imix
Apr 26	1 Chuen	Jun 3	1 Ix
May 9	1 Kan	Jun 16	1 Manik'
May 22	1 Caban	Jun 29	1 Ahau
Jun 4	1 Oc	Jul 12	1 Ben
Jun 17	1 Akb'al	Jul 25	1 Cimi
Jun 30	1 Cib	Aug 7	1 Cauac
Jul 13	1 Muluc	Aug 20	1 Eb
Jul 26	1 Ik'	Sep 2	1 Chicchan
Aug 8	1 Men	Sep 15	1 Etznab
Aug 21	1 Lamat	Sep 28	1 Chuen

GREGORIAN DATE	MAYAN DATE	GREGORIAN DATE	MAYAN DATE
Oct 11	1 Kan	Dec 1	1 Ahau
Oct 24	1 Caban	Dec 14	1 Ben
Nov 6	1 Oc	Dec 27	1 Cimi
Nov 19	1 Akb'al		
Dec 2	1 Cib	**1975**	
Dec 15	1 Muluc	Jan 9	1 Cauac
Dec 28	1 Ik'	Jan 22	1 Eb
		Feb 4	1 Chicchan
1974		Feb 17	1 Etznab
Jan 10	1 Men	Mar 2	1 Chuen
Jan 23	1 Lamat	**Mar 3–Mayan Year 2 Eb**	
Feb 5	1 Imix	Mar 15	1 Kan
Feb 18	1 Ix	Mar 28	1 Caban
Mar 3	1 Manik'	Apr 10	1 Oc
Mar 3–Mayan Year 1 Manik'		Apr 23	1 Akb'al
Mar 16	1 Ahau	May 6	1 Cib
Mar 29	1 Ben	May 19	1 Muluc
Apr 11	1 Cimi	Jun 1	1 Ik'
Apr 24	1 Cauac	Jun 14	1 Men
May 7	1 Eb	Jun 27	1 Lamat
May 20	1 Chicchan	Jul 10	1 Imix
Jun 2	1 Etznab	Jul 23	1 Ix
Jun 15	1 Chuen	Aug 5	1 Manik'
Jun 28	1 Kan	Aug 18	1 Ahau
Jul 11	1 Caban	Aug 31	1 Ben
Jul 24	1 Oc	Sep 13	1 Cimi
Aug 6	1 Akb'al	Sep 26	1 Cauac
Aug 19	1 Cib	Oct 9	1 Eb
Sep 1	1 Muluc	Oct 22	1 Chicchan
Sep 14	1 Ik'	Nov 4	1 Etznab
Sep 27	1 Men	Nov 17	1 Chuen
Oct 10	1 Lamat	Nov 30	1 Kan
Oct 23	1 Imix	Dec 13	1 Caban
Nov 5	1 Ix	Dec 26	1 Oc
Nov 18	1 Manik'		

GREGORIAN DATE	MAYAN DATE	GREGORIAN DATE	MAYAN DATE
*1976		Feb 1	1 Ben
Jan 8	1 Akb'al	Feb 14	1 Cimi
Jan 21	1 Cib	Feb 27	1 Cauac
Feb 3	1 Muluc	**Mar 2–Mayan Year 4 Ik'**	
Feb 16	1 Ik'	Mar 12	1 Eb
Feb 29	1 Men	Mar 25	1 Chicchan
Mar 2–Mayan Year 3 Caban		Apr 7	1 Etznab
Mar 13	1 Lamat	Apr 20	1 Chuen
Mar 26	1 Imix	May 3	1 Kan
Apr 8	1 Ix	May 16	1 Caban
Apr 21	1 Manik'	May 29	1 Oc
May 4	1 Ahau	Jun 11	1 Akb'al
May 17	1 Ben	Jun 24	1 Cib
May 30	1 Cimi	Jul 7	1 Muluc
Jun 12	1 Cauac	Jul 20	1 Ik'
Jun 25	1 Eb	Aug 2	1 Men
Jul 8	1 Chicchan	Aug 15	1 Lamat
Jul 21	1 Etznab	Aug 28	1 Imix
Aug 3	1 Chuen	Sep 10	1 Ix
Aug 16	1 Kan	Sep 23	1 Manik'
Aug 29	1 Caban	Oct 6	1 Ahau
Sep 11	1 Oc	Oct 19	1 Ben
Sep 24	1 Akb'al	Nov 1	1 Cimi
Oct 7	1 Cib	Nov 14	1 Cauac
Oct 20	1 Muluc	Nov 27	1 Eb
Nov 2	1 Ik'	Dec 10	1 Chicchan
Nov 15	1 Men	Dec 23	1 Etznab
Nov 28	1 Lamat		
Dec 11	1 Imix	**1978**	
Dec 24	1 Ix	Jan 5	1 Chuen
		Jan 18	1 Kan
1977		Jan 31	1 Caban
Jan 6	1 Manik'	Feb 13	1 Oc
Jan 19	1 Ahau	Feb 26	1 Akb'al

GREGORIAN DATE	MAYAN DATE	GREGORIAN DATE	MAYAN DATE
Mar 2–Mayan Year 5 Manik'		Apr 5	1 Cimi
Mar 11	1 Cib	Apr 18	1 Cauac
Mar 24	1 Muluc	May 1	1 Eb
Apr 6	1 Ik'	May 14	1 Chicchan
Apr 19	1 Men	May 27	1 Etznab
May 2	1 Lamat	Jun 9	1 Chuen
May 15	1 Imix	Jun 22	1 Kan
May 28	1 Ix	Jul 5	1 Caban
Jun 10	1 Manik'	Jul 18	1 Oc
Jun 23	1 Ahau	Jul 31	1 Akb'al
Jul 6	1 Ben	Aug 13	1 Cib
Jul 19	1 Cimi	Aug 26	1 Muluc
Aug 1	1 Cauac	Sep 8	1 Ik'
Aug 14	1 Eb	Sep 21	1 Men
Aug 27	1 Chicchan	Oct 4	1 Lamat
Sep 9	1 Etznab	Oct 17	1 Imix
Sep 22	1 Chuen	Oct 30	1 Ix
Oct 5	1 Kan	Nov 12	1 Manik'
Oct 18	1 Caban	Nov 25	1 Ahau
Oct 31	1 Oc	Dec 8	1 Ben
Nov 13	1 Akb'al	Dec 21	1 Cimi
Nov 26	1 Cib		
Dec 9	1 Muluc	***1980**	
Dec 22	1 Ik'	Jan 3	1 Cauac
		Jan 16	1 Eb
1979		Jan 29	1 Chicchan
Jan 4	1 Men	Feb 11	1 Etznab
Jan 17	1 Lamat	Feb 24	1 Chuen
Jan 30	1 Imix	**Mar 1–Mayan Year 7 Caban**	
Feb 12	1 Ix	Mar 8	1 Kan
Feb 25	1 Manik'	Mar 21	1 Caban
Mar 2–Mayan Year 6 Eb		Apr 3	1 Oc
Mar 10	1 Ahau	Apr 16	1 Akb'al
Mar 23	1 Ben	Apr 29	1 Cib

GREGORIAN DATE	MAYAN DATE	GREGORIAN DATE	MAYAN DATE
May 12	1 Muluc	Jun 19	1 Eb
May 25	1 Ik'	Jul 2	1 Chicchan
Jun 7	1 Men	Jul 15	1 Etznab
Jun 20	1 Lamat	Jul 28	1 Chuen
Jul 3	1 Imix	Aug 10	1 Kan
Jul 16	1 Ix	Aug 23	1 Caban
Jul 29	1 Manik'	Sep 5	1 Oc
Aug 11	1 Ahau	Sep 18	1 Akb'al
Aug 24	1 Ben	Oct 1	1 Cib
Sep 6	1 Cimi	Oct 14	1 Muluc
Sep 19	1 Cauac	Oct 27	1 Ik'
Oct 2	1 Eb	Nov 9	1 Men
Oct 15	1 Chicchan	Nov 22	1 Lamat
Oct 28	1 Etznab	Dec 5	1 Imix
Nov 10	1 Chuen	Dec 31	1 Manik'
Nov 23	1 Kan	Dec 18	1 Ix
Dec 6	1 Caban	Dec 31	1 Manik'
Dec 19	1 Oc		

1981

		1982	
Jan 1	1 Akb'al	Jan 13	1 Ahau
Jan 14	1 Cib	Jan 26	1 Ben
Jan 27	1 Muluc	Feb 8	1 Cimi
Feb 9	1 Ik'	Feb 21	1 Cauac
Feb 22	1 Men	**Mar 1–Mayan Year 9 Manik'**	
Mar 1–Mayan Year 8 Ik'		Mar 6	1 Eb
Mar 7	1 Lamat	Mar 19	1 Chicchan
Mar 20	1 Imix	Apr 1	1 Etznab
Apr 2	1 Ix	Apr 14	1 Chuen
Apr 15	1 Manik'	Apr 27	1 Kan
Apr 28	1 Ahau	May 10	1 Caban
May 11	1 Ben	May 23	1 Oc
May 24	1 Cimi	Jun 5	1 Akb'al
Jun 6	1 Cauac	Jun 18	1 Cib
		Jul 1	1 Muluc

GREGORIAN DATE	MAYAN DATE	GREGORIAN DATE	MAYAN DATE
Jul 14	1 Ik'	Aug 21	1 Chicchan
Jul 27	1 Men	Sep 3	1 Etznab
Aug 9	1 Lamat	Sep 16	1 Chuen
Aug 22	1 Imix	Sep 29	1 Kan
Sep 4	1 Ix	Oct 12	1 Caban
Sep 17	1 Manik'	Oct 25	1 Oc
Sep 30	1 Ahau	Nov 7	1 Akb'al
Oct 13	1 Ben	Nov 20	1 Cib
Oct 26	1 Cimi	Dec 3	1 Muluc
Nov 8	1 Cauac	Dec 16	1 Ik'
Nov 21	1 Eb	Dec 29	1 Men
Dec 4	1 Chicchan		
Dec 17	1 Etznab	***1984**	
Dec 30	1 Chuen	Jan 11	1 Lamat
		Jan 24	1 Imix
1983		Feb 6	1 Ix
Jan 12	1 Kan	Feb 19	1 Manik'
Jan 25	1 Caban	**Feb 29–Mayan Year 11 Caban**	
Feb 7	1 Oc	Mar 3	1 Ahau
Feb 20	1 Akb'al	Mar 16	1 Ben
Mar 1–Mayan Year 10 Eb		Mar 29	1 Cimi
Mar 5	1 Cib	Apr 11	1 Cauac
Mar 18	1 Muluc	Apr 24	1 Eb
Mar 31	1 Ik'	May 7	1 Chicchan
Apr 13	1 Men	May 20	1 Etznab
Apr 26	1 Lamat	Jun 2	1 Chuen
May 9	1 Imix	Jun 15	1 Kan
May 22	1 Ix	Jun 28	1 Caban
Jun 4	1 Manik'	Jul 11	1 Oc
Jun 17	1 Ahau	Jul 24	1 Akb'al
Jun 30	1 Ben	Aug 6	1 Cib
Jul 13	1 Cimi	Aug 19	1 Muluc
Jul 26	1 Cauac	Sep 1	1 Ik'
Aug 8	1 Eb	Sep 14	1 Men

GREGORIAN DATE	MAYAN DATE	GREGORIAN DATE	MAYAN DATE
Sep 27	1 Lamat	Nov 4	1 Chuen
Oct 10	1 Imix	Nov 17	1 Kan
Oct 23	1 Ix	Nov 30	1 Caban
Nov 5	1 Manik'	Dec 13	1 Oc
Nov 18	1 Ahau	Dec 26	1 Akb'al
Dec 1	1 Ben		
Dec 14	1 Cimi	**1986**	
Dec 27	1 Cauac	Jan 8	1 Cib
		Jan 21	1 Muluc
1985		Feb 3	1 Ik'
Jan 9	1 Eb	Feb 16	1 Men
Jan 22	1 Chicchan	**Feb 28–Mayan Year 13 Manik'**	
Feb 4	1 Etznab	Mar 1	1 Lamat
Feb 17	1 Chuen	Mar 14	1 Imix
Feb 28–Mayan Year 12 Ik'		Mar 27	1 Ix
Mar 2	1 Kan	Apr 9	1 Manik'
Mar 15	1 Caban	Apr 22	1 Ahau
Mar 28	1 Oc	May 5	1 Ben
Apr 10	1 Akb'al	May 18	1 Cimi
Apr 23	1 Cib	May 31	1 Cauac
May 6	1 Muluc	Jun 13	1 Eb
May 19	1 Ik'	Jun 26	1 Chicchan
Jun 1	1 Men	Jul 9	1 Etznab
Jun 14	1 Lamat	Jul 22	1 Chuen
Jun 27	1 Imix	Aug 4	1 Kan
Jul 10	1 Ix	Aug 17	1 Caban
Jul 23	1 Manik'	Aug 30	1 Oc
Aug 5	1 Ahau	Sep 12	1 Akb'al
Aug 18	1 Ben	Sep 25	1 Cib
Aug 31	1 Cimi	Oct 8	1 Muluc
Sep 13	1 Cauac	Oct 21	1 Ik'
Sep 26	1 Eb	Nov 3	1 Men
Oct 9	1 Chicchan	Nov 16	1 Lamat
Oct 22	1 Etznab	Nov 29	1 Imix

GREGORIAN DATE	MAYAN DATE	GREGORIAN DATE	MAYAN DATE
Dec 12	1 Ix	*1988	
Dec 25	1 Manik'	Jan 6	1 Kan
		Jan 19	1 Caban
1987		Feb 1	1 Oc
Jan 7	1 Ahau	Feb 14	1 Akb'al
Jan 20	1 Ben	Feb 27	1 Cib
Feb 2	1 Cimi	**Feb 28–Mayan Year 2 Caban**	
Feb 15	1 Cauac	Mar 11	1 Muluc
Feb 28–Mayan Year 1 Eb		Mar 24	1 Ik'
Feb 28	1 Eb	Apr 6	1 Men
Mar 13	1 Chicchan	Apr 19	1 Lamat
Mar 26	1 Etznab	May 2	1 Imix
Apr 8	1 Chuen	May 15	1 Ix
Apr 21	1 Kan	May 28	1 Manik'
May 4	1 Caban	Jun 10	1 Ahau
May 17	1 Oc	Jun 23	1 Ben
May 30	1 Akb'al	Jul 6	1 Cimi
Jun 12	1 Cib	Jul 19	1 Cauac
Jun 25	1 Muluc	Aug 1	1 Eb
Jul 8	1 Ik'	Aug 14	1 Chicchan
Jul 21	1 Men	Aug 27	1 Etznab
Aug 3	1 Lamat	Sep 9	1 Chuen
Aug 16	1 Imix	Sep 22	1 Kan
Aug 29	1 Ix	Oct 5	1 Caban
Sep 11	1 Manik'	Oct 18	1 Oc
Sep 24	1 Ahau	Oct 31	1 Akb'al
Oct 7	1 Ben	Nov 13	1 Cib
Oct 20	1 Cimi	Nov 26	1 Muluc
Nov 2	1 Cauac	Dec 9	1 Ik'
Nov 15	1 Eb	Dec 22	1 Men
Nov 28	1 Chicchan		
Dec 11	1 Etznab	1989	
Dec 24	1 Chuen	Jan 4	1 Lamat
		Jan 17	1 Imix

GREGORIAN DATE	MAYAN DATE	GREGORIAN DATE	MAYAN DATE
Jan 30	1 Ix	**Feb 27–Mayan Year 4 Manik'**	
Feb 12	1 Manik'	Mar 9	1 Caban
Feb 25	1 Ahau	Mar 22	1 Oc
Feb 27–Mayan Year 3 Ik'		Apr 4	1 Akb'al
Mar 10	1 Ben	Apr 17	1 Cib
Mar 23	1 Cimi	Apr 30	1 Muluc
Apr 5	1 Cauac	May 13	1 Ik'
Apr 18	1 Eb	May 26	1 Men
May 1	1 Chicchan	Jun 8	1 Lamat
May 14	1 Etznab	Jun 21	1 Imix
May 27	1 Chuen	Jul 4	1 Ix
Jun 9	1 Kan	Jul 17	1 Manik'
Jun 22	1 Caban	Jul 30	1 Ahau
Jul 5	1 Oc	Aug 12	1 Ben
Jul 18	1 Akb'al	Aug 25	1 Cimi
Jul 31	1 Cib	Sep 7	1 Cauac
Aug 13	1 Muluc	Sep 20	1 Eb
Aug 26	1 Ik'	Oct 3	1 Chicchan
Sep 8	1 Men	Oct 16	1 Etznab
Sep 21	1 Lamat	Oct 29	1 Chuen
Oct 4	1 Imix	Nov 11	1 Kan
Oct 17	1 Ix	Nov 24	1 Caban
Oct 30	1 Manik'	Dec 7	1 Oc
Nov 12	1 Ahau	Dec 20	1 Akb'al
Nov 25	1 Ben		
Dec 8	1 Cimi	**1991**	
Dec 21	1 Cauac	Jan 2	1 Cib
		Jan 15	1 Muluc
1990		Jan 28	1 Ik'
Jan 3	1 Eb	Feb 10	1 Men
Jan 16	1 Chicchan	Feb 23	1 Lamat
Jan 29	1 Etznab	**Feb 27–Mayan Year 5 Eb**	
Feb 11	1 Chuen	Mar 8	1 Imix
Feb 24	1 Kan	Mar 21	1 Ix

GREGORIAN DATE	MAYAN DATE	GREGORIAN DATE	MAYAN DATE
Apr 3	1 Manik'	May 10	1 Oc
Apr 16	1 Ahau	May 23	1 Akb'al
Apr 29	1 Ben	Jun 5	1 Cib
May 12	1 Cimi	Jun 18	1 Muluc
May 25	1 Cauac	Jul 1	1 Ik'
Jun 7	1 Eb	Jul 14	1 Men
Jun 20	1 Chicchan	Jul 27	1 Lamat
Jul 3	1 Etznab	Aug 9	1 Imix
Jul 16	1 Chuen	Aug 22	1 Ix
Jul 29	1 Kan	Sep 4	1 Manik'
Aug 11	1 Caban	Sep 17	1 Ahau
Aug 24	1 Oc	Sep 30	1 Ben
Sep 6	1 Akb'al	Oct 13	1 Cimi
Sep 19	1 Cib	Oct 26	1 Cauac
Oct 2	1 Muluc	Nov 8	1 Eb
Oct 15	1 Ik'	Nov 21	1 Chicchan
Oct 28	1 Men	Dec 4	1 Etznab
Nov 10	1 Lamat	Dec 17	1 Chuen
Nov 23	1 Imix	Dec 30	1 Kan
Dec 6	1 Ix		
Dec 19	1 Manik'	**1993**	
		Jan 12	1 Caban
*1992		Jan 25	1 Oc
Jan 1	1 Ahau	Feb 7	1 Akb'al
Jan 14	1 Ben	Feb 20	1 Cib
Jan 27	1 Cimi	**Feb 26–Mayan Year 7 Ik'**	
Feb 9	1 Cauac	Mar 5	1 Muluc
Feb 22	1 Eb	Mar 18	1 Ik'
Feb 27–Mayan Year 6 Caban		Mar 31	1 Men
Mar 6	1 Chicchan	Apr 13	1 Lamat
Mar 19	1 Etznab	Apr 26	1 Imix
Apr 1	1 Chuen	May 9	1 Ix
Apr 14	1 Kan	May 22	1 Manik'
Apr 27	1 Caban	Jun 4	1 Ahau

GREGORIAN DATE	MAYAN DATE	GREGORIAN DATE	MAYAN DATE
Jun 17	1 Ben	Jul 25	1 Cib
Jun 30	1 Cimi	Aug 7	1 Muluc
Jul 13	1 Cauac	Aug 20	1 Ik'
Jul 26	1 Eb	Sep 2	1 Men
Aug 8	1 Chicchan	Sep 15	1 Lamat
Aug 21	1 Etznab	Sep 28	1 Imix
Sep 3	1 Chuen	Oct 11	1 Ix
Sep 16	1 Kan	Oct 24	1 Manik'
Sep 29	1 Caban	Nov 6	1 Ahau
Oct 12	1 Oc	Nov 19	1 Ben
Oct 25	1 Akb'al	Dec 2	1 Cimi
Nov 7	1 Cib	Dec 15	1 Cauac
Nov 20	1 Muluc	Dec 28	1 Eb
Dec 3	1 Ik'		
Dec 16	1 Men		
Dec 29	1 Lamat		

1995

		Jan 10	1 Chicchan
		Jan 23	1 Etznab
		Feb 5	1 Chuen

1994

		Feb 18	1 Kan
Jan 11	1 Imix	**Feb 26–Mayan Year 9 Eb**	
Jan 24	1 Ix	Mar 3	1 Caban
Feb 6	1 Manik'	Mar 16	1 Oc
Feb 19	1 Ahau	Mar 29	1 Akb'al
Feb 26–Mayan Year 8 Manik'		Apr 11	1 Cib
Mar 4	1 Ben	Apr 24	1 Muluc
Mar 17	1 Cimi	May 7	1 Ik'
Mar 30	1 Cauac	May 20	1 Men
Apr 12	1 Eb	Jun 2	1 Lamat
Apr 25	1 Chicchan	Jun 15	1 Imix
May 8	1 Etznab	Jun 28	1 Ix
May 21	1 Chuen	Jul 11	1 Manik'
Jun 3	1 Kan	Jul 24	1 Ahau
Jun 16	1 Caban	Aug 6	1 Ben
Jun 29	1 Oc	Aug 19	1 Cimi
Jul 12	1 Akb'al		

GREGORIAN DATE	MAYAN DATE	GREGORIAN DATE	MAYAN DATE
Sep 1	1 Cauac	Oct 8	1 Ik'
Sep 14	1 Eb	Oct 21	1 Men
Sep 27	1 Chicchan	Nov 3	1 Lamat
Oct 10	1 Etznab	Nov 16	1 Imix
Oct 23	1 Chuen	Nov 29	1 Ix
Nov 5	1 Kan	Dec 12	1 Manik'
Nov 18	1 Caban	Dec 25	1 Ahau
Dec 1	1 Oc		
Dec 14	1 Akb'al	**1997**	
Dec 27	1 Cib	Jan 7	1 Ben
		Jan 20	1 Cimi
*1996		Feb 2	1 Cauac
Jan 9	1 Muluc	Feb 15	1 Eb
Jan 22	1 Ik'	**Feb 25–Mayan Year 11 Ik'**	
Feb 4	1 Men	Feb 28	1 Chicchan
Feb 17	1 Lamat	Mar 13	1 Etznab
Feb 26–Mayan Year 10 Caban		Mar 26	1 Chuen
Mar 1	1 Imix	Apr 8	1 Kan
Mar 14	1 Ix	Apr 21	1 Caban
Mar 27	1 Manik'	May 4	1 Oc
Apr 9	1 Ahau	May 17	1 Akb'al
Apr 22	1 Ben	May 30	1 Cib
May 5	1 Cimi	Jun 12	1 Muluc
May 18	1 Cauac	Jun 25	1 Ik'
May 31	1 Eb	Jul 8	1 Men
Jun 13	1 Chicchan	Jul 21	1 Lamat
Jun 26	1 Etznab	Aug 3	1 Imix
Jul 9	1 Chuen	Aug 16	1 Ix
Jul 22	1 Kan	Aug 29	1 Manik'
Aug 4	1 Caban	Sep 11	1 Ahau
Aug 17	1 Oc	Sep 24	1 Ben
Aug 30	1 Akb'al	Oct 7	1 Cimi
Sep 12	1 Cib	Oct 20	1 Cauac
Sep 25	1 Muluc	Nov 2	1 Eb

GREGORIAN DATE	MAYAN DATE	GREGORIAN DATE	MAYAN DATE
Nov 15	1 Chicchan	**1999**	
Nov 28	1 Etznab	Jan 5	1 Imix
Dec 11	1 Chuen	Jan 18	1 Ix
Dec 24	1 Kan	Jan 31	1 Manik'
		Feb 13	1 Ahau
1998		**Feb 25–Mayan Year 13 Eb**	
Jan 6	1 Caban	Feb 26	1 Ben
Jan 19	1 Oc	Mar 11	1 Cimi
Feb 1	1 Akb'al	Mar 24	1 Cauac
Feb 14	1 Cib	Apr 6	1 Eb
Feb 25–Mayan Year 12 Manik'		Apr 19	1 Chicchan
Feb 27	1 Muluc	May 2	1 Etznab
Mar 12	1 Ik'	May 15	1 Chuen
Mar 25	1 Men	May 28	1 Kan
Apr 7	1 Lamat	Jun 10	1 Caban
Apr 20	1 Imix	Jun 23	1 Oc
May 3	1 Ix	Jul 6	1 Akb'al
May 16	1 Manik'	Jul 19	1 Cib
May 29	1 Ahau	Aug 1	1 Muluc
Jun 11	1 Ben	Aug 14	1 Ik'
Jun 24	1 Cimi	Aug 27	1 Men
Jul 7	1 Cauac	Sep 9	1 Lamat
Jul 20	1 Eb	Sep 22	1 Imix
Aug 2	1 Chicchan	Oct 5	1 Ix
Aug 15	1 Etznab	Oct 18	1 Manik'
Aug 28	1 Chuen	Oct 31	1 Ahau
Sep 10	1 Kan	Nov 13	1 Ben
Sep 23	1 Caban	Nov 26	1 Cimi
Oct 6	1 Oc	Dec 9	1 Cauac
Oct 19	1 Akb'al	Dec 22	1 Eb
Nov 1	1 Cib		
Nov 14	1 Muluc	***2000**	
Nov 27	1 Ik'	Jan 4	1 Chicchan
Dec 10	1 Men	Jan 17	1 Etznab
Dec 23	1 Lamat	Jan 30	1 Chuen

GREGORIAN DATE	MAYAN DATE	GREGORIAN DATE	MAYAN DATE
Feb 12	1 Kan	Mar 21	1 Manik'
Feb 25	1 Caban	Apr 3	1 Ahau
Feb 25–Mayan Year 1 Caban		Apr 16	1 Ben
Mar 9	1 Oc	Apr 29	1 Cimi
Mar 22	1 Akb'al	May 12	1 Cauac
Apr 4	1 Cib	May 25	1 Eb
Apr 17	1 Muluc	Jun 7	1 Chicchan
Apr 30	1 Ik'	Jun 20	1 Etznab
May 13	1 Men	Jul 3	1 Chuen
May 26	1 Lamat	Jul 16	1 Kan
Jun 8	1 Imix	Jul 29	1 Caban
Jun 21	1 Ix	Aug 11	1 Oc
Jul 4	1 Manik'	Aug 25	1 Akb'al
Jul 17	1 Ahau	Sep 6	1 Cib
Jul 30	1 Ben	Sep 19	1 Muluc
Aug 12	1 Cimi	Oct 2	1 Ik'
Aug 25	1 Cauac	Oct 15	1 Men
Sep 7	1 Eb	Oct 28	1 Lamat
Sep 20	1 Chicchan	Nov 10	1 Imix
Oct 3	1 Etznab	Nov 23	1 Ix
Oct 16	1 Chuen	Dec 6	1 Manik'
Oct 29	1 Kan	Dec 19	1 Ahau
Nov 11	1 Caban		
Nov 24	1 Oc	**2002**	
Dec 7	1 Akb'al	Jan 1	1 Ben
Dec 20	1 Cib	Jan 14	1 Cimi
		Jan 27	1 Cauac
2001		Feb 9	1 Eb
Jan 2	1 Muluc	Feb 22	1 Chicchan
Jan 15	1 Ik'	**Feb 24–Mayan Year 3 Manik'**	
Jan 28	1 Men	Mar 7	1 Etznab
Feb 10	1 Lamat	Mar 20	1 Chuen
Feb 23	1 Imix	Apr 2	1 Kan
Feb 24–Mayan Year 2 Ik'		Apr 15	1 Caban
Mar 8	1 Ix	Apr 28	1 Oc

GREGORIAN DATE	MAYAN DATE	GREGORIAN DATE	MAYAN DATE
May 11	1 Akb'al	Jun 18	1 Cimi
May 24	1 Cib	Jul 1	1 Cauac
Jun 6	1 Muluc	Jul 14	1 Eb
Jun 19	1 Ik'	Jul 27	1 Chicchan
Jul 2	1 Men	Aug 9	1 Etznab
Jul 15	1 Lamat	Aug 22	1 Chuen
Jul 28	1 Imix	Sep 4	1 Kan
Aug 10	1 Ix	Sep 17	1 Caban
Aug 23	1 Manik'	Sep 30	1 Oc
Sep 5	1 Ahau	Oct 13	1 Akb'al
Sep 18	1 Ben	Oct 26	1 Cib
Oct 1	1 Cimi	Nov 8	1 Muluc
Oct 14	1 Cauac	Nov 21	1 Ik'
Oct 27	1 Eb	Dec 4	1 Men
Nov 9	1 Chicchan	Dec 17	1 Lamat
Nov 22	1 Etznab	Dec 30	1 Imix
Dec 5	1 Chuen		
Dec 18	1 Kan		
Dec 31	1 Caban		

2004

GREGORIAN DATE	MAYAN DATE
Jan 12	1 Ix
Jan 25	1 Manik'

2003

GREGORIAN DATE	MAYAN DATE
Jan 13	1 Oc
Jan 26	1 Akb'al
Feb 8	1 Cib
Feb 21	1 Muluc

Feb 24–**Mayan Year 4 Eb**

Mar 6	1 Ik'
Mar 19	1 Men
Apr 1	1 Lamat
Apr 14	1 Imix
Apr 27	1 Ix
May 10	1 Manik'
May 23	1 Ahau
Jun 5	1 Ben

2004 (continued)

Feb 7	1 Ahau
Feb 20	1 Ben

Feb 24–**Mayan Year 5 Caban**

Mar 4	1 Cimi
Mar 17	1 Cauac
Mar 30	1 Eb
Apr 12	1 Chicchan
Apr 25	1 Etznab
May 8	1 Chuen
May 21	1 Kan
Jun 3	1 Caban
Jun 16	1 Oc
Jun 29	1 Akb'al
Jul 12	1 Cib

GREGORIAN DATE	MAYAN DATE	GREGORIAN DATE	MAYAN DATE
Jul 25	1 Muluc	Sep 1	1 Eb
Aug 7	1 Ik'	Sep 14	1 Chicchan
Aug 20	1 Men	Sep 27	1 Etznab
Sep 2	1 Lamat	Oct 10	1 Chuen
Sep 15	1 Imix	Oct 23	1 Kan
Sep 28	1 Ix	Nov 5	1 Caban
Oct 11	1 Manik'	Nov 18	1 Oc
Oct 24	1 Ahau	Dec 1	1 Akb'al
Nov 6	1 Ben	Dec 14	1 Cib
Nov 19	1 Cimi	Dec 27	1 Muluc
Dec 2	1 Cauac		
Dec 15	1 Eb		
Dec 28	1 Chicchan		

2006

		Jan 9	1 Ik'
		Jan 22	1 Men
2005		Feb 4	1 Lamat
Jan 10	1 Etznab	Feb 17	1 Imix
Jan 23	1 Chuen	**Feb 23–Mayan Year 7 Manik'**	
Feb 5	1 Kan	Mar 2	1 Ix
Feb 18	1 Caban	Mar 15	1 Manik'
Feb 23–Mayan Year 6 Ik'		Mar 28	1 Ahau
Mar 3	1 Oc	Apr 10	1 Ben
Mar 16	1 Akb'al	Apr 23	1 Cimi
Mar 29	1 Cib	May 6	1 Cauac
Apr 11	1 Muluc	May 19	1 Eb
Apr 24	1 Ik'	Jun 1	1 Chicchan
May 7	1 Men	Jun 14	1 Etznab
May 20	1 Lamat	Jun 27	1 Chuen
Jun 2	1 Imix	Jul 10	1 Kan
Jun 15	1 Ix	Jul 23	1 Caban
Jun 28	1 Manik'	Aug 5	1 Oc
Jul 11	1 Ahau	Aug 18	1 Akb'al
Jul 24	1 Ben	Aug 31	1 Cib
Aug 6	1 Cimi	Sep 13	1 Muluc
Aug 19	1 Cauac	Sep 26	1 Ik'

GREGORIAN DATE	MAYAN DATE	GREGORIAN DATE	MAYAN DATE
Oct 9	1 Men	Nov 29	1 Chuen
Oct 22	1 Lamat	Dec 12	1 Kan
Nov 4	1 Imix	Dec 25	1 Caban
Nov 17	1 Ix		
Nov 30	1 Manik'	***2008**	
Dec 13	1 Ahau	Jan 7	1 Oc
Dec 26	1 Ben	Jan 20	1 Akb'al
		Feb 2	1 Cib
2007		Feb 15	1 Muluc
Jan 8	1 Cimi	**Feb 23–Mayan Year 9 Caban**	
Jan 21	1 Cauac	Feb 28	1 Ik'
Feb 3	1 Eb	Mar 12	1 Men
Feb 16	1 Chicchan	Mar 25	1 Lamat
Feb 23–Mayan Year 8 Eb		Apr 7	1 Imix
Mar 1	1 Etznab	Apr 20	1 Ix
Mar 14	1 Chuen	May 3	1 Manik'
Mar 27	1 Kan	May 16	1 Ahau
Apr 9	1 Caban	May 29	1 Ben
Apr 22	1 Oc	Jun 11	1 Cimi
May 5	1 Akb'al	Jun 24	1 Cauac
May 18	1 Cib	Jul 7	1 Eb
May 31	1 Muluc	Jul 20	1 Chicchan
Jun 13	1 Ik'	Aug 2	1 Etznab
Jun 26	1 Men	Aug 15	1 Chuen
Jul 9	1 Lamat	Aug 28	1 Kan
Jul 22	1 Imix	Sep 10	1 Caban
Aug 4	1 Ix	Sep 23	1 Oc
Aug 17	1 Manik'	Oct 6	1 Akb'al
Aug 30	1 Ahau	Oct 19	1 Cib
Sep 12	1 Ben	Nov 1	1 Muluc
Sep 25	1 Cimi	Nov 14	1 Ik'
Oct 8	1 Cauac	Nov 27	1 Men
Oct 21	1 Eb	Dec 10	1 Lamat
Nov 3	1 Chicchan	Dec 23	1 Imix
Nov 16	1 Etznab		

GREGORIAN DATE	MAYAN DATE	GREGORIAN DATE	MAYAN DATE
2009		Feb 12	1 Caban
Jan 5	1 Ix	**Feb 22–Mayan Year 11 Manik'**	
Jan 18	1 Manik'	Feb 25	1 Oc
Jan 31	1 Ahau	Mar 10	1 Akb'al
Feb 13	1 Ben	Mar 23	1 Cib
Feb 22–Mayan Year 10 Ik'		Apr 5	1 Muluc
Feb 26	1 Cimi	Apr 18	1 Ik'
Mar 11	1 Cauac	May 1	1 Men
Mar 24	1 Eb	May 14	1 Lamat
Apr 6	1 Chicchan	May 27	1 Imix
Apr 19	1 Etznab	Jun 9	1 Ix
May 2	1 Chuen	Jun 22	1 Manik'
May 15	1 Kan	Jul 5	1 Ahau
May 28	1 Caban	Jul 18	1 Ben
Jun 10	1 Oc	Jul 31	1 Cimi
Jun 23	1 Akb'al	Aug 13	1 Cauac
Jul 6	1 Cib	Aug 26	1 Eb
Jul 19	1 Muluc	Sep 8	1 Chicchan
Aug 1	1 Ik'	Sep 21	1 Etznab
Aug 14	1 Men	Oct 4	1 Chuen
Aug 27	1 Lamat	Oct 17	1 Kan
Sep 9	1 Imix	Oct 30	1 Caban
Sep 22	1 Ix	Nov 12	1 Oc
Oct 5	1 Manik'	Nov 25	1 Akb'al
Oct 18	1 Ahau	Dec 8	1 Cib
Oct 31	1 Ben	Dec 21	1 Muluc
Nov 13	1 Cimi		
Nov 26	1 Cauac	**2011**	
Dec 9	1 Eb	Jan 3	1 Ik'
Dec 22	1 Chicchan	Jan 16	1 Men
		Jan 29	1 Lamat
2010		Feb 11	1 Imix
Jan 4	1 Etznab	**Feb 22–Mayan Year 12 Eb**	
Jan 17	1 Chuen	Feb 24	1 Ix
Jan 30	1 Kan	Mar 9	1 Manik'

GREGORIAN DATE	MAYAN DATE	GREGORIAN DATE	MAYAN DATE
Mar 22	1 Ahau	Apr 28	1 Akb'al
Apr 4	1 Ben	May 11	1 Cib
Apr 17	1 Cimi	May 24	1 Muluc
Apr 30	1 Cauac	Jun 6	1 Ik'
May 13	1 Eb	Jun 19	1 Men
May 26	1 Chicchan	Jul 2	1 Lamat
Jun 8	1 Etznab	Jul 15	1 Imix
Jun 21	1 Chuen	Jul 28	1 Ix
Jul 4	1 Kan	Aug 10	1 Manik'
Jul 17	1 Caban	Aug 23	1 Ahau
Jul 30	1 Oc	Sep 5	1 Ben
Aug 12	1 Akb'al	Sep 18	1 Cimi
Aug 25	1 Cib	Oct 1	1 Cauac
Sep 7	1 Muluc	Oct 14	1 Eb
Sep 20	1 Ik'	Oct 27	1 Chicchan
Oct 3	1 Men	Nov 9	1 Etznab
Oct 16	1 Lamat	Nov 22	1 Chuen
Oct 29	1 Imix	Dec 5	1 Kan
Nov 11	1 Ix	Dec 18	1 Caban
Nov 24	1 Manik'	Dec 31	1 Oc
Dec 7	1 Ahau		
Dec 20	1 Ben	**2013**	
		Jan 13	1 Akb'al
*2012		Jan 26	1 Cib
Jan 2	1 Cimi	Feb 8	1 Muluc
Jan 15	1 Cauac	**Feb 21–Mayan Year 1 Ik'**	
Jan 28	1 Eb	Feb 21	1 Ik'
Feb 10	1 Chicchan	Mar 6	1 Men
Feb 22–Mayan Year 13 Caban		Mar 19	1 Lamat
Feb 23	1 Etznab	Apr 1	1 Imix
Mar 7	1 Chuen	Apr 14	1 Ix
Mar 20	1 Kan	Apr 27	1 Manik'
Apr 2	1 Caban	May 10	1 Ahau
Apr 15	1 Oc	May 23	1 Ben

GREGORIAN DATE	MAYAN DATE	GREGORIAN DATE	MAYAN DATE
Jun 5	1 Cimi	Jul 13	1 Muluc
Jun 18	1 Cauac	Jul 26	1 Ik'
Jul 1	1 Eb	Aug 8	1 Men
Jul 14	1 Chicchan	Aug 21	1 Lamat
Jul 27	1 Etznab	Sep 3	1 Imix
Aug 9	1 Chuen	Sep 16	1 Ix
Aug 22	1 Kan	Sep 29	1 Manik'
Sep 4	1 Caban	Oct 12	1 Ahau
Sep 17	1 Oc	Oct 25	1 Ben
Sep 30	1 Akb'al	Nov 7	1 Cimi
Oct 13	1 Cib	Nov 20	1 Cauac
Oct 26	1 Muluc	Dec 3	1 Eb
Nov 8	1 Ik'	Dec 16	1 Chicchan
Nov 21	1 Men	Dec 29	1 Etznab
Dec 4	1 Lamat		
Dec 17	1 Imix	**2015**	
Dec 30	1 Ix	Jan 11	1 Chuen
		Jan 24	1 Kan
2014		Feb 6	1 Caban
Jan 12	1 Manik'	Feb 19	1 Oc
Jan 25	1 Ahau	**Feb 21–Mayan Year 3 Eb**	
Feb 7	1 Ben	Mar 4	1 Akb'al
Feb 20	1 Cimi	Mar 17	1 Cib
Feb 21–Mayan Year 2 Manik'		Mar 30	1 Muluc
Mar 5	1 Cauac	Apr 12	1 Ik'
Mar 18	1 Eb	Apr 25	1 Men
Mar 31	1 Chicchan	May 8	1 Lamat
Apr 13	1 Etznab	May 21	1 Imix
Apr 26	1 Chuen	Jun 3	1 Ix
May 9	1 Kan	Jun 16	1 Manik'
May 22	1 Caban	Jun 29	1 Ahau
Jun 4	1 Oc	Jul 12	1 Ben
Jun 17	1 Akb'al	Jul 25	1 Cimi
Jun 30	1 Cib	Aug 7	1 Cauac

GREGORIAN DATE	MAYAN DATE	GREGORIAN DATE	MAYAN DATE
Aug 20	1 Eb	Sep 26	1 Men
Sep 2	1 Chicchan	Oct 9	1 Lamat
Sep 15	1 Etznab	Oct 22	1 Imix
Sep 28	1 Chuen	Nov 4	1 Ix
Oct 11	1 Kan	Nov 17	1 Manik'
Oct 24	1 Caban	Nov 30	1 Ahau
Nov 6	1 Oc	Dec 13	1 Ben
Nov 19	1 Akb'al	Dec 26	1 Cimi
Dec 2	1 Cib		
Dec 15	1 Muluc		
Dec 28	1 Ik'	**2017**	
		Jan 8	1 Cauac
		Jan 21	1 Eb
*2016		Feb 3	1 Chicchan
Jan 10	1 Men	Feb 16	1 Etznab
Jan 23	1 Lamat	**Feb 20–Mayan Year 5 Ik'**	
Feb 5	1 Imix	Mar 1	1 Chuen
Feb 18	1 Ix	Mar 14	1 Kan
Feb 21–Mayan Year 4 Caban		Mar 27	1 Caban
Mar 2	1 Manik'	Apr 9	1 Oc
Mar 15	1 Ahau	Apr 22	1 Akb'al
Mar 28	1 Ben	May 5	1 Cib
Apr 10	1 Cimi	May 18	1 Muluc
Apr 23	1 Cauac	May 31	1 Ik'
May 6	1 Eb	Jun 13	1 Men
May 19	1 Chicchan	Jun 26	1 Lamat
Jun 1	1 Etznab	Jul 9	1 Imix
Jun 14	1 Chuen	Jul 22	1 Ix
Jun 27	1 Kan	Aug 4	1 Manik'
Jul 10	1 Caban	Aug 17	1 Ahau
Jul 23	1 Oc	Aug 30	1 Ben
Aug 5	1 Akb'al	Sep 12	1 Cimi
Aug 18	1 Cib	Sep 25	1 Cauac
Aug 31	1 Muluc	Oct 8	1 Eb
Sep 13	1 Ik'	Oct 21	1 Chicchan

GREGORIAN DATE	MAYAN DATE	GREGORIAN DATE	MAYAN DATE
Nov 3	1 Etznab	Dec 11	1 Imix
Nov 16	1 Chuen	Dec 24	1 Ix
Nov 29	1 Kan		
Dec 12	1 Caban	**2019**	
Dec 25	1 Oc	Jan 6	1 Manik'
		Jan 19	1 Ahau
2018		Feb 1	1 Ben
Jan 7	1 Akb'al	Feb 14	1 Cimi
Jan 20	1 Cib	**Feb 20–Mayan Year 7 Eb**	
Feb 2	1 Muluc	Feb 27	1 Cauac
Feb 15	1 Ik'	Mar 12	1 Eb
Feb 20–Mayan Year 6 Manik'		Mar 25	1 Chicchan
Feb 28	1 Men	Apr 7	1 Etznab
Mar 13	1 Lamat	Apr 20	1 Chuen
Mar 26	1 Imix	May 3	1 Kan
Apr 8	1 Ix	May 16	1 Caban
Apr 21	1 Manik'	May 29	1 Oc
May 4	1 Ahau	Jun 11	1 Akb'al
May 17	1 Ben	Jun 24	1 Cib
May 30	1 Cimi	Jul 7	1 Muluc
Jun 12	1 Cauac	Jul 20	1 Ik'
Jun 25	1 Eb	Aug 2	1 Men
Jul 8	1 Chicchan	Aug 15	1 Lamat
Jul 21	1 Etznab	Aug 28	1 Imix
Aug 3	1 Chuen	Sep 10	1 Ix
Aug 16	1 Kan	Sep 23	1 Manik'
Aug 29	1 Caban	Oct 6	1 Ahau
Sep 11	1 Oc	Oct 19	1 Ben
Sep 24	1 Akb'al	Nov 1	1 Cimi
Oct 7	1 Cib	Nov 14	1 Cauac
Oct 20	1 Muluc	Nov 27	1 Eb
Nov 2	1 Ik'	Dec 10	1 Chicchan
Nov 15	1 Men	Dec 23	1 Etznab
Nov 28	1 Lamat		

GREGORIAN DATE	MAYAN DATE

*2020

Jan 5	1 Chuen
Jan 18	1 Kan
Jan 31	1 Caban
Feb 13	1 Oc

Feb 20–Mayan Year 8 Caban

Feb 26	1 Akb'al
Mar 10	1 Cib
Mar 23	1 Muluc
Apr 5	1 Ik'
Apr 18	1 Men
May 1	1 Lamat
May 14	1 Imix
May 27	1 Ix
Jun 9	1 Manik'
Jun 22	1 Ahau
Jul 5	1 Ben
Jul 18	1 Cimi
Jul 31	1 Cauac
Aug 13	1 Eb
Aug 26	1 Chicchan
Sep 8	1 Etznab
Sep 21	1 Chuen
Oct 4	1 Kan
Oct 17	1 Caban
Oct 30	1 Oc
Nov 12	1 Akb'al
Nov 25	1 Cib
Dec 8	1 Muluc
Dec 21	1 Ik'

Bibliographical Note

Very little has been written in English about the practice of day sign astrology among the contemporary Maya. In order to learn it, I had to go there and quite literally sit at the feet of those who knew.

There are a few books worth reading. First and foremost, there is *The Book of Destiny*, by Carlos Barrios, translated by Lisa Carter (New York, HarperCollins, 2009). The second half of the book deals with the astrology of the twenty day signs and covers the essentials of the Mayan Cross (but without the numbers). Barrios writes within the mainstream contemporary tradition as it is now practiced in Guatemala.

A great deal of hard-to-find information about variant (i.e. non-K'iche') traditions can be obtained from *Mayan Calendar User's Guide*, by former journalist Shay Addams (Antigua, Casa Caos, 2011). The insights gleaned from the Tz'utujil tradition around Lake Atitlan are especially noteworthy.

Other books that include lists of the day signs of the *tzolk'in* with their meanings are *The Ancient Spirituality of the Modern Maya*, by Thomas Hart (Albuquerque, University of New Mexico, 2008), *The Living Maya: Ancient Wisdom in the Era of 2012*, by Robert Sitler (Berkeley, North Atlantic Books, 2010), and *Contemporary Maya Spirituality: The Ancient Ways Are Not Lost*, by Jean Molesky-Poz (Austin, University of Texas, 2006), although in the case of the latter, it should be noted that at some time during the book's production, confusion arose between the Yucatec Maya terms "Kan" and "Chicchan" and the K'iche' Maya terms "K'at" and "Kan."

As I have noted previously, there is no harm in mixing Western astrology with Mayan day sign astrology; the Maya themselves were doing it at least as early as the 18th century. One intriguing venture into the field is *How to Practice Mayan Astrology*, by Bruce Scofield and Barry C. Orr (Rochester, VT, Bear and Co., 2006). For those who want to experience the blend of the two systems "straight from the horse's mouth" and who are not intimidated by scholarly footnotes, there is *An Encounter of Two Worlds: The Book of Chilam Balam of Kaua*, by Victoria Bricker and Helga-Maria Miram (New Orleans, Middle American Research Institute, 2002).

Finally, no one with a serious interest in the contemporary lore of the Mayan Calendar should be without Barbara Tedlock's extraordinary *Time and the Highland Maya* (Albuquerque, University of New Mexico, 1982, 2nd ed. 1994), a true classic in every sense of the word.

Resources

BOOKS

13 B'aktun—Mayan Visions of 2012 and Beyond
Gaspar Pedro González

2012: Science and Prophecy of the Ancient Maya
Mark Van Stone, PhD

The Ancient Spirituality of the Modern Maya
Thomas Hart

The Book of Destiny: Unlocking the Secrets of the Ancient Maya
Carlos Barrios

Breaking the Maya Code
Michael D. Coe

Contemporary Maya Spirituality: The Ancient Ways Are Not Lost
Jean Molesky-Poz

How to Read Maya Hieroglyphs
John Montgomery

Jaguar Wisdom: an Introduction to the Mayan Calendar
Kenneth Johnson

The Living Maya: Ancient Wisdom in the Era of 2012
Robert Sitler, PhD

Maya 2012: A Guide to Celebrations in Mexico, Guatemala, Belize & Honduras
Joshua Berman

Maya Cosmos: Three Thousand Years on the Shaman's Path
David Freidel, Linda Schele, and Joy Parker

Popol Vuh: The Definitive Edition of the Mayan Book of the Dawn of Life and the Glories of Gods and Kings
Dennis Tedlock

The Serpent and the Jaguar: Living in Sacred Time
Birgitte Rasine

Time and the Highland Maya
Barbara Tedlock

MOBILE APPS

MCP Mayan Tzolkin (iPhone and Android)
Get your Tzolk'in Energy of the Day reading, plus descriptions
of the day signs, numbers, and deities. This is the award-winning
official mobile app of the Mayan Calendar Portal.

My Mayan Match (iPhone and Android)
Discover the nature of your compatibility with the people in your
life. This app is based on the little-known personal compatibility
matrix embedded in the sacred Tzolk'in calendar.

WEB SITES

European Association of Mayanists: **www.wayeb.com**

Foundation for the Advancement of Mesoamerican Studies:
www.famsi.org

Jaguar Wisdom: **www.jaguarwisdom.org**

Mayan Calendar Portal: **www.maya-portal.net**

Mayan Majix: **www.mayanmajix.com**

The Mesoamerica Center: **www.utmesoamerica.org**

Mesoweb: **www.mesoweb.com**

Mundo Maya online: **www.mayadiscovery.com**

About the Author

The first person to publish information about the five-sign Mayan Cross horoscope in English (1997), Kenneth Johnson has continued his studies with Mayan Daykeepers throughout the years, and has now created a complete manual of Mayan astrological practice. All the material in this unique new book is based upon information obtained from shamanic Mayan astrologers in Guatemala; there are no "New Age" inventions or "interpretations."

The presenter of numerous talks and seminars on the Mayan Calendar and its astrological systems, Ken has also designed several webinars, or online workshops, for the Mayan Calendar Portal (**www.maya-portal.net**); these webinars remain among the most appreciated by MCP audiences.

Ken holds a B.A. in Comparative Religions from California State University Fullerton. He obtained his Master of Arts in Eastern Studies (with an emphasis in Classical Sanskrit) from St. John's College, Santa Fe. He is the author of numerous books and magazine articles, of which *Jaguar Wisdom: An Introduction to the Mayan Calendar* is the best known. His other titles include the *Mythic Astrology* series (with Arielle Guttman), and *Mansions of the Moon: The Lost Zodiac of the Goddess*. A student of Mayan spirituality and languages, he divides his time between the United States and Guatemala.

Ken's web site is **www.jaguarwisdom.org**.

Endnotes

Chapter 1. An Introduction to the Sacred Calendar

1. The term *ch'ol q'ij* is itself an abbreviated rendering of the more correct *ch'ol b'al q'ij*.

2. Tedlock, Barbara, *Time and the Highland Maya* (Austin, University of Texas, 2nd ed. 1994). This legendary book should be on the shelves of anyone who is serious about the study of the Mayan Calendar. In fact, I have sometimes found the Spanish language edition on the shelves of Mayan traditionalists themselves.

3. These are, of course, the same four elements familiar to many of us from Greek philosophy and Western astrology. It seems unlikely that the Maya would have happened upon just these same elements; one would expect quite a different cosmovision, as we find with the Chinese. Are the four elements adopted from Western civilization? Some Maya Daykeepers assert that the tradition of the four elements was known to them since the ancient times. In any case, if they were "borrowed," they have certainly been a part of Mayan culture for a very long time.

Chapter 2. The Day Signs

1. Klein, Ceceilia F., "Woven Heaven, Tangled Earth: A Weaver's Paradigm of the Mesoamerican Cosmos," in Aveni, Anthony, and Gary Urton, eds., *Ethnoastronomy and Archaeo-astronomy in the American Tropics* (New York, New York Academy of Sciences, 1982), pp. 1-35.

2. This day sign was symbolized by a monkey among the Aztecs, and the word *b'atz'* literally means "howler monkey" in K'iche', but contemporary K'iche' Daykeepers are more likely to perceive this day sign as a thread, as if it were spelled *batz*, which does in fact mean "thread."

3. This creation myth is from a colonial manuscript known as *The Book of Chilam Balam of Chumayel*. The most recent translation is by Munro Edmonson, published under the title *Heaven Born Merida and its Destiny* (Austin, University of Texas Press, 1986). The creation story is on pp. 120-6.

4. Prechtel, Martin, *Stealing Benefacio's Roses* (Berkeley, North Atlantic Books, 2002), pp. 26-101.

5. Tedlock, Dennis, trans. *Popol Vuh: The Mayan Book of the Dawn of Life* (New York, Simon & Schuster, 1986), p. 181.

6. Some scholars feel that the "Maker and Modeler" represents a polarity of the Divine which is substantially different from that described as "Heart of Sky, Heart of Earth." Others feel that these two terms describe the same universal polarity; essentially, there is no difference.

7. Edmonson, *op. cit.*

8. For the occasional use of Eastern religious terminology in this book, see my comments on p. 13 of Chapter 1.

9. Several Juan No'j stories can be found in Hart, Thomas, *The Ancient Spirituality of the Modern Maya* (Albuquerque, University of New Mexico Press, 2008), pp. 145-51.

10. Lem Batz, *Nik: Filosofía de los Numeros Mayas* (Chimaltenango, Editorial Rukemik Na'ojil, 2005), pp. 9-27.

11. Among the Yucatec Maya, the "flower" in question was almost certainly the frangipani or plumeria (*nicte* in Yucatec). Among the Aztecs, it appears to have been the marigold, still used in Mexican ceremonies during the Days of the Dead.

12. Technically, the crocodile so well known to us from the Aztec version of the day signs ought to be a caiman, which is the member of the crocodilian species common in southern Mesoamerica.

13. Hart, *op. cit.*, p. 43.

14. Adrian Chavez translates Tz'aqol B'itol into Spanish as *Arquitecto, Formador*, which I have rendered as "Architect and Maker." Most Daykeepers prefer the Chavez translation of the *Pop Wuj* above all

others; Chavez was himself an initiated Daykeeper, originally from the K'iche' community of San Francisco el Alto. See *Pop Wuj: Poema Mitico-Historico K'iche'*, trans. Adrian Ines Chavez (Quetzaltenango, Ligo Maya Guatemala, 2007). Dennis Tedlock's English translation, *Popol Vuh: The Mayan Book of the Dawn of Life* (New York, Simon & Schuster, 1985), is also deeply respected; Tedlock, also a Daykeeper, worked with the assistance of the well-known Momostecan sage Andres Xiloj. Tedlock translates the phrase as "Maker and Modeler."

15. The other English word commonly acknowledged to be derived from the Mayan languages is "shark," which is xoc in Mayan. This term most likely originated with buccaneers who sailed off the coasts of Yucatan and present-day Belize.

16. Almost all my oral sources agree in referring to this day sign as "dawn," despite the fact that aq'ab means "night." K'iche' people often speak in a mixed dialect of Spanish and K'iche'. The names for most, perhaps all, day signs have Spanish language equivalents, though I am not familiar with all of them, since I was focused upon K'iche'. I have, however, heard the name of the day sign Aq'ab'al referred to in conjunction with the Spanish word madrugada, which refers to the time of fading darkness and incipient light.

17. Prechtel, *Stealing Benefacio's Roses*, pp. 259-60.

18. Hart, *op. cit.*, p. 44.

19. Barrios, Carlos, *The Book of Destiny*, translated by Lisa Carter (New York, HarperCollins, 2009), pp. 261-2.

20. Much of the information in this and the next paragraph is based on Prechtel, Martin, *Long Life, Honey in the Heart* (Berkeley, North Atlantic Books, 2004), pp. 91-3, 364-6.

21. Lem Batz, *op. cit.*, p. 27-31, as well as personal conversation with my K'iche' language teacher, Don Ricardo Zarate Guix, Momostenango, 2010-11.

22. In our culture, we see a "man" in the moon; the Aztecs and the Maya saw a rabbit.

23. Edmonson, Munro, *op. cit.*, pp. 120-6. The translator dates this piece to *k'atun* 11 Ahau (1539-59).

Chapter 3. The Numbers

1. Tarn, Nathaniel, and Martin Prechtel, "Constant Inconstancy: The Feminine Principle in Atiteco Mythology," in *Symbol and Meaning beyond the Closed Community: Essays in Mesoamerican Ideas*, ed. Gary H. Gossen (Albany, SUNY, 1986), pp. 173-84.

2. Bricker, Victoria R. and Helga-Maria Miram, *An Encounter of Two Worlds: The Book of Chilam Balam of Kaua* (New Orleans, Middle American Research Institute, 2002), p. 36.

3. Shay Addams, citing Walburga Rupflin Alvarado in *El Tzolkin es Más Que un Calendario* (Guatemala City, Fundación Cedim, 1995), p.197, records a different K'iche' tradition in which the four special 13 days are 13 Aj, 13 Tz'ikin, 13 Kan and 13 Kej. Addams, *Mayan Calendar User's Guide* (Antigua, Casa Caos, 2011), p. 133.

Chapter 6. Sun and Moon

1. The *k'atun* was comprised of twenty *tuns*. A *tun* is not the same thing as a solar year; while the solar year has 365 days, a *tun* is a mathematical year of 360 days. Thus the actual length of a Mayan *k'atun* is equivalent to 19.7 solar years. This is almost exactly the length of a Jupiter-Saturn cycle. The cycle of Jupiter and Saturn was used by Arabic and medieval astrologers to assess trends in human history; contemporary astrologers still treat it as an important factor in political astrology. Susan Milbrath, in *Star Gods of the Maya* (Austin, University of Texas, 1999), p. 230, argues that the Mayan *k'atun* is also based ultimately on the Jupiter–Saturn cycle.

2. *Op. cit.*, p 35.

Chapter 8. Path of Feathered Serpent

1. See Chapter 3 on "The Numbers" for an explanation of why 9 and 7 represent life and death, respectively.

2. Bricker, Victoria R. and Helga-Maria Miram, *An Encounter of Two Worlds: The Book of Chilam Balam of Kaua* (New Orleans, Middle American Research Institute, 2002).

THE VISIONARY
literary fiction

Light and Time. Two great universal forces unite all living things, binding them by biology, physiology, and evolution, and impact every facet of human civilization.

A work of unrelenting poetic prose, "The Visionary" pierces the veil of delusion and denial we've been weaving in our minds and hearts about every aspect of our lives and shines a glaring yet guiding light onto a much simpler, and deeper, path.

Coming Fall 2014 in print on Amazon, Barnes & Noble, and in digital (eBook) format on iTunes, Amazon, Barnes & Noble, and Kobo.

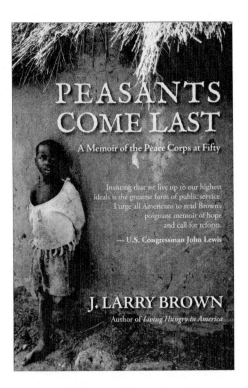

Printed in Great Britain
by Amazon